Childhood and Human Nature

Childhood and Human Nature,

The Development of Personality

Sula Wolff

WITHDRAWI

R
Routledge
London and New York

First published in 1989
by Routledge
11 New Fetter Lane, London EC4P 4EE
29 West 35th Street, New York, NY 10001

© 1989 Sula Wolff

Phototypeset in 10pt Times
by Mews Photosetting, Beckenham, Kent
Printed in Great Britain by
Billings & Sons Limited, Worcester

British Library Cataloguing in Publication Data

Wolff, Sula
    Childhood and human nature: the development
    of personality.
    1. Personality.   Development
    I. Title
    155.2'5

Library of Congress Cataloging in Publication Data

Wolff, Sula, 1924–
    Childhood and human nature: the development of personality /
    Sula Wolff.
    p.   cm.
    Bibliography: p.
    Includes index.
    1. Personality development. 2. Personality development — Case
    studies. I. Title.
    BF723.P4W65   1989
    155.4'18–dc19   89-3453
                                                                          CIP

ISBN 0-415-01128-0
      0-415-01129-9 (pbk)

'The childhood shows the man as morning shows the day'

John Milton, *Paradise Regained*

Contents

Author's note

Many children and parents are quoted in this book. Their names are fictitious and their life circumstances have been altered to guard their privacy. To all of them I am grateful for helping me to get to know them so well. It has been a privilege.

I want to thank Charles Clark and Ron Davie for initiating this venture and for their comments on an early version. Steven Wolkind and Henry Walton read the final draft and I greatly appreciated their suggestions. Special thanks go to Susan Whitson and Patricia Rose for much patient secretarial help.

Acknowledgements are due to Sigmund Freud Copyrights Ltd, The Institute of Psycho-Analysis, and The Hogarth Press for permission to quote from *The Standard Edition of the Complete Psychological Work of Sigmund Freud*, translated and edited by James Strachey, and to Penguin Books Ltd for permission to reproduce a passage from C. Rycroft (ed.) *Psychoanalysis Observed*.

Introduction

How do we make sense of people? Empathy and mutual understanding are universal human attributes present even in the very young (Hoffman 1975 and 1984). A few people, psychotic adults and autistic children for example, lack such interpersonal skills and in some solitary scientists and artists they may be poorly developed. But most of us have innate abilities to imagine how others feel and to respond to them as they would like. We are after all made to live in human groups. To understand another person well we need to know his biography, both as it is and as he or she sees it. Empathic understanding is further improved by knowledge about developmental processes and the likely impact of life events and circumstances. For accurate empathy with children we must in addition appreciate how at different ages they tend to perceive their lives and to think and reason about the world.

An example of events this book sets out to explain

William came to a child psychiatric clinic aged 8 because of constant trouble in and out of school. He was restless, with a poor attention span. He stole and repeatedly took risks such as running in front of cars. He was attractive, outgoing, and with many friends. He was also extremely intelligent, better at verbal than at practical tasks.

He had been a premature and small baby. He had had severe whooping cough in infancy, and in his second year his overactivity contributed to three traumatic events: he scalded himself with hot tea; he fell into a fire; he fell and seriously hurt his forehead. At 6 he had meningitis.

The mother, meticulous about her appearance and highly competent both at home and at work, had been reared as the youngest of twelve. She discovered only at puberty that she was illegitimate and that her 'mother' was in fact her grandmother. She had never been really close to either of her mothers. Throughout her life she felt insecure; appearances were very important for her and she needed constant demonstrations of approval from others. For her, William's misbehaviour, which showed her up in public, was especially painful.

The father, from a united but socio-economically deprived family, described himself as 'harum scarum'. Proud of his wife's superior social standards, he nevertheless, jokingly but repeatedly, undermined these; and he confused his sons by often telling them it was 'all right' to do forbidden things, so long as 'you're not found out'.

William's older brother presented no problems. He, too, had been premature, but he was neither restless nor distractable, and had been raised more strictly and consistently by his mother.

Both parents and William worried constantly about his possible delinquency. The parents warned and punished him repeatedly. But, the more anxious William was, the more risks he took, while always afraid he might lose control.

A family-based behavioural treatment programme combined with individual interviews with William and with the parents as a couple, led to only intermittent improvement. Residential schooling by relieving the parents of the full burden of responsibility and providing for William a stimulating environment and non-judgemental external controls to augment his own real efforts, resulted in several years of peaceful development. Back in the community, however, and in a large secondary school where misbehaviour evoked 'common sense' responses of punishment and warning, his symptoms escalated once more and, once he was in trouble, his anxious parents found themselves reverting to their old patterns of reproaching and reprimanding him and quarrelling with each other.

It was important here to understand how each family member felt, but also to recognize the causes for William's troublesome conduct.

A fundamental difficulty in the discussion of personality development arises from the two separate modes of explaining and understanding human behaviour: the introspective and purposive, exemplified by the psychoanalytic schools, and the scientific, based on the data and theories of ethologists, developmental psychologists and other social scientists. These two viewpoints are often set against each other as if one must be false if the other is true. Much misunderstanding is avoided if we can be clear that both approaches are valid but that their premises, methods and uses are different. The nature of these two kinds of explanation current in the social sciences and reflecting a psychosocial dualism has been helpfully discussed (Toulmin 1970) in terms of *reasons* and *causes*. The way reasons determine conduct is different from causal mechanisms, such as those underlying physical processes.

We use reasons to justify our actions after the event and to signal our intentions for the future: 'I hope to become a psychologist *because* I want to protect other children from the miseries I had as a child.' Reasons are part of the subjective continuity of our self-reflective lives and help us make sense of ourselves and others. They are psychological explanations, crucial in all human encounters, and form the cognitive tools, accompanying empathy, for understanding and skilfully responding to other people.

Causal explanations, on the other hand, form the scientific basis of knowledge. They relate to more objectively observable phenomena or facts including behaviour, and help us within statistical limits to predict future events: we now know that children brought up in children's homes in their first three years are at risk of later personality difficulties. Scientific knowledge is indispensable for the decisions affecting groups of people that have to be made in medicine, social work, education and politics. Scientific knowledge is essential too for professional interventions in the lives of individuals, by indicating the probable outcome of one measure rather than another. When decisions for action have to be taken, psychological understanding is not enough.

This book is concerned with both objective and subjective aspects of personality development in childhood and aims to convey, with examples from clinical practice, how scientifically-observed developmental processes and transformations may be experienced and appraised subjectively by an individual person. It is about those personal qualities, inner processes and life circumstances of children which influence what sort of people they turn into in later life. It is written for the practitioner in child care in the belief that no single theoretical viewpoint and no simple formula for action is helpful.

At every stage, a child is not only himself now, with particular capacities in a particular social setting. He or she already contains residual influences from the past and potentialities for the future. The adult too brings his or her life history to whatever the current predicament. Doctors take this for granted in beginning each clinical enquiry with the development of the complaints, and cherishing the lifelong contact a family doctor can achieve with patients. Social workers, too, use a historical perspective both in assessment and casework. While a 'here and now' approach is perfectly legitimate in a medical or social crisis, or when the focus, as between teacher and pupil, is on interests and competence in the public world, all intimate understanding of another person must encompass both the present and the past.

Although human behaviour is immensely varied, there are limits to this variability, and within the range of what is possible there are constraints on the behaviour of individuals. These come, for example, from a person's age, from physical competence and intelligence, but also from sickness and handicap, quite apart from cultural and socio-economic influences.

The different professions are on the whole concerned with different constraints. Teachers help the young to increase their understanding and competence within the limits set by maturational processes on intelligence and physical skills; social workers are primarily concerned with material and socio-cultural constraints on behaviour; doctors and nurses with those imposed by sickness and handicap both physical and psychiatric. All professionals, however, need the capacity to look beyond their particular area of expertise in order to assess the causes of adaptive failure (that is, of excessive behavioural constraint) and to choose the most promising intervention. Doctors must be alert to the health hazards of socio-cultural privation; social workers to the family and social disorganization brought about, for example, by depressive illness or alcoholism; and teachers to the educational failures caused by physical and social handicap.

An accurate diagnosis of the nature of behavioural constraints also sharpens our judgement as to the amount of active care a person needs and how much responsibility for his predicament he is able to take himself. There is no argument about the need for care of children and the very old. Physical handicap present for all to see also poses no problem. But there is frequent controversy about the responsibility for their own conduct of people with impaired intelligence, with person-ality disorders or temporary mental illnesses. Are we right, some might even ask, to hospitalize a depressed and suicidal patient against her will although, once recovered, her wish to die has gone and she does not resent her doctors? What is commonly needed is a dual or alternating approach of fostering autonomy while ready to offer care.

Theories about personality development are often presented in a partisan way as if inevitably they conflict with each other. It is my belief that to understand human behaviour and experience, we need multiple and flexible viewpoints: the historical and the here-and-now; the scientific and the empathic. Professionals are most helpful to people in trouble when they can look at maladaptive responses from a developmental, educational, social, and medical perspective, and are prepared simultaneously to ensure safety while maintaining concerned respect.

The twentieth century has seen an enormous investment in the study of children, reflected in a fast-growing literature on child development, bewildering for the beginner. We have a better understanding now of children and of childhood influences in later life, as well as of adaptive failure at any stage. Knowledge about personality development in childhood is essential in three important domains: in the appraisal of deviant behaviour at all ages; in the development of social policy for children; and in therapeutic interventions for children and their families.

This book begins with some definitions of personality and its components, and with an outline of inborn and constitutional aspects of intelligence and temperament. It continues with descriptions of the developmental processes determining infant sociability; the acquisition of intelligence and emotional maturity; and the influences of the social environment. In the final chapter we discuss what can be done to safeguard the personality development of children. Our concern is as much with the preservation of an environment in which children can fulfil their urge to become civilized and creative, as with the less easily accomplished tasks of making good deficiencies.

Inevitably each chapter can deal with only limited aspects of development so that the integration of different areas of knowledge and of different viewpoints, which this book aims to bring about, will be the reader's own. Inevitably too justice cannot be done to all the many theories of personality structure and development which have emerged from naturalistic and experimental studies and from therapeutic explorations of human experience. Instead, this book will focus on those facts and theories which seem most relevant to the understanding of individual differences between people, and especially of disturbed children and their parents.

Part I

Inborn aspects of personality and development

Chapter one

A biological view of personality

What is personality?

The definitions of personality are bewildering in their variety. Some psychologists use the word to refer only to observable behaviour; others include communications about introspective self-knowledge; some the organization of an individual's patterns of thought, motives and feelings; some the internal integration or external adjustment of the person. All agree that personality refers to more *enduring and hence predictable qualities*. It can be no biological accident that we are all in part predictable. We can guess how we are likely to cope in different circumstances and we have some choice, at least as adults, about the settings to which we expose ourselves. The more enduring aspects of our natures also foster mutual adaptation between people: we attune what we say and do to the anticipated reactions of others.

Some definitions of personality exclude intelligence and aptitudes. Some focus only on individual differences, that is on features which distinguish one person from another. Sometimes the concept is not used at all for children because they are held to be so changeable and unpredictable that to talk of childhood personality is thought to be meaningless.

I shall use the term for all behaviour and self-reports of thoughts and feelings that have some permanence, recognizing that a great deal of behaviour is universal to the human race, much is common to all members of a particular culture or subculture, some is familial, and only a portion is unique. In childhood, predictable behaviour changes remarkably with age, from infancy to adult life. These transformations of behaviour patterns in the course of development are shared by all children. But for each child, the interactions between his or her particular constitution, culture and personal environment, including life events, contribute to the evolving personality and to the individual and unique patterns of his or her responses.

Components of personality

It has been helpful both in the study of personality and in the clinical understanding of people with personal troubles to think about three interdependent components of personality: (1) motivation and emotions; (2) temperament; (3) intelligence.

Motivation and emotions give direction, determining the *what and why* of behaviour. The content of our thoughts, the things in life that matter to us, our moral standards and our more public lives, our beliefs, attitudes and opinions, our goals, hopes and ambitions, the things we fear and those we reject, our joys and griefs, all make up this most important part of our personality which we identify as our self, and which psychoanalysts have called 'identity' (Erikson 1968).

Temperament, or style, concerns the *how* of behaviour. It has been described (Allport 1961:34) as 'the characteristic phenomena of an individual's emotional nature, including his susceptibility to emotional stimulation, his customary strength and speed of responses, the quality of his prevailing mood, and all peculiarities of fluctuation and intensity in mood'.

Intelligence refers to levels of achievement and in childhood to rates of development. Intelligence defines *how much* an individual can do.

The complexity of our inner life and the excellence of our performance in thought and action depend in large measure, although not entirely, on our intelligence. How we react to our surroundings and our style of self-expression reflect our temperament. And both intelligence and temperament have, as we shall see, firm biological roots. But our affective motivational self, although animated and coloured by these other parts of our personality, is most open to influence by the events and circumstances of our lives. Our behaviour is patterned by the family who brings us up, by our school, by the culture within which we live. We learn from our interactions with these environmental influences and from the events that befall us; and the patterns of this learning, the connections between the outer influences and the changes in our manifest behaviour at different stages of life, can be traced and laws established which govern these relationships.

Biological determinants have been identified even in this field, especially in relation to the development of that part of affective behaviour which is common to all human beings, for example, the child's attachment to his mother, the teenager's search for a sexual partner and the nurturing activities of parents. Later chapters in this book will be concerned with the development during childhood of this socio-emotional part of the human personality and with the effects on individuals of growing up under different life circumstances.

Much human behaviour is universal

It is sometimes overlooked that the differences between people may be smaller than what they have in common. Much human behaviour and experience and a great deal of the human environment is shared by everyone. Indeed, in some aspects of our personality, of our social environment, especially in early childhood, and of the developmental processes of infancy, we resemble the higher vertebrates. Perhaps the wordless, empathic understanding we can reach with animals of certain species through eye contact, gesture and tone of voice, phenomena we tend totally to take for granted, reflect such similarities.

All behaviour is the outcome of complex interactions between our constitutional make-up, largely genetically determined, and the social and inanimate environment in which we grow up. The extent to which we resemble each other reflects both a common gene pool and a common environment to which we have, through evolutionary processes, become adapted. Developmental processes, too, are shared by everyone. And in many studies of child development groups of babies or children have been observed at different ages or under different circumstances without regard to their individual differences. Such studies of the 'universal' infant or child have illuminated general processes of intellectual and socio-emotional development. In contrast, in studies designed to shed light on individual differences, including pathology, children are compared who differ in the qualities under investigation but who are otherwise as similar as possible.

Biological perspective: heredity, environment and constitution

There is no getting away from the fact that we live in our bodies and that our anatomy and physiology are prerequisites for all our actions and experience. Social processes alone cannot explain human behaviour. The increasing fascination in recent decades with the intelligence and sociability of the human baby, heightened when comparative studies revealed developmental similarities in animal infants, has revived a general interest in the biological basis of behaviour in childhood. Doctors and psychologists concerned with abnormalities of development and behaviour believe that assessments of individual children, and indeed of patients of all ages, must include biological aspects such as genetic predisposition, nutrition, organic illness and physical handicap. Biological determinants are important both for our understanding of personality development in general and of how individual differences and pathology can come about.

Charles Darwin demonstrated a structural continuity between species. His theory of biological evolution on the basis of *natural selection* (Plomin *et al*. 1980) was that characteristics, mental as well as physical, promoting survival of a species were passed on from one generation to the next, while harmful characteristics, interfering with the organism's adaptation to its environment, led to its extinction, either because affected individuals did not survive to pass them on or because they failed to find a mate and beget offspring. The Augustinian monk, Gregor Mendel, discovered the basis for biological variability and its hereditary transmission during his researches on peas. Each inherited trait depends on two elements, one coming from each parent. These elements, or genes, located on chromosomes, remain discrete, and different traits are inherited independently of each other. Individual variability is thus ensured by ever new combinations of genes in each individual person. In addition, new characteristics arise by mutation, that is by spontaneous changes occurring in a gene. Evolutionary theory rests on two tenets: genetic variation and selection. The modification and increasing complexity of living beings is, according to Darwinian theory, attributable to non-random survival (i.e. selection) of random variabilities.

Biological evolution also implies a changing environment calling for new adaptive patterns with consequent modification of the species over the eons. It is a very slow process as far as the species as a whole is concerned, and anatomically and physiologically man has changed little in 30,000 years. At the same time, as we shall see, genetic variations are of extreme importance for individuals, and genetic abnormalities can be devastating in their effects.

Biological evolution depends on the hereditary transmission of genes from parents to child. Parents do not choose each other at random. Marital choice, based on opportunities for meeting and on mutual selection, is called *assortative mating*. Parents resemble each other in many ways and the effect of assortative mating is to maintain the spread within a population especially of traits based on multigenic inheritance (Scarr and Kidd 1983).

Our genetic heritage affects not only how we are constructed and the way we function at any one stage of life, but determines also the actual processes of maturation and ageing in the course of our life span. And these include the changes with age of our potential for action and experience. Genes constitute a programme, implemented via biochemical bodily processes, for performance in time. But the manifestations of genetic influence are open to enormous variation as a result of the environment in which we live, with which we interact and which is increasingly man-made. The changing social environment of the human species in general, to which the activities and products of people themselves contribute most of all, is the basis for *cultural evolution*. Just as the genes transmit our biological heritage from one generation to the next, so language, written language and the other artefacts created by man transmit his cultural heritage.

Each one of us contains a complement of genes made up of those which all human beings share, that is those which determine our common biological potential, as well as genes which contribute to the characteristics of groups and individuals. Our environment too contains universal ingredients (called the *environment of human adaptedness* or our *common expectable environment*) as well as characteristics shared by cultures and families, and those that are unique.

Geneticists have discovered that some characteristics depend on a single gene, for example, eye colour and some inborn errors of metabolism such as phenylketonuria which can cause serious mental retardation. Some chromosomal aberrations have also been identified as the causes of specific syndromes of mental handicap: Down's syndrome and Fragile X abnormality. Other human characteristics depend on the combined effect of very many genes (multigenetic inheritance) in interaction with the environment, for example height and intelligence. The patterns of inheritance of these characteristics vary, as does their distribution in the community.

Much has been learnt about the genetic basis of human attributes from the study of twins, since twins are of two kinds: identical or *monozygotic twins* formed by the division of a fertilized egg cell into two identical cells and giving rise to two genetically identical fetuses, and fraternal or *dizygotic twins* derived from two separate fertilized egg cells developing side by side from the start. The latter are genetically no more similar than ordinary brothers and sisters. Siblings resemble each other as they do their parents because they have a part of their genetic heritage in common, but also because they share a family culture. When we find similarities between members of a family we cannot know whether this reflects the effects of the family environment, or an interaction between this and a common genetic make-up. On the other hand, when we hear that for a given characteristic, for example intelligence, the similarities between monozygotic twins differ from those between same-sex dizygotic twins far more than do those of dizygotic twins from those of ordinary siblings, we can be sure that, whatever else determines the feature under investigation, it also has a genetic basis and is not merely brought about by the way in which families differentially react to identical twin partners, non-identical twins, and to ordinary brothers and sisters.

Robert Shields some years ago studied pairs of twins reared together and pairs reared because adopted or fostered in early infancy (Shields 1962). These twins were often very eager to meet up with each other, and twin partners were traced through television. Shields found that identical twins reared apart were almost as similar in intelligence as those reared together, while on some tests of temperament (extraversion and neuroticism) there were greater differences when monozygotic partners were brought up apart, but the differences between monozygotic twins overall were still less than between dizygotic twins. Another approach to the study of the genetic contribution to human attributes has been opened by the natural experiments of adoption and fostering. The extent to which adopted people resemble their biological parents rather than the parents who brought them up reflects the genetic rather than the environmental contributions to the quality of personality or physique or the illness or deviation in question.

The development of personality, like physical growth, is based on interactions of organism and environment. Here the concept of *constitution* is important. It means the structure of the individual at any one time. From the moment of conception each person with his or her particular genetic potential is open to influence by their surroundings and, in turn, exerts an effect to bring about change in these surroundings. Environmentally induced changes alter the individual's constitution and this now differently constituted being then interacts with an environment slightly altered through his influence.

Scarr and McCartney developed an important theory to link genetic differences between people with individual differences in how these are expressed (Scarr and McCartney 1983). The effect can be a *direct* expression of the genetic predisposition, as in the case of a single gene abnormality like phenylketonuria, or a chromosome abnormality like Down's syndrome, where the environment is of little importance. More commonly, the effect is *indirect*, via three types of possible interactions with the environment. (1) The first environmental mechanism is *passive*, through the upbringing provided by biologically related parents. It should not be overlooked that highly intelligent parents, for example, are not only likely to have children genetically predisposed to giftedness but to provide a more varied and stimulating environment for their children, thereby further enhancing these children's intellectual progress. (2) The second mode of gene-environmental effects on behaviour is *evoked*, through the responses elicited from other people by genetically determined qualities in the child such as his appearance, temperament, or intelligence. Constitutionally cheerful babies are more likely to attract attention even in unfavourable conditions, unavoidable for example in a children's home, and this extra nurturing care will then contribute further to their social responsiveness. (3) The third is *active*, through the selection of different environments or different aspects of the environment by genetically differently constituted children.

Quite apart from the single gene or chromosome abnormalities which we have mentioned, some circumstances present before birth can have profound effects on later personality. Biological accidents such as an attack of German measles early in pregnancy or the thalidomide tragedy of twenty years ago can so alter the constitution of genetically healthy babies that their development, including that of personality, is indelibly changed. Babies malnourished in the womb are born small and at increased risk of birth injury. They are also at risk of not developing their full genetic intelligence because of impaired brain growth.

It is unrealistic and indeed harmful to overlook constitutional personality impairments of children or parents which, although often inconspicuous, nevertheless, and especially under adverse conditions, impose severe constraints on adaptive capacities. Everyone accepts that not all children are equally capable at school learning. What is not always realized is that aspects of temperament, too, for example the restless distractibility of a developmentally impaired child, or the aloof withdrawal of a child with schizoid personality traits, may have a constitutional basis.

One other biological influence needs to be mentioned: the timing of physical maturity. In a longitudinal study (Magnusson 1988), girls who reached puberty early were found to have rather different social experiences at adolescence within an older peer group, to leave school early, establish their families at a younger age, and to be less career oriented in adult life.

Normality and abnormality

When people are ill, physically or mentally, the practical recognition of their disorder is usually not difficult. A change for the worse has come about and there are complaints (the symptoms) and observations (the signs) which identify the disorder. In childhood, psychiatric disturbance often consists of behaviour all children may transiently display, and a child is identified as disturbed only when his difficulties have assumed distressing or handicapping proportions (Rutter *et al*. 1970). But in children, too, psychiatric disorder represents a discontinuity in development or adaptation.

The concept of abnormality or pathology as applied to personality on the other hand, where such discontinuity of behaviour and experience is very rare, is a more difficult one. Of course we can identify what is unusual, that is statistically abnormal, especially when we deal with measureable qualities. We can also identify attributes of personality that handicap an individual in his or her particular life situation. In highly industrialized societies with compulsory education, relatively slight deficiencies in intelligence are handicapping when in a different cultural setting they are not. During the school years when conformity and gregariousness are expected, a schizoid, withdrawn boy preoccupied with solitary pursuits and uncomfortable in crowds is at a serious disadvantage, while during his pre-school years in an understanding family, and later in a congenial occupation, he copes well.

In practice, when people repeatedly engage in behaviour that is self-destructive or destructive of other people, we can be sure they would act differently if they could. Our task then is to identify the nature of the constraints impeding personality functioning; to gauge how fixed the disorder is likely to be and to decide on the most fruitful methods of intervention. The question: pathology or healthy personality development? is often of more academic than practical importance except in relation to the law and criminal responsibility. It is then sometimes extremely difficult to reach a conclusion. Unless intellectual deficit, genetic abnormalities or brain injury can be demonstrated, one has to fall back on generally accepted professional practices both of personality description and diagnosis and of professional treatment approaches, rather than on more objective criteria of pathology.

Continuity and discontinuity of behaviour and experience

There has been much debate, some astonishingly bitter, about the permanance or otherwise of childhood behaviour. In particular, the notion that there are biologically determined *sensitive periods of development* in which children are especially prone to long-lasting personality damage if either traumatized or deprived of normal environmental opportunities for learning, has caused controversy (Clarke and Clarke 1976; Rutter 1981). The recovery of language and other intellectual skills in individual children who had been most seriously neglected and deprived of human care and contact in their early years has been cited as evidence to counter such ideas. To these issues we shall return later. Here only three general points will be made.

Living organisms are robust

There is no question that all living things are in part biologically protected against adversity. If one function fails, another can take over; if we miss out on development at one stage of life, it is possible to catch up at another. There is a 'self-righting' tendency in many aspects of growth (Scarr and Kidd 1983). Although normal babies learn many social skills through vision, they are equipped for social learning through other senses if vision fails. While it is easiest to pick up language in early childhood, we can be taught much later, but with greater effort. The fact that learning and behavioural change can occur at all ages does not argue against sensitive periods in which we are especially ready for certain kinds of learning, for example to become attached to our parents, to acquire language, to learn the rules of society, to fall in love, with consequent profound and enduring changes in our being.

The maintenance of individual differences is biologically adaptive

If we were endlessly open to influence, if experiences had no indelible effects at all, individual differences of personality would be washed out. It can be argued that the maintenance of individual variability between people, through genetic inheritance (reinforced by marital choice), and through the enduring effects of organism-environment interchanges, protects the survival of our species. Individual differences guarantee that in a complex society there will be people equipped to fill many different social and work roles; individual differences also ensure that there will always be people ready to adapt to the transformations that occur over time in our natural and especially in our cultural environment.

Different processes contribute to maintain stability of personality and to preserve individual differences between people

A number of distinct processes combine to maintain a continuity of behavioural patterns in each one of us, sometimes even enhancing the differences between people. *Genetic predisposition*, which as we shall see affects especially our intellectual aptitudes and qualities of temperament, is one such process. *Transactional effects* between people also tend to maintain and reinforce the qualities of personality already present. Most, although not all, gifted children grow up in an environment which fosters their abilities. Less able children are often educationally disadvantaged too, and this can magnify their difficulties. Children who have lost parents early in life often become emotionally disturbed and this makes it hard, although again not impossible, for substitute parents to give affectionate, non-critical care. Then, too, there is the fact that for most of us *the family, the type of school, and the neighbourhood in which we grow up stay, if not the same, at least similar throughout our childhood*. The personalities of our parents influence us for much of our life; they respond to us repeatedly in similar ways, and this makes for continuity in our experiences and behaviour. Finally, and this is often ignored by researchers who place value only on objective phenomena, there are the memories we each have of our earlier selves, of the events and circumstances we experienced and of the thoughts and emotions we then had. While of course this *internal biography* is not fixed, and with increasing maturity and exposure to life we reinterpret our past history, nevertheless we each have within ourselves a firm thread of continuity of experience and sense of self which contributes to the enduring nature of our personality.

Chapter two

Intelligence and achievement

It is a curious fact that, as we move into the post-industrial era in which machines not only substitute for muscle but for brain power, and in which, while many of us can master the use of computers, only a minority of very clever people understand how they work, differences of intelligence between people are almost taboo and intelligence tests in disrepute. Yet, however much we may wish that we were all equally talented or at least almost equally so, we do not help children by denying that individual differences in ability exist, or by failing to recognize those children who are either exceptionally gifted or intellectually handicapped in some way.

This chapter does not aim to give an account of the varieties of mental handicap in childhood, nor of the many different types of specific educational retardation, their causes and management. Instead, the focus will be on more general aspects of intelligence and educational retardation as these impinge on and form a part of the developing personalities of children.

Even before their first birthday, babies enjoy their own competence in exploring the world, and throughout life intelligence and attainments are important sources of emotional satisfaction, linked inextricably with self-esteem. Ability and achievement can compensate emotionally and socially disadvantaged children. On the other hand, global or specific retardation of intellectual development is stressful; many less able children wish they were 'more brainy'; and there are often secondary emotional or behavioural difficulties.

A 6-year-old, for example, nice-looking and physically well developed, had been excluded from his second year at primary school because of violent outbursts and physical attacks on other children and his teacher. As part of an overall psychological assessment, his intelligence was tested and found to be equivalent to that of a 3½-year-old child. Transferred to a smaller class of slow learning children, he became a welcomed member of the group.

What is intelligence?

The concept of intelligence has defied definition in any uniformly acceptable way, and the tests to measure it are less than perfect. Yet an individual's capacity for thought and action and a child's rate of development compared with other children are notions which in practice we cannot do without. Although ability level is greatly influenced by learning and the exercise of skills, and changes with fluctuations in health and well-being, it is one of the most predictable aspects of behaviour. Ability level is not fixed, but it is a good deal more stable than affective-motivational components of personality, and much more easily recognized because it is measurable in terms of performance.

Every child at school knows, even if no one tells him so, whether he can accomplish the assignments of the class, whether he does so easily and well or whether he struggles with difficulties of comprehensio1 or execution, attempting to copy, but without success, what others do. Parents are aware from the start of their children's developmental progress, proud of an alert, attentive baby, who experiments with his limbs and with the things around him with engrossed inventiveness. They worry when language is slow to develop or comprehension lacking. All parents have standards of what children at different ages should be able to do based on their observations of other children and on what they hear or read about child development. Against these standards they measure their own offspring.

Intelligence tests

In 1904 the Ministry of Public Instruction of Paris appointed a commission to study the education of mentally subnormal children attending school. Binet and Simon accepted the task of finding ways of predicting school performance in Parisian children. They constructed a series of thirty tasks or problems thought to require imagery, memory, comprehension, judgement and reasoning. These tasks were chosen so that they could be understood and done by children without school experience, and they varied widely in difficulty. The first observation was that the performance on these tasks improved with age; the second that it correlated with school teachers' independent assessment of a child's intelligence and with his school grades. This was a measure of the *validity* of the tasks. Binet and Simon observed the percentage of correct answers given by children of different ages and they grouped together problems correctly solved by the average child, that is by 50 per cent of all tested children, aged 3; by the average child aged 4, and so forth. They had constructed the first *intelligence test* and they now proceeded to invent the concepts of *mental age* and *IQ*.

If a child passed all the tests an average eight-year-old can do but none of those tests the average nine-year-old can do, his mental age is 8. If his actual (chronological) age is also 8, then his intelligence quotient ($IQ = \frac{MA}{CA} \times 100\%$) is 100. If his chronological age is ten, his IQ is 80; if his chronological age is only 6, his IQ is 133 (Eysenck 1962).

As they grow up, children can do more and more difficult tasks. Their intelligence grows rapidly at first, more slowly after the age of 12 and reaches a peak at around 15. Intelligence declines gradually in early and middle adult life and more rapidly during senescence. After the age of 12 to 15 the definition of IQ as the ratio between mental and chronological age is no longer applicable. Instead a scale is constructed on the basis of the proportions of the population who can correctly perform tests of varying difficulty. An individual's IQ is thus measured against the performance of the population from which he comes.

The interpretation of a child's intelligence test results, just as the administration of the tests themselves, is a matter for experts. But it is important that everyone concerned with child development has some idea of the snags and complexities. No test is totally *reliable*. The best tests will vary by an average of 5 per cent from one measurement to another. When tests are closely spaced there is in addition a practice effect, so that the second result is likely to be a little higher. When children are tested at longer intervals their IQs vary, especially when the initial test was done in very early childhood. Although intelligence tests have predictive value, they actually measure current performance. Under the age of 5 their constancy, that is their capacity to predict future ability, is not high and under 6 months it is non-existent. This is in part due to individual differences in maturation rates, in part to different learning experiences children have, but in part it is due to the fact that intelligence tests do not measure any one global quality. They consist of problems which tap a variety of capacities some of which, e.g. language, the very young do not yet have at all (Rutter 1970).

Psychologists have identified *components of intelligence* which to some degree vary independently. Examples are verbal ability, numerical ability, spatial ability, perceptual ability, memory, inductive reasoning. Some 3-year-olds with excellent motor skills and a great deal of social competence have little language, and a few may never be as proficient in the use of words as in the rest of their performance. Others are relatively clumsy and poor at tasks requiring visuo-motor abilities while excellent linguistically. The tasks set by intelligence tests have been designed to tap abilities and not knowledge or skills acquired through education. But they are never totally free from educational bias, so that people not exposed to the same cultural influences as the population against which the test was calibrated, or *standardized*, are at a disadvantage.

The same principles on which intelligence tests were constructed were used later in devising *tests of school attainments*. These are measures of individual children's performance in, for example, reading, spelling, writing, and arithmetic, compared with the average attainments of children of different ages in the same cultural environment. The distinction between measures of educational attainments and intelligence is, as we shall see, very important from an educational point of view.

Is intelligence innate or acquired?

It is a truism that both heredity and environment contribute to individual differences in human intelligence. At a time of greater inequality of educational opportunity in Britain, Cyril Burt stressed the importance of intelligence tests so that bright children from disadvantaged homes could be singled out for better schooling (Burt 1946, 1975). Even today, socio-economically deprived including black children do not get the best out of their schooling, in part because of differential qualities of the schools themselves, in part because of adverse family and social environments. It is the more regrettable that intelligence tests are often deliberately abandoned because their results are thought to be stigmatizing.

The unpopularity of the idea that intelligence has a genetic basis rests on at least two misconceptions. The first is that genetic endowment imposes some kind of straitjacket on human potential and could spoil our efforts to create a better world. While it is true that genes set limits to what is possible, for example in physical growth and the development of intelligence, in practice the ceiling of our possibilities is rarely reached, and never for the community as a whole. Environmental improvements continue to be worthwhile. In Europe and America, for example, the growth of children of all ages accelerated steadily during the last century (although not before) as a result of nutritional and other health improvements (Tanner 1984). Second, it is held that genetic and constitutional disadvantages are inherently less treatable and their outlook less hopeful than conditions caused by life events or circumstances. This is not so. Although we know a great deal about the personality deficits resulting from nutritional, emotional and educational privations in early childhood, and this has little to do with genetics, we have not yet discovered how to guarantee that such privations are prevented or compensated for. Nor are we good at helping parents to manage their relationships with each other better, although we know that parental discord does children harm. Yet all babies are now tested at birth for the presence of phenylketonuria, a genetic inborn error of metabolism causing mental handicap, because early treatment with a special diet effectively prevents the loss of intelligence.

The tested intelligence quotients of a population, like its height, fall along what is called a 'normal' curve; that is, most people have an average or mean score and decreasing proportions of the population have scores increasingly different from this mean. All characteristics with such a distribution in the population are known to be due to multiple causes and, if genetically determined, to multigenic inheritance. Apart from cases of severe mental handicap, brought about by single gene or chromosome abnormalities (such as phenylketonuria, Down's syndrome and Fragile X chromosome abnormality), or by early brain damage or disease, most deviations of intelligence whether handicapping or contributing to giftedness are attributable to polygenic inheritance in interaction with environmental opportunities.

The genetic basis for variability in intelligence has been studied by comparing the measured intelligence of biologically related people, especially monozygotic and dizygotic twins, ordinary brothers and sisters, and parents and children. Such studies have shown that the closer the biological relationship between relatives, that is the more similar their genetic make-up, the closer they were also in tested intelligence. Adoption studies, in which the intelligence of children could be compared with their birth parents who did not bring them up and with their adoptive parents who did, have consistently demonstrated greater similarities of tested intelligence between children and their biological parents (Henderson 1982; Plomin *et al.* 1980).

All such studies have, despite their often vociferous detractors, revealed a significant contribution of heredity to intelligence. But how much individual differences within a population are due to heredity and how much to environmental effects is not yet certain. What is more, this ratio will vary from society to society and from time to time, depending on the prevailing culture. When educational opportunities are poor or inequably distributed, variations in intelligence will depend more on environmental opportunities, that is on access to educational experiences. When opportunities for the intellectual development of children are generally good and accessible to all, individual differences in intelligence will, on the contrary, be more dependent on genetic factors. Moreover, estimates of the relative contributions to such individual differences of heredity and environment tell one little about their influence on the intellectual development of the individual child.

In an excellent review paper Michael Rutter argues that within a normal environment, environmental effects on IQ are modest (Rutter 1985). Only under conditions of extreme disadvantage, such as occasionally occur when children of grossly abnormal parents are hidden away and reared for many childhood years with a minimum of human contact, or under conditions of national disaster such as famine and migration, is the intelligence of children depressed by environment causes. Much of the supposed relationship found between children's intelligence and the qualities of their unbringing may be spurious because, as we saw in the last chapter, the environment in which children are brought up reflects in large measure the intelligence of their parents. As Rutter says, one has to consider the possibility that the apparent psycho-social influences on intelligence are in fact genetically determined.

A recent series of studies, relating aspects of the home environment to intellectual competence in the first five years of life, has shown the parents' own educational level and the mothers' tested intelligence to be strongly related to the children's tested abilities from the age of 18 months onwards, but certain qualities of the home environment, especially the variety of stimulating experiences, made an independent contribution (Gottfried 1984).

One other issue, painful for those who wish for an egalitarian society, has to be faced. Intellectually less able people tend on the whole to get less well paid jobs or, when unemployment rates are high, no jobs at all. Assortative mating has the effect of enabling brighter children of intellectually dull parents to marry more intelligent partners and move out of their socio-economically more deprived subculture. Less able children on the other hand tend to find similar partners and to remain socio-economically disadvantaged. This means that, under conditions of social inequality, the resources they have for providing an intellectually rewarding environment for their children are more limited, as is their access to good schooling. In a society with large income differentials and increasing constraints on public spending on education and other freely available high-standard services for children, class-related differentials of material resources are magnified, and this will reinforce the developmental disadvantages of children of intellectually less able parents.

Ethnic origin, intelligence and school performance

Arguments against the use of intelligence tests for children and against the notion of a genetic basis for intelligence sprang up as a reaction to the ideas of Jensen, first published in 1969, that American Black children had genetically determined lower IQs than Whites, that there were ethnic differences in intelligence, and that the educational sights for underfunctioning Black children should be lowered (Jensen 1980). While there is no inherent reason why different ethnic groups should not for genetic reasons have different types of intellectual capacities, just as their appearance is so obviously varied, Jensen's explanations for the difference in intelligence between American Blacks and Whites are limited and he deliberately excluded from his calculations the possible effects of intermarriage on the IQ of Black Americans (Jensen 1981). The late Jack Tizard argued cogently that we cannot draw conclusions about the extent to which genetic differences contribute to observed differences between cultural groups growing up in different environments (Tizard 1975).

Some studies have in fact found intellectual and educational differences between ethnic groups. Asian children have higher IQs than American White children; and a recent study of Japanese, Chinese and White American children tested in their own countries showed that when IQ was held constant, Japanese children in senior school performed better at mathematics and science than the other two groups. Whether teaching in Japanese schools was more effective or whether the students were especially gifted in mathematics and science is not known. The fact that Chinese children were found to be especially poor verbally in their early school years compared with the other two groups was attributed to less encouragement for young Chinese children to speak and express their views (Stevenson *et al.* 1985).

Intelligence, educational failure, and disturbed personality development

Rutter and his colleagues in their population studies on the Isle of Wight (Rutter *et al*. 1970) and in inner London (Rutter *et al*. 1975) were the first to reveal the important relationships between intelligence, school performance, and mental health in childhood. Children with low intelligence were about four times as likely to be disturbed as normally intelligent children, their disturbance could take the form of emotional or antisocial behaviour, and boys and girls were equally at risk. In contrast, children whose intelligence was average or above but who were educationally retarded, that is whose attainment tests showed them to be functioning below what was expected at their age and IQ level, were mainly boys and their associated disturbance was most often a conduct disorder. Around 4 per cent of 10 to 11-year-old children on the Isle of Wight were conduct disordered, and about 4 per cent had serious reading retardation. But fully one-third of retarded readers were conduct disordered, and one-third of conduct-disordered children were retarded readers.

While most often educational failure was but one factor contributing to an antisocial development, and while other features of the antisocial child could have contributed to educational failure, nevertheless there is some evidence, especially from the intervention studies we will shortly describe, that school failure itself can contribute to antisocial conduct in childhood and to personality disorder in later life.

Childhood conduct disorder is one of the most worrying childhood disturbances. It is common and, when serious, frequently persists into adult life as personality disorder and delinquency (Robins 1966). While there are many causal strands within the child and his or her life experience within the family and neighbourhood which interact with school performance and experience to bring such a development about, there is also now abundant evidence that educational retardation can to some extent be prevented and that, if this is achieved, the risk of later antisocial personality disorder may be reduced.

The protective value of educational success

The early British longitudinal studies of a national cohort of children documented how social and educational processes reinforced the educational disadvantages of socio-economically deprived children so that the school performance of such children declined progressively compared with that of children of the same levels of intelligence who came from more advantaged backgrounds (Douglas 1964; Douglas *et al.* 1968). Poor children, especially boys, were perceived by their teachers as less able and as less well behaved than they actually were; and streaming in schools, whereby the less successful were taught separately from the more successful, had a discouraging effect on the poor performers. Subsequently, in an important schools' study to which we will return, Rutter and his colleagues showed that in schools with very high concentrations of less able, more disturbed, and socially disadvantaged children, such children made less educational and social progress than in schools where they formed a minority (Rutter *et al.* 1979).

Contemporaneously with the first longitudinal study of a national cohort of British children, Americans became concerned with the progressive school failure of socially disadvantaged black city children. Numerous Headstart Programs were initiated in the 1960s for pre-school children to prevent such a decline. The underlying ideas were that black American toddlers growing up in poor and crowded families were understimulated in an intellectually barren home environment so that they arrived at school with poor verbal skills. It was thought that their tested intelligence on school entry was depressed by their upbringing, and because of this they could not benefit from their classroom experiences. Moreover, their intellectual performance declined progressively with increasing years at school. The special programmes were varied and some did not succeed at all. But others, especially when they placed emphasis on encouraging children's language, and involved mothers in home-based programmes, did fulfil the researchers' initial aim to boost the children's IQ: children in the programmes had higher IQs on school entry than controls, although the test results of both groups before the intervention had been the same.

Some years later there was much disappointment because the IQ gains disappeared over time once the special programmes ceased (Bronfenbrenner 1974). More recently this gloom has lifted with a further detailed reassessment in later life of children who had taken part in the Perry Preschool Program in Ypsilanti, Michigan. The children's tested IQs in later school years were no different from those of controls who had not been in the special programme. But their work achievements continued to be better, as was their teachers' assessment of their work and behaviour, the children's motivation, and even their social conduct. Fewer of these children had to repeat a school year, fewer were in special classes, and fewer became delinquent in their early teens (Berrueta-Clement *et al*. 1984; for a summary, see also Farrington 1985). What could explain such effects? It is likely that the temporary boost in IQ on school entry had made the children more self-confident about their work and that this in turn induced their teachers to expect future success. A chain reaction of mutually reinforcing classroom transactions between successful children and approving and encouraging teachers then promoted further more confident educational progress than that achieved by children who had not had the benefit of intensive preschool education. Michael Rutter suggests that the first teacher a child encounters at school can similarly, through her attitudes and expectations, tip the balance between indifferent school progress and confidence and success in later school years (Rutter 1985).

An intimate study of the conversations of middle- and working-class 4-year-olds at home and at school has shed further light on the possible underlying processes which determine the progress of young children at school in Britain (Tizard and Hughes 1984). Only girls were studied. Differences were found in the measured IQ of the two groups of children and in the styles, but not in the numbers and lengths of their conversations with their mothers at home. Working-class girls used language for less complex purposes, asked fewer 'curiosity' questions of their mothers and engaged in fewer 'passages of intellectual search'. Working-class girls were also more often in dispute with their mothers. More striking, however, were the very different language behaviours observed between the two groups of children in the nursery school setting. Here middle-class girls found familiar toys and furnishings and teachers who spoke rather like their own mothers. This was not so for the working-class girls, often warned by their mothers beforehand to behave well and obey their teachers. While the middle-class children were surprisingly assertive with their teachers, the working-class girls were subdued in the nursery setting and presented themselves as more immature than they were observed to be at home. Teachers in turn clearly underestimated these children's capacities, responded to them with less complex linguistic statements, and made fewer linguistic demands on them.

It may well be that the successful Headstart Programs had helped in part by overcoming some of the class barriers between socio-economically disadvantaged children and primary school teachers, enabling the children to present themselves at school more confidently and with fewer social and linguistic constraints.

The effect of positive school experiences, especially for disadvantaged children, can be profound. A small piece of evidence for a protective effect on later personality functioning comes from Quinton and Rutter's (1988) study of the adult adjustment of girls who had spent long years of their childhood in children's homes. Compared with women matched for age and social background who had not had such disruptive and depriving childhood experiences, the women who had been in care much more often made early marriages to equally deprived and disturbed young men after very short acquaintances. They had their children younger, often lost their partners, and were more often unable to care for their children consistently and well. More of them also showed other features of personality disorder at follow-up. But not all had such a poor outcome. Some of the women, although brought up in care, had married supportive and stable husbands. When this had happened their adult adjustment, including the care of their children, was good. The important further finding was that a happy marriage was neither a coincidence nor a mere reflection of a girl's lesser emotional disturbance. Instead, it was related to her having had positive school experiences. While in this disadvantaged group of girls such rewarding memories were only rarely associated with high educational achievements, they were related to their teachers' acknowledgements of hard work or of competence in sport or artistic endeavours, as well as to happy relationships with other children. All such positive school experiences, thought to foster self-esteem and confidence in one's own capacity to influence one's life, had evidently compensated some of the girls in this study for the potentially harmful years spent amid family strife and in children's homes, and contributed to their effective marital choice.

What causes educational retardation?

When children's school achievements fail to match up to the competence expected for their age and IQ, two sometimes interacting groups of causes are usually responsible: those associated with the socio-emotional environment, and specific, constitutional developmental delays.

The first group of contributory factors include the child's social class of origin with its particular values and constraints vis-à-vis a more middle-class school setting; the more limited material resources at home in terms of space, books and play objects; larger family size with constraints on the time parents can spend in intimate interactions with each of their children; the greater emphasis on out-door play and rough and tumble rather than on quiet, constructive activities. Such influences, as Tizard and Hughes have shown (Tizard and Hughes 1984), determine a child's presentation of self at school and in turn the teacher's evaluation of and reactions to the child. But in economically deprived sections of society the levels of medical and social pathology are also high, with profound effects on the children. Even brief hospital admissions, if repeated, can lead to educational failure (Rutter *et al*. 1970), especially in mathematics, when children miss crucial lessons and are not helped to catch up. Frequent moves of school and changes of teaching methods also unsettle learning. And the anxieties brought about by family illness, discord, and disruption can effectively prevent children from getting the best out of their schooling. Then, too, the quality of the schools themselves are often worse in urban-deteriorating areas, with high pupil and teacher turn over (Rutter *et al*. 1975) and low educational standards.

The second group of constraints and causes include specific developmental delays, for example in language and language-related skills; in motor or perceptual functions; and in mathematical abilities. Such developmental delays always affect more boys than girls; they are often multiple; and may be accompanied by delays in achieving bladder and bowel control. Frequently a child slow to start to speak, and slower still to speak clearly, arrives at school fluent and clear but then turns out to have difficulty in learning to read or spell. Often developmental delays run in families; occasionally they are associated with evidence of birth injury; and sometimes with unusual, either hyperkinetic or schizoid, patterns of temperament to be described in the next chapter.

A recent study of the intelligence and attainments of 104 pairs of monozygotic twins and 118 pairs of same-sex dizygotic twins (Stevenson *et al*. 1987) showed, as before, a significant heritability of IQ and of educational retardation. But, in this study of children all aged 13 years, the heritability of spelling retardation was much greater than that of IQ or specific reading difficulty. Environmental influences, especially in the twins' *common environment* (that is, the environmental differences of social class, schooling, parent interest in education, etc., that differentiate *between families*), played a considerable part in the causation of individual differences in reading and IQ at this age. *Specific environmental influences* (that is, environmental differences between individual children within families, such as birth injury, illness, relationships with teachers, etc.) had the greatest effect on individual differences in reading skill rather than IQ or spelling. An interesting finding was that heritability of IQ and of reading retardation was reduced at very low levels of IQ and reading skill, suggesting that environmental factors, perhaps involving brain damage, were now the most important. The main conclusions of this study were that there is no blanket effect on all literacy-related difficulties and that by the age of 13 genetic factors are no longer the major cause of reading retardation, but do contribute greatly to spelling difficulties.

Specific educational delays are always frustrating for the children themselves and, unless recognized, also for their parents and teachers. Their effect on later personality however will vary according to the events and circumstances in the young person's life and his or her temperament.

Andrew, of superior intelligence, had a serious and at first unrecognized specific developmental delay in reading and spelling, a disability which had ruined his mother's school life. He was referred to a child psychiatrist at 8 because of constant complaints by his teacher about his work. He was anxious, unhappy, isolated, and teased at school. He was an only child and both parents were ill. The mother, with recurrent depressions, developed a drink problem, and at one stage the father too became profoundly depressed, made a serious suicide attempt, and nearly died. At 12, Andrew transferred to a residential school for maladjusted children both to give him distance from the family upheavals and to provide the individually-geared remedial education he needed. He now began to make friends, worked well but, not surprisingly, never quite fulfilled his intellectual potential. At 17 he reported that he thought what had helped him was to get away from the family upsets. Meanwhile the mother, with treatment, had stopped drinking and the father remained well. Andrew continued to be a poor speller, but he had become a skilled underwater diver and had recently made his first solo flight. He had plans to work abroad in a children's holiday camp. In his early 20s he qualified in dentistry and married. Although his personality development had been at risk because of the psychiatric disorders of both parents and his own serious educational retardation, the positive factors in his life were his parents' unfailing affection for him despite their own troubles, and his easy temperament: he had a sunny disposition and a placid, rather quiet nature; always ready for adventure, he adapted to new circumstances easily.

A 7-year-old, Michael, living alone with his mother, was referred because of refusal to go to school. His IQ was 163. He was extremely articulate in conversation but his reading age was just 7, he could barely write or spell, and his drawings were immature even for his chronological age. He reported having had sad feelings, especially in the mornings, for some weeks. He also complained of headaches: 'I get an unusual feeling, a sensation you get before you're sick. It comes on suddenly.' About his school work he said 'My brain went flying and my hand was left behind.' His library books were about science and science fiction. He found school boring: 'The only improvement that could be made is a more advanced teacher.' He reported other children to have different interests from his own: 'I have a different brain, I'd say (and) I don't play many games. I'm not a good runner. I'm short for my age and I'm definitely overweight.' He *was* obese, and also placid and rather detached in temperament.

He had been born by Caesarian section for fetal distress, and this may have accounted for the developmental delays in his case. The parents, now separated, were of superior intelligence, especially his father. The father also had unusual personality features: he was emotionally detached, unempathic, occasionally paranoid and highly litigious during subsequent divorce proceedings. The mother was subject to recurrent depression, but she was exceptionally imaginative about augmenting her son's rather unsatisfactory experiences as a gifted boy who was failing educationally in his ordinary primary school. He continued to have depressive episodes with non-attendance at school.

At 8 he declared a special interest in chemistry and physics; his mother had established a regular friendship for him with the curator of the local museum; and Michael reported playing with children up to 13 and 14-years-old. He told the children he learnt more at home than at school and this did not go down well with the teacher when she came to hear of it. She felt the boy was deliberately asking her difficult questions to attract attention.

At 10 Michael transferred to a small school catering for a mixed age group of children with varied abilities, all working at their own level on individual programmes with much teacher assistance. Michael described the school as 'great' and said he was 'never bored for a minute'.

By 11, with hardly a day off school during the preceding year, his reading age had risen to 17 years, in keeping with his current verbal ability. His arithmetic age was 14½, but his spelling still only at a 9-year-old level, and his writing very poor. Good teaching had clearly helped to advance his reading and mathematical skills. The spelling difficulty, as would have been predicted from the work of Stevenson *et al.* (1987) (see p. 30), was less open to environmental influence. He was, however, now able to put his ideas on paper and felt generally less frustrated. A home computer also helped a great deal.

Yet, as a group, children of superior intelligence are not more likely than others to have educational or emotional problems: the reverse. Lewis Terman (Terman and Oden 1959) in his classical thirty-five-year follow-up of gifted children found these to be healthier, physically more advanced in childhood, and with fewer emotional and behavioural difficulties than less intelligent children. They had wider interests in sports and the arts, as well as in purely intellectual pursuits, and they remained fitter and better adjusted well into middle age.

Joan Freeman more recently studied children whose parents had joined the National Association for Gifted Children (Freeman 1983). She compared these children with classmates of similarly high intelligence whose parents had not joined this organization, and with children of average abilities. She found a slight excess of behavioural and emotional difficulties in the first group but none in the second in comparison with the children of average ability. It seems that when there are problems parents, understandably, are more likely to join an organization which may be able to help them. But intellectually gifted children as a group are not especially prone to become disturbed. When they do, they need a careful educational assessment. An improvement in the school setting often helps such children even when, as the two boys described above illustrate, there are other important causes for their difficulties either within themselves or their families. Freeman points to the interesting fact that fewer girls tend to be selected as 'gifted', although there are no sex differences in intelligence; and she also stresses that, just as among children with more limited abilities, gifted boys are more prone than gifted girls to be underachieving.

Very high intelligence is not the only form of giftedness which may need special educational consideration.

A 14-year-old, Anna, was on the point of suspension from school. After a long period of minor misbehaviour she had incited her friends to throw flour and eggs at the school staff during an end-of-term ceremony. She was of just average intelligence with modest attainments, and her teachers thought her own musical aspirations and her parents' pride in her piano-playing altogether excessive. A psychiatric referral followed an episode when, together with another girl, Anna was rescued by her family from a banana boat about to leave for the West Indies. She was then an open, friendly, plump and somewhat impulsive girl with very poor self-esteem, a rather distant relationship with her more intellectual parents, and a definite love of music. The parents exerted themselves to find the resources to get her into a music school and there, after some initial turbulence, she did extremely well, becoming a competent instrumentalist. Her psychiatric troubles did not return; she worked well at her music, married and remained on good terms with her parents.

In each of the illustrative cases, the child's temperament influenced outcome in an important way. To this topic the next chapter is addressed.

Chapter three

Temperament

Temperament, body build, and disease

Behavioural style has long been linked to body build and susceptibility to illness. Hippocrates (460–377 BC), the father of medicine, associated a short, thick body type, the *Habitus apoplecticus*, with liability to heart disease; and a long, thin body type, the *Habitus pthisicus*, with respiratory illness. Galen (201–130 BC) evolved a classification of both physical and personality types related to disease pictures (Ackerknecht 1968). For several hundred years medicine was ruled by the theory of the four humours or body juices and their relation to four temperaments: the sanguine, choleric, melancholic, and phlegmatic.

The correlation of body measurements with the disorders of mental hospital patients led Kretschmer to develop his ideas of three types of physique and temperament, two of these to be found in patients with two specific forms of mental illness. People of lean and slender build, *asthenics*, predominated among schizophrenic patients and had often had *schizoid personality* traits before their illness. Kretschmer describes the schizoid personality type vividly (Kretschmer 1925:146–7):

> Schizoid men have a surface and a depth. Cuttingly brutal, dull and sulky, bitingly sarcastic, or timidly retiring, like a mollusc without a shell — that is the surface. Or else the surface is just nothing; we see a man who stands in our way like a question mark, we feel that we are in contact with something flavourless, boring and yet with a certain problematic taste about it. . . There are schizoid men, with whom one can live for ten years, and yet we may not say for certain that we know them. A shy girl, pious and lamblike serves for months in the town: she is gentle and tractable with everyone. One morning

the three children of the house lie murdered. The house is in flames. She has not lost her senses, she understands everything. She smiles uncertainly when she realises her act. A young man dreams away the lonely days of his youth. He is so clumsy and loutish that one could shake him. If he is set upon a horse he falls off at once. He smiles in an embarrassed way, rather ironical. He says nothing. One day there appears a volume of poetry he has written; exquisite feeling for nature; and every blow, that some fat lout has given him as he passed by is moulded into an inner tragedy; and the polished rhythms flow on full of quiet.

Thick and stocky people, *pyknics*, Kretschmer held to be commoner among patients with manic-depressive psychoses and a pre-illness *cycloid temperament* of friendly, trustful sociability, full of practical good sense, associated with swings of mood from depression to elation. Associations of types of body build and temperament were later confirmed in normal people without psychotic illnesses (Sheldon 1942).

Dimensions of personality

Much work has been done on devising reliable and valid questionnaire measures of different persisting personality traits and, by means of intercorrelations of such traits in a population, discovering *dimensions of personality*. The hope has been that an individual's score on such dimensions would then meaningfully describe important aspects of his or her personality. Some dimensions, like extraversion, introversion and neuroticism (Eysenck 1967), are very general, while others, perhaps of more clinical relevance, are more specific, for example schizoidness or 'schizotypy' (Claridge 1985). Two assumptions underlie much of this work: first, that there is a biological basis for these characteristics; and second, that they are normal variations occurring to a greater or lesser degree in everyone. We must be clear that, while certain mental illnesses may be specifically associated with certain types of pre-illness temperament, this tells us nothing about the risk for later illness carried by these personality features. It may be very small.

Broad dimensions of temperament or constitutional type have contributed to the understanding of aspects of adult personality and pathology. So far they have not been especially helpful in illuminating the disorders of children. But the tracing of narrower aspects of childhood reactivity has been very fruitful indeed. In a recent discussion of temperament, personality and personality disorder, Rutter suggests that the term temperament should be used to describe a rather limited number of simple, non-motivational, non-cognitive, stylistic features (Rutter 1987). Of these, emotionality, activity level, and sociability have so far been best substantiated, and may yet be found to have a quite specific neurobiological basis.

The New York Longitudinal Study

A landmark of research on temperament in childhood is the New York Longitudinal Study (Thomas *et al.* 1963; Chess and Thomas 1984). It arose from the observations that even at birth one baby is different from another and retains his or her characteristics at least for some time. The New York researchers accumulated detailed descriptions from mothers of their children's daily activities at regular intervals. The children came from a homogeneous middle-class background to reduce differences between them due to variations in their life circumstances.

A content analysis on the first batch of descriptive protocols led to the definitions of nine categories of reactivity which could be reliably rated by independent raters. These were: level of motor activity, intensity of response, sensitivity to stimuli (threshold), mood (whether predominantly positive or negative), approach or withdrawal in novel situation, adaptability, rhythmicity (regularity of the biological functions of sleeping, eating, elimination), persistence (in the face of frustration), and distractibility. Behavioural observations of the same children in a standard situation when recorded and similarly rated agreed well with the mothers' reports. While children differed from each other in their scores on these characteristics, each child's profile maintained some constancy, especially from the age of 3 onwards (McDevitt 1986).

By the time the children were 7, a number had developed emotional or behavioural difficulties and it was then possible to look back and see whether these disturbed children had been different in their responses at the age of 3 from those who remained well adjusted. Statistically significant differences were indeed found and led to the idea that some children are harder to bring up than others because of qualities of temperament present so early in life that they are likely to be constitutional. These were a predominantly negative mood, intense responses, irregular biological functioning, and slow adaptability (Rutter *et al.* 1964). Although the profiles of temperament did not remain totally stable, children changing in personality in response to their life experiences,

37

nevertheless these particular early characteristics had clearly initiated transactional patterns between some children and their parents which fostered the later development of problem behaviour. Subsequent twin studies have found greater similarities between monozygotic and dizygotic twins for activity level, sociability and impulsivity in childhood, and also for neuroticism and extraversion, supporting the notion of a genetic contribution to temperament (Scarr and Kidd 1983).

The 133 children of the New York Longitudinal Study have now been followed up for over twenty years (Chess and Thomas 1984) and their adjustment in young adult life compared with their early childhood characteristics and circumstances. Three temperamental constellations were statisically derived from scores on the nine categories at the age of 3 years: 48 per cent of the sample were *easy* children, regular, with positive approach, adaptable, mild in intensity, and largely positive in mood; 10 per cent had a *difficult child syndrome*, being irregular, withdrawing from novelty, non-adaptable, and with intense reactions and negative mood; 15 per cent, with a combination of withdrawal from novelty but mild intensity, slow adaption, but regularity of biological functions, were called *slow-to-warm-up*.

Both ratings of 'difficult/easy' temperament and of global adjustment at 3 years (which correlated with each other) predicted adult adjustment and temperamental style. Conflict between the parents at 3 also predicted a poor adult adjustment and was more powerfully harmful than a difficult temperament. The authors, imaginatively, looked at the exceptions to the rule. What, they asked themselves, had protected high-risk children, that is those with a difficult child syndrome and parental conflict at 3 years, from a poor adult outcome; and what factors were associated with a poor outcome for children reared in harmonious homes and without temperamental difficulties? A successful adult outcome for high-risk children was associated with work success in adolescence, with the development of a special gift or career commitment, with distancing of the young person from the inappropriate demands of his or her parents, and with a positive relationship with someone outside the family. A poor outcome for low-risk children was found when these children had had a definite constitutional impairment such as brain damage or recurrent depressive illnesses.

On the whole women did better than men, and those families offered guidance for childhood psychiatric disorders of the children did better when the main contributing factor had been the child's difficult temperament rather than conflict between parents. Chess and Thomas stress the impact on children's development of life events and circumstances, such as discord between parents, the death of a father, a good relationship with someone outside the family, the development of a gift or talent; and they acknowledge the significance of the child's inner life in making sense of his or her experiences and influencing his or her life choices.

The New York Longitudinal Study emphasises the importance of a transactional view of child development. Childhood behaviour disorders and adult maladjustment are seen as the outcome of a poor fit between a child's temperament and other constitutional attributes on the one hand, and the expectations and demands of his or her environment, especially the parents, on the other.

In their observational studies of young children at home and in the nursery school, Stevenson-Hinde and Hinde have clearly demonstrated the reality of such transactions (Stevenson-Hinde and Hinde 1986). They differ at different ages, and for boys and girls, and are in part determined by the social expectations of the wider culture. A negative mood in 50-month-old boys, for example, is correlated with having a more irritable mother and with more hostility on the part of the nursery teacher. At this age high ratings of shyness in girls are associated with frequent, warm interactions with mothers at home, but with infrequent, although not hostile, social contacts with teachers and other children at school. High activity levels in girls, especially when associated with a negative mood, evokes more hostile responses. In contrast, 50-month-old boys when excessively shy elicit more negative interactions from both parents, from siblings, teachers and peers. Some mothers complain that by that age their sons should have outgrown their shyness, regarded by these mothers as a feminine characteristic. High activity levels in boys were approved of by fathers although, as in girls, negatively responded to by mothers.

Behavioural style in childhood is individual but there are also important differences between children of different ages, from different cultures, and between boys and girls. Some differences are biologically based, but it is often difficult to disentangle these from personality attributes due to social expectations, that is to the different responses boys and girls at different ages and in different cultures elicit from other people. Nevertheless, we take it for granted that the baby quivers as he gropes uncertainly to explore his surroundings, that smiles appear slowly and he is easily startled; that the toddler's attention span is short and his impulse control limited; that children in middle childhood have boundless energy; and that adolescents are labile in mood.

Biological factors contribute to cultural difference in temperament

The way a society brings up its children helps to fit them into the social world that awaits them in adult life, and which they in turn will influence. But there is evidence, too, that the pressures of child rearing do not act on a universal infant. Children from different ethnic groups are born with constitutionally different temperaments. American Chinese and American White babies, for example, within a few days of birth react differently to minor frustrations. Chinese babies calmly tolerate having their face covered with a cloth or being laid flat down on their faces, while Caucasian babies are observed to squirm and struggle more, rapidly dislodging the cloth or turning their face to the side. This difference in what has also been called 'inhibition' between Chinese and Caucasian babies has been confirmed in a longitudinal study in which Chinese and White American children were observed in standard situations at intervals between 4 and 29 months (Kagan *et al.* 1986).

Oriental stoicism has been observed also in Japanese infants and in Navaho Indian babies (Freedman 1979). It may well contribute to the methods of child rearing, to adult personality and even to the socio-political arrangements within these cultures. In contrast, African and Black American babies are more motorically active and also more advanced in motor development than White or Asian babies, even when only a few days old. Like Australian Aborigines they can lift their heads and look about them after birth, skills not attained by other infants until they are a month old.

Sex differences in temperament

Sex differences in temperament have also been described in infancy (Hutt 1972), girls being more sensitive and boys more active, more vigorous and more impulsive. Manning and her colleagues demonstrated sex differences in styles of aggressive behaviour in nursery children, 3-year-old boys engaging in more rough and tumble play aggression than girls (Manning *et al.* 1977). Increased aggressiveness in the male has also been found in animals and it is known that female animals can be made more aggressive artificially by injecting their mothers with male hormones during pregnancy.

Recent work has shed further light on the effects on later behaviour of levels of sex hormones in children's pre-birth environment. Gender identity, that is which sex the person believes herself or himself to be, depends on assigned sex, that is, on whether children are being brought up as girls or boys. Pre-natal levels of male hormones have no effect. Gender-role behaviour on the other hand, that is play and imitative behaviour in which girls and boys differ from each other, are affected by pre-birth male sex hormone levels (Meyer-Bahlburg *et al*. 1986).

Temperamental differences between boys and girls influence their interactions with other people and with their inanimate world. Transformed by life experiences, especially in childhood and adolescence, they contribute to adult personality. In childhood sex differences in temperament also contribute to problem behaviour: aggression and acting-out behaviour predominate among disturbed boys; anxiety, inhibition, and depression among disturbed girls.

Constitutional determinants of problem behaviour and personality disorder

Aggression

Excessive aggression is one of the most worrying childhood disturbances. Boys are more often affected than girls; the behaviour tends to persist over time; it evokes coercive responses from others that often serve to reinforce it; and it is frequently a forerunner of delinquency and antisocial personality disorders. While the causes for such developments, to be described in later chapters, are multiple and largely environmental, several studies have pointed to constitutional predispositions too, and these will here be briefly mentioned.

Both twin and adoption studies support a genetic contribution to delinquency (Mednick *et al*. 1986). More recently, high levels of male sex hormones in the blood have been found in adolescent boys to correlate with self-reports of verbal and physical aggression, especially in response to provocation and threat, and with a low frustration tolerance (Olweus 1986). Male sex hormones may act by stimulating increased muscularity and athleticism, distinguishing features of delinquent boys noted long ago by Sheldon and Eleanor Glueck, the veterans of research into juvenile delinquency (Glueck and Glueck 1950). The greater susceptibility of motorically very active boys to develop aggressive behaviour in response to their social experiences in a nursery setting when compared with more passive boys (Patterson *et al*. 1967) may be one intervening step in this association. In addition, extraversion with low arousal and a constant need for thrills, as well as lack of impulse control, are thought to foster aggressive and delinquent risk-taking behaviour (Olweus 1986).

Hyperkinesis

The rare and much debated syndrome of *hyperkinesis* (Taylor 1986) is mentioned here, not because it is regarded as a variant of temperament, as are the more commonly identified traits of hyperactivity, but because there is evidence that it is constitutionally based rather than a response to adversity, and because its effects on later personality development are long-lasting. It is often accompanied by intellectual retardation, by specific developmental delays, by mild neurological abnormalities, and sometimes by isolated schizoid personality traits. It is commoner in boys than girls, and identified by UK clinicians in fewer than 1 per cent of children in the general population. Its main features are pervasive disinhibited and poorly organized overactivity in all settings, short attention span, distractability, and impulsivity.

The more commonly recognised traits of *hyperactivity*, in contrast, consist of unfocused overactivity, distractability, and short attention span, often situationally determined. Both hyperkinesis and hyperactivity are frequently associated with aggressive and antisocial behaviour.

While the clinical management of children with these two groups of difficulties is different, the actual overactivity, distractability, and poor attention span they have in common may well respond to drug treatment.

Mary, the second child of professional parents, had been clumsy since a toddler. Speech was early but always slurred. From the age of 3 she was overactive in all settings, with poor concentration and attention. In an ordinary primary school she stood out because of her restless inability to settle down to any task. She wandered about the classroom, apparently unconcerned at reprimands. She scratched and punched other children, she swore at them, and occasionally took their sweets. She was of average tested intelligence but by 8 years, while only mildly retarded in reading, had barely made a start in spelling, and her pencil and paper skills were poor. Medical examination revealed definite neurological signs of brain damage, presumably sustained at birth.

Mary was expressionless and emotionally detached. Her interview responses were mechanical and she voiced no worries or miseries other than that she would prefer short hair to her ponytail. She was insensitive to social cues, unable to empathize accurately with the feelings of others, and she managed her social relationships according to the 'rules' her mother had taught her. The mother reported improvement of Mary's restlessness with age, and her own relief to have the child's difficulties attributed to a neurological defect: 'It's made a difference knowing there is a cause and [that it's] not just awkwardness.'

Mary transferred to a special school where, in a small class, a remedial teaching programme was started. She began to make friends, enjoyed regular 'speech and drama' classes, and her behaviour improved but, by the age of 10, her attainments in spelling and arithmetic were still only those of a 7-year-old. Anti-hyperkinetic medication, methyl phenydate, improved her restless distractibility and impulsiveness. By 13, she was quiet and shy, happy and well accepted by other children but still emotionally detached. She remained poorly co-ordinated, and with impaired concentration. Difficulties in spelling and arithmetic persisted. But her speech was now clear, and she had become a great reader and a passionate cook.

On leaving school Mary joined a special training centre for young people run on Rudolf Steiner lines. There she continued with schoolwork, worked in the centre's shop and attended a further education college for cookery classes. By 18, she had developed considerable social poise. She was now off medication and no longer overactive. Three years later she had moved into a flat with a friend and was working voluntarily in a bakery. Her parents, still surprised at her competent independence, maintained a non-intrusive but supportive watch on progress.

Not all hyperkinetic children do so well. Under conditions of family strife or socio-economic disadvantage, hyperkinetic children, especially boys, are at increased risk of becoming conduct disordered and of an antisocial development of personality in later life (Weiss *et al*. 1985).

In the course of a follow-up study, Mr Alec Sikowsky, now 26, was interviewed in prison. His story illustrates the importance of childhood data for making sense of adult personality disorders, in this case, sociopathy. It is not good enough to label antisocial people as criminal. This moral category excludes them from the social group and denies them the empathic understanding that could ensure, if not cure and release from prison, at least a life in more decent conditions than currently exist.

Alec was first seen at 9 because of uncontrollable temper outbursts at school during which he shouted obscenities. The episodes, which never occurred at home, were always followed by remorse. Neurological examination showed mild but definite abnormalities, including an abnormal EEG, a marked tremor and over-brisk reflexes. He, too, had had a developmental speech delay and psychological testing showed him to be of low normal overall intelligence with serious educational retardation in reading, spelling and arithmetic, so that schoolwork caused much frustration. His birth and developmental milestones had been normal, but he had always been clumsy and overactive, with a poor attention span. His school failure aroused not only frustration but a paranoid feeling that the teachers picked on him and other children teased him: 'One of the boys annoys me. He blows his nose and the stuff runs and he comes after you with it in a hanky and wipes it on people. . . and he kicks you and trips you up and annoys you and we start a fight. . . and I shout and swear.' He felt too guilty to mention the swear words he used. He was a serious boy, who made good contact; and his 'three magic wishes' were 'One, to grow up and be intelligent; to get on with people; and to stay at home with my mum.'

Alec was moved to a small day school for maladjusted children and then, despite his educational retardation, coped well in a rather gentle ordinary primary school. But once at secondary school, his adjustment again broke down. Unable to face school, he ran out of class repeatedly. At the end of holidays, he also ran away from home. His aggressive behaviour led to school exclusion. When I saw him at almost 13, his school attainments were at only a 6½-year-old level. The mother, now clinically depressed, had recurrent worries about his future: 'If we get on to him, he runs. He was missing for 24 hours and slept in a hut.' The father said: 'We've got to get to the bottom of it.' The mother was sure he 'knows right from wrong', but he cannot stand criticism, especially from his father. He still got on well with his brothers and neighbourhood friends, but at school he swore non-stop, began to mix with delinquent children, and at 13 started shop-lifting.

Whenever he was in trouble, the mother now reacted both with depression and asthma; the father, to support his wife, became increasingly more critical and restrictive of Alec, and Alec the more bitter. A charge of breaking and entering was followed by social work supervision.

Follow-up at 19 found him, still illiterate, married but separated, his two younger brothers still at home and the parents' marriage and social integration intact. Alec was withdrawn and unhappy. Illiteracy, which he tried to hide, had been a major obstacle in finding work. A succession of brief jobs were followed by unemployment, at times without getting benefit because he could not read to fill in the forms. His wife had left because of unpaid bills, but she was still fond of Alec and got on well with his parents. His bouts of anger persisted, and at times he lashed out, even at her.

Recurrent thefts and assaults had, seven years later, led to a long prison sentence. When interviewed then, he was clinically depressed (his younger brother had recently been killed in a street accident), and deeply remorseful. His divorced wife, parents, and surviving brother were regular visitors.

The causes of hyperkinesis are not yet established. In some cases, as in Alec's, brain damage is involved; in others there is an association only with mental retardation or with specific developmental delays of language, of motor or of perceptional functioning. While a genetic predisposition may exist, its nature is by no means clear.

Schizoid personality (Asperger's syndrome)

In contrast, the personality type now to be described has always been noted to run in families, although no formal genetic studies have yet been done. Nor is it known whether, as Claridge believes, the personality features are to be regarded as traits present to a greater or lesser degree in everyone (Claridge 1985), or whether they affect only some people, admittedly in varying degrees of severity. The personality syndrome was first described by the Viennese paediatric psychiatrist Hans Asperger, and has subsequently been studied in the UK by Lorna Wing and myself (Wing 1981; Wolff 1987; Wolff and Chick 1980; Wolff and Cull 1986).

When severe enough to cause trouble, the features of schizoid personality disorder in childhood are as follows: the children are 'loners'; they lack empathy, finding it difficult to put themselves into other people's shoes; they may be very sensitive, even suspicious; they develop special interest patterns, e.g. in electronics, dinosaurs, collections, story writing, drawing, which they pursue to the exclusion of other activities; and they have unusual patterns of communication. They tend to be rigid, unable to shift once their mind is made up. Some children are verbose, even tactlessly open, and use surprising metaphors and made-up words. Others are secretive and uncommunicative, and a few present with *elective mutism*: they speak only to their families at home, never to the teacher or even other children at school. The Silent Twins, reported on by Marjorie Wallace, who had these characteristics in a very severe degree, did not even speak to their family, only to each other (Wallace 1986).

The conformity demanded at school for participation in noisy groups and in activities imposed by others is painful for schizoid children, and they often react with rage or tears, incomprehensible to others. Problems arise during the school years when the pressures on these eccentric individualists are greatest, and it is then that psychologists and psychiatrists tend to be called upon for help. Prior to school, most parents learn to adjust to their schizoid child; and after school, especially when the young people are gifted, they can find their own niche in, for them, congenial work settings.

Boys are more often affected than girls; the children may be intellectually gifted but can also, much more rarely, be mentally handicapped. Specific developmental disorders and evidence of neurological impairments are common, as is a family history of similar personality traits. On the other hand, environmental adversity and stressful life events are not often found and can certainly not account for the difficulties.

The condition, as a ten-year follow-up has shown, is very long-lasting; the children, especially the boys, remaining solitary and unempathic, but their career achievements are occasionally high.

It is important to distinguish schizoid personality from introversion, shyness, and neurotic inhibition. *Introversion*, as measured on Eysenck's Personality Inventory (Eysenck 1970), is not at all correlated with schizoidness, and indeed schizoid people can be very withdrawn and inward or, alternatively, quite outgoing. *Shyness and neurotic inhibition* are, unlike schizoid personality, commoner in girls than boys. Affected people usually wish they could mix with others more easily, longing to be able to cast off their constitutional or self-imposed constraints. Schizoid people, in contrast, often feel content in their social isolation, although the pressures on them for greater sociability can be irksome and even painful.

James was referred at 14 because of school failure and because he lived in a fantasy world. His room was littered with papers and apparently useless objects. School teachers found him able but 'lazy', and he was bottom of his class in all subjects except maths and science.

School essays contained repetitive and macabre themes. He had hated school, especially ball games, from the start. At 5 he invented an inhabited island on the ocean bed and his stories about its imaginary inhabitants, including a professor, preoccupied him for over two decades. The mother saw him as 'introverted', like herself, and thought he resembled her own father who was 'brilliant but eccentric' and had left her mother. James was of very superior intelligence. He got by in school because his teachers followed advice to reduce the pressures on him for conformity, and allowed him to go his own way. He started a school electronics club.

When seen at 28 years, he had obtained three degrees and become an Oxbridge scientist. But he was as solitary as ever and suffered from this. He dressed all in black, and rarely talked to anyone, even his parents. He was still writing rambling stories full of invented words and metaphors and he longed to live in the wilds.

By the age of 37, still all in black and with long hair, he was happily married with two young children. He said of himself 'I'm still much the same. Basically I'm a private person. There are private areas my wife and I don't share . . . but we get on very well.'

He also said 'I feel I've had a charmed life . . . I've never really had any bad experience . . . I think I had a very lucky childhood.' He thought his mother 'finds me bewildering. She and I find our hearts are in the right place but we don't communicate very well . . . marriage [my wife] made a bridge between us.' His story writing is temporarily in abeyance. About his past use of neologisms he said 'I try to invent less words because it puts people off . . . and English is full of weird words. There's no real excuse for inventing words. I could write just fabricated words and I'd enjoy that but it would be a pointless exercise.'

He feels his oldest daughter is similar to himself. 'She has the same sort of sinister bent. She likes dark and strange things . . .' He also described one brother, less able than himself, as a solitary drifter, now taking 'low level courses in psychology and massage'. He said 'I can understand what goes on in his mind.' And of his maternal grandfather he said, 'If we'd been contemporaries, we'd have got on rather well.'

As Kretschmer suggested sixty years ago, schizoid people can vary greatly from each other. Schizoid girls may more often than boys be quite outgoing and superficially sociable. Some schizoid children become conduct disordered. When this happens, inexplicable aggression and pathological lying, associated with an unusual fantasy life, are the distinguishing features rather than a background of family discord and socio-economic disadvantage that is so common in other conduct-disordered children (Wolff and Cull 1986).

The following boy illustrates the association of schizoid traits with a specific language disorder and with a serious antisocial development at adolescence. This boy too came from a well functioning family.

Ian was referred by his teacher aged 9, because of temper outbursts, head banging, and verbal and physical attacks on other children from whom he totally isolated himself. Because of a serious language delay — so that, while understanding well what others said, he was unable to talk fluently — he attended a special remedial school with small classes.

His father and two sisters had also had early language delays but they were conscientious, warm, and socially responsive people. The mother, subject to depressions, was vague in her talk and mildly out of touch emotionally. But she managed a part-time job and her household competently, and the marriage was harmonious.

When first seen, Ian was emotionally detached and avoided eye contact. He described himself objectively. He preferred to be alone. His intelligence was good average, and he read well but had a very serious spelling delay.

At school he remained rigid about his routines, over sensitive to slights, even suspicious, and threw chairs during paroxysmal rages. A behavioural approach was initiated and succeeded in reducing his outbursts, to his own satisfaction. Because no suitable day-school was available to meet his special educational needs he went to a special boarding school. Here he was happy at first. But during the last school year when, contrary to advice, he was encouraged to participate in self-exploratory group discussions with staff and other youngsters, his explosive outbursts recurred. He attacked a staff member and also another boy, quite seriously.

By 15 he had developed an interest in the 'occult' and in sexy magazines. He said, 'I'm bored and I start annoying people for no reason at all.' He lacked guilt about his assaults on others and said, 'It must have been the circumstances; I got bored. There's nothing at the school to fit my needs . . . no programme.' He longed for a 'rota'.

By 16 he saw the school staff as having it in for him and they in turn viewed his behaviour as 'bizarre', for example, when he argued with the TV newscaster. He now become preoccupied with violence and at home he amassed a collection of newspaper accounts and photographs of a violent criminal. He was dressed in black leather and remained solitary and secretive. The parents were extremely concerned about his potential for aggression: 'in case the next time there'll be a death.'

Of course, schizoid traits are seen in people of all ages. While most schizoid adults cope well with marriage and the upbringing of their children, especially when more mildly affected and supported by a warm, flexible, and empathic partner, others do not. When children are referred to professionals with emotional or behaviour problems, it is important that the parents' difficulties are accurately diagnosed and that realistic treatment goals are set. Expectations for change should be limited to what is possible and exploratory treatment methods to what is tolerable for such parents.

Occasionally after a divorce an exceptionally litigious, paranoid parent is found to have schizoid traits which impede any reasonable compromises over financial or access arrangements for the children. A more ominous situation is when a parent lacks all feeling for one of the children, or sees some special handicap or ill intent in a particular child, scapegoating and persecuting this child for years. When such a child is actually injured physically, improvement in the parent over time is likely to be minimal.

In this chapter we have reviewed those variations of normal and abnormal temperament that are largely constitutional in origin and contribute to individual differences of personality, and to some pathological developments. In the next section of this book we shall be concerned with universal developmental processes and their vicissitudes from infancy to adult life. How these contribute to our personalities depends of course on the family and cultural environment in which we are brought up and on the events that befall us. But our individual biological equipment for cognitive development and temperament determines in an important way how we each start out on and negotiate our particular life path.

Part II

Developmental processes

Chapter four

Sociability in infancy

No one remembers his or her first year of life. Some people, exceptionally open to experience, recollect isolated moments of very early childhood before they could speak, but most of us have childhood memories going back only to when we were 2 or 3, and can form chains of recollections only from 4 or 5 years onwards. Infancy is evanescent and even small children cannot remember what it was like. The human baby is the more strange and remarkable, evoking powerful emotions in us all.

It will be one of my aims to stress the continuity between infants and children, children and adults. While the inner experience of continuity of the person stops short of infancy, the outer continuity of our lives begins at the moment of conception. Despite the many possible changes in developmental direction with changes of circumstances and life experiences, decisions about babies are decisions about the children, the future citizens and the parents which these babies will in turn become. I also believe that the good clinician, of whatever professional discipline, chooses his or her interventions in the lives of children with a view of their possible future paths as grown-up people in mind, and approaches their parents and other adults who may be in trouble with the aim of understanding not only their present predicament but their childhood selves; that is, the legacies in them now of the particular circumstances and life events they experienced from earliest youth.

Systematic observations of infants and young children have revolutionized our understanding of developmental processes affecting sociability and intelligence, of the interactions between children and parents, and of the biological significance of the patterns of early human relationships.

From concern with deprived children to infant observation

Charles Darwin wrote:

> This infant smiled at 45 days, a second infant when 46 days old; and these were true smiles, indicative of pleasures, for their eyes brightened and eyelids slightly closed. The smiles arose chiefly when looking at their mother, and were probably of mental origin; but this infant often smiled then, and for some time afterwards, from some inward pleasurable feeling, for nothing was happening which could have in any way excited or amused him. When 110 days old he was exceedingly amused by a pinafore thrown over his face and then suddenly withdrawn; and so he was when I suddenly uncovered my own face and approached his. . . Surprise was the chief cause of amusement, as is the case to a large extent with the wit of grown-up persons, . . . I was at first surprised at humour being appreciated by an infant only a little above three months old, but we should remember how very early puppies and kittens begin to play.
>
> (Darwin 1877)

Despite the detailed but isolated accounts of their own very young children by Taine (1877), Darwin (1877) and Preyer (1888) a hundred years ago, and the theories of early developmental psychologists such as Baldwin (1897), often to prove surprisingly accurate, systematic studies of early sociability began much later and got their impetus from the concern evoked by parentless infants. Spitz described a state of depression, developmental arrest, physical illness and often death in babies reared in the excessively hygienic orphanages of his day, deprived of opportunities for social contact, play and even mobility (Spitz 1945). He was among the first to study the baby's smiling response, a source of delight to later researchers who spent many hours as self-invited guests in the homes of mothers and young children, observing and recording their interactions under different conditions and at different stages of the infant's life.

Bowlby's early work

John Bowlby's first publication on maternal deprivation (1951) arose out of international concern for children whose lives had been disrupted by the evacuations, migrations, and parent loss that occurred during the Second World War. His research review, commissioned by the World Health Organization, stressed for the first time that experiences in infancy directly affect later development. More specifically, Bowlby evolved the thesis that if children are deprived of continuous mothering between 6 months and 3 years of age, their future capacity for human relationships and for intellectual performance, especially language, can be permanently stunted.

This work had two major effects: on child-care policy, and on research. It revolutionized the institutional care of young children who, for reasons of illness or family breakdown, have to be looked after away from their parents. Free visiting was gradually introduced in children's hospitals; parents were invited to live in paediatric wards and share in the nursing of children under 4; and when children needed public care because of family breakdown, the alternatives were far more carefully chosen in the light of the children's perceived emotional needs.

The impact of Bowlby's monograph on scientific progress has been even more profound. His ideas, sometimes misrepresented, stimulated researchers to try to confirm or refute his thesis. The finding that children brought up in institutions from 6 months to 3 years, compared with similarly abandoned children who had been adopted from these institutions in early infancy, were indiscriminate in their social attachments, unable to form deep and lasting relationships, often had behavioural problems, were retarded in language development, and more often failed at school (Goldfarb 1945) was attributed to the poor quality of the orphanages of the 1940s. And indeed, later studies (Tizard *et al.* 1972; Tizard and Rees 1976) did show that in well-run residential nurseries the intellectual and linguistic progress of young children can be preserved. On the other hand, the emotional impairments which had followed prolonged periods of very early group care, without opportunities for selective and continuous attachments, although modifiable by later experiences, remained (Tizard 1972; Tizard 1979). These issues were well reviewed by Rutter who made it clear that 'maternal deprivation' is too global a term, and that a much more discriminating approach is needed both to child development and to disentangling the effects on children of different kinds of privations at different ages (Rutter 1980).

One area in which research has flourished during the past four decades is in the detailed exploration of what actually goes on between mothers and babies in the earliest weeks and months of life. It became clear that, with maturation of the central nervous system, the baby becomes capable not only of increasingly more complex behaviour, but also of observing different aspects of his environment and construing what he observes differently. The apparent meaning for him of the world changes as he grows up. The baby's smile and reactions to novelty and strangers are indicative of changes of meaning with age. In addition, the social responses of babies differ, not only according to their differing temperamental styles, but as a result of their personal life experiences; for example, how many different people look after them, whether or not they had been separated from those they knew best, and what the nature of their relationships with their parents were.

More recently researchers have focused on the mutuality of infant-parent social interchanges; on how their quality varies with different circumstances; and what the later effects on the child's development are of different types of early family interactions. A major contribution to the study of infant sociability came from the ideas and methods of animal ethologists.

Ethological approaches

Ethologists are concerned with observing the behaviour of animals within their natural environment from a biological viewpoint. How, they ask themselves, are the behaviour patterns of a particular species adapted to the environment of that species? How have they evolved in that species? How do they develop in the individual members of the species? As the methods of the baby watchers have come to resemble those of animal ethologists, and techniques for analysing human behaviour have developed, so increasingly we are helped to understand how our species resembles and differs from others, and also what all babies have in common.

A cognitive developmental viewpoint

Rudolph Schaffer, who has greatly advanced our understanding of human infant development, takes the view that each individual from the start actively organizes his experiences and selectively exposes himself to stimuli from the environment (Schaffer 1971). Moreover, he or she can store information as memory, and behaviour changes over time, even under similar circumstances. Schaffer suggests we cannot do without postulating cognitive structures in the mind which mediate between external stimuli and our responses to them. Such cognitive structures are shaped by our genetic endowment and by neurological maturation as well as by our past experiences, and they include internal representations both of the present and the past.

The sequence of early social development

Neonatal responses

The newborn enters the world with a set of ready-made social responses to human stimuli which seems designed to captivate the parents. When awake and attentive, he can follow a bright object or human face with his eyes; make fleeting eye-contact with his mother; follow the gaze of another person (Klaus *et al.* 1975); respond by turning his head towards a human voice, especially if high pitched (usually female); within a few days of birth, recognize his mother's voice; and at 5 days even know her breast by its smell (McFarlane 1975). We have as yet insufficient observations over time to know for how long such skills persist. Some of them seem to fade out, only to reappear more firmly in later weeks. But the baby's most compelling first activity is his cry.

Richard Bell described mothers as at the mercy of their baby's cry during his or her first month of life (Bell 1974). By the third month, crying has usually decreased to a level parents can tolerate. When, at 3 months, Bell asked mothers about their subjective feelings of attachment to their babies, he found that the mothers of infants who maintained high levels of crying beyond their first month and were inconsolable when held had experienced a decline of motherly feelings for their baby and ignored him or her more. Which came first in this sequence of mutually reinforcing interactions, the baby's noisy irritability or the mother's inattentiveness, is not clear. But we do know that even mild obstetric difficulties and also anoxia at birth are associated with infant irritability and sleeplessness (Bernal 1973); and that post-natal depression, so common in mothers, is often accompanied by maternal irritability and at times by emotional withdrawal from the child. It may well be that even mild pathology in mother or child can, especially if the partner in the relationship is also vulnerable, trigger adverse mother-infant interactions in these early months of life.

The smile of the baby: a paradigm for social development

From the start, the baby's smile has the expressive qualities of a social smile, and the earliest facial movements and gestures uncannily resemble those used purposefully by much older people (Trevarthen 1974). From birth, parents endow what their babies do with meaning; mothers attribute intentions even to their newborn, responding to them as if they were already more mature (Hinde 1976). This is thought to help babies not only to become aware of their possible effects on others, but to discover meaning in their own actions (Newson 1979).

Within a few weeks of birth, definite patterns of mutual interaction between parents and infants develop about which parents are quite unselfconscious. A regularity of approach and withdrawal has been observed. As the baby looks at and gestures towards the mother, she holds back, watches and waits. When he stops, she begins to become actively stimulating, often imitating what he has just done, and then stops to let him have his turn again. These interchanges, totally absorbing for both partners, have the rhythmic sequences of true conversations and are thought to be their forerunners (Schaffer 1977a and b).

The early eye-contact babies achieve after birth is soon lost, but reappears at around 3–4 weeks. Babies now also look longer at patterns resembling eyes, and this spontaneous development of selective attention to human eyes has been likened to the evolution in birds of certain social responses essential for survival. Human babies are biologically programmed to respond to the features of people during their second month of life, displaying what Schaffer has called a *primary attraction to social objects* (Schaffer 1971). Between 6 and 8 weeks infants smile selectively at human faces, even at masks, and at 4 months they look longer at true pictures of faces than at pictures of faces with eyes, nose and mouth scrambled.

This early undifferentiated sociability Schaffer has likened to the anonymous social interactions of some animal species, such as insects. All animals associate with each other, some only for procreation. Others, like insects, engage in complex joint activities but with no preferences for the companionship of any particular members of their group.

In higher vertebrates and birds, *selective attachments* are seen: between parents and offspring, between mates and between other subgroups of the flock or herd. Konrad Lorenz studied the selective bonds that tied fledglings to their mother bird and discovered that young birds are biologically programmed to become attached to and follow the first moving object they encounter after hatching, usually their mother (Lorenz 1935). There is a photograph of Professor Lorenz swimming in a pond, followed by a flock of goslings for whom *he* had been this first object. To this process of attachment in lower animals the term 'imprinting' has been applied. The capacity for imprinting is at its height shortly after birth, and the period during which it is most easily established has been called *a sensitive period* (Schaffer 1971).

Such rapid processes attaching infants to their parents are clearly essential in helping animals protect and nurture their young, when these are born immature, unable to fend for themselves, and yet mobile on their feet. For human babies, unable to move about, there is less urgency (and hence less risk) in forming basic social bonds.

A most important change occurs between the third and fifth months of the baby's life: indiscriminate social smiling is replaced by selective smiling at people he or she knows best. *Differential smiling at familiar people* is a sign of the development of *specific or focused attachments* (Yarrow 1972). This is the first major, socially important learnt response, and it depends of course on some capacity for memory. Once she can hold an image of her mother in her mind against which to match other people she sees, the baby can respond differently to her than to a stranger.

When normal babies are brought up in families, they learn to distinguish between familiar and unfamiliar people. But under some conditions of handicap or privation, differential smiling and the growth of specific attachments are delayed.

Congenitally blind babies, for example, pass through all the stages of attachment to parents at a slower pace. Vision is the most important sensation mediating both social interactions and cognitive development in very early life. Because blind babies cannot look at people, they elicit less social stimulation (Fraiberg 1974). Even small children will exert themselves to catch a baby's eye, and in doing so will talk to, touch and move the infant about. When a baby's eyes are not seeing, such exertions cease. Blind babies not only lack the normal equipment for sociability; they also fail to evoke it adequately from others.

Social and cognitive development in infancy go hand in hand. Both can be delayed, as we shall see, under conditions of group care when, inevitably, the infant's attempts to form selective attachments are repeatedly frustrated by the routines and rotas of a large and changing child-care staff. Yet the development of specific attachments does not require a mother's full-time attendance. Kibbutz infants, with regular but time-limited contact with their parents, develop normally.

Although babies begin to know and become attached to their parents at around 3 to 5 months, their notions even of their mothers are as yet quite strange. Bower in an ingenious experiment showed that when, on weekly visits to his laboratory, babies were exposed to multiple reflections of their mother seen in mirrors, they became even more cheerful and animated than in her unreflected presence (Bower 1974). But quite suddenly, at about 5 months, a change occurred. The baby now screamed in terror when instead of one mother, he appeared to be facing four. Clearly up to that time, while able to recognize his mother, he found nothing incongruous in seeing several of her at a time. This means that he did not then know that he had only one mother, and might well think that the one who leaves the room, while similar, is not the same as the one who returns to attend to him a little while later. At 5 months he knows she is unique, so that to be faced by multiple mirror images of her does not match his maturing expectations and is frightening.

Specific attachments and the fear of strangers

An early and crucial investigation (Schaffer and Callender 1959) showed that under 7 months children react quite differently to brief separations from their mothers than children over 7 months. Babies under a year were observed during and after brief hospital admissions when they were no longer seriously ill and were visited by their mothers daily. All babies cried a great deal in hospital but the younger ones were as responsive to nurses as to their mothers, crying when left alone, but consoled when someone reappeared. On coming home, these young infants were at first totally preoccupied with their domestic environment, staring at everything, but unresponsive to their mothers. This reaction, lasting at most two days, was interpreted as a response to relief from the perceptual monotony of the hospital ward.

After 7 months, quite different patterns were seen. Babies now responded selectively to their mothers at visiting times, cried and fretted when the mothers left, and could not be consoled by strange nurses. For up to two weeks after returning home, these infants were excessively clinging to their mothers, following them constantly with their eyes, or creeping after them if old enough. Even brief domestic absences now caused distress. Sleep was often interrupted and appetite poor.

Clearly a major change had come about at the start of the second half of the first year of life in what the child perceived as important. In a further study of sixty Glasgow infants, Schaffer and Emerson confirmed that specific attachments begin at this age (Schaffer and Emerson 1964). Babies observed regularly in their own homes over time suddenly developed protest crying at brief domestic separations from their mothers in the third quarter of the first year of life, when this had not happened before. Often babies formed attachments to a number of familiar people, usually but not always including the mother, although it was she who almost invariably provided food and nurturing care. Schaffer and Callender thought that not food but social gratification mediated attachment, and that the care-giver to whom babies become most strongly attached is the one most sensitively responsive to the infant.

Within a few weeks of the first signs of specific attachments, most babies showed wary withdrawal from strangers. This *stranger response* occurred later in babies who had been exposed to a wide social circle than in babies who rarely met anyone other than their parents. But there are also constitutional differences between babies in the timing, strength, and style, both of their attachments and their fear of strangers. This was shown in a study of monozygotic and dizygotic twins, in which the former were found to be much more alike than the latter (Freedman and Keller 1963).

When babies are separated from parents, the nature of the intervening care determines how easily selective attachments are formed or re-established once the child returns home. Seven out of 9 infants admitted to a children's home where they had much social contact with care-givers, and returned home after the age of 7 months, established selective attachments to their families within two weeks of reunion. On the other hand, of 11 children admitted to hopsital, with much less social care, 10 took over 4 weeks and some several months to do so (Schaffer 1971). This has profound implications for child care. It is in line with the vividly filmed demonstrations by the Robertsons (Robertson and Robertson 1967–72) that, when children under 2 have to be separated from their mother, sensitive and individualized substitute care can, in contrast to group care in a residential nursery, minimize a child's distress and his difficulties on reunion with her.

The crucial step towards specific attachments at 6 months, followed in most babies by a temporary recoil from strangers, has many developmental and practical implications. Babies now clearly have more durable memory traces of what they have seen before, against which they match what they now encounter. The question: same or different? can be seen to exercise the baby of this age, as he looks repeatedly from face to face for cues about how to respond. The very antics that make him laugh when performed by the mother: tickling and bouncing him or creating a surprising spectacle by turning herself upside down, or pulling a funny face, engender terror when done by a stranger (Bruner 1972).

The second half of the first year

While in the early weeks and months of life the baby arouses his parents' commitment to his care, the child himself experiences his first human relationship only in the second half of the first year, when the parent becomes a real person to whom he is attached. The infant's needs in the first 6 months of life are different from those in the second, and this has evident implications for the kind of care babies should have if for any reason their own parents cannot look after them.

When babies are separated from their families at around 3 months of age and looked after in institutions, their intellectual development is affected by the amount of general stimulation and social attention they get. Schaffer showed that on coming home after two to nine months of institutional care, the developmental quotient of some babies increases significantly, a sign that in the institution their development had been retarded and, now they were home again, they were catching up (Schaffer 1965). This was especially so for babies who had spent the weeks away from home in the then unstimulating and socially barren environment of a hospital ward. In the more sociable and interesting environment of a children's home, such intellectual retardation did not occur in these very young children. Since then hospital has greatly changed. Children's wards are now colourful, babies if well enough are propped up to get a view of what goes on, and parents are encouraged to spend much time with their offspring. But the fact remains that from early infancy onwards children require stimulating surroundings which they can actively explore, and they also need sensitively responsive human contact. After 6 months, however, this is no longer enough. Babies now need, in addition, the regular company of those few people, especially their mothers, to whom they are selectively attached and on whom they rely to give meaning to their world.

Increasingly studies of children brought up by their mothers emphasize the baby's role in initiating social interactions, and how much mothers adapt their behaviour to suit their children's individual needs. Mothers find themselves responding quite differently to each of their babies.

Mothers also influence their children's reactions to the outside world, and from a surprisingly early age: again the second half of the first year. Feinman and Lewis showed that this is the time when children begin to look to their mothers for cues about how to treat other people (Feinman and Lewis 1983). In an experimental setting mothers were asked to react to a stranger in three different ways while with their 10-month-old babies: with neutrality; with positive verbal and gestural expression;

and with positive talk and gestures to the child *about* the stranger. Babies were most friendly to this third person when the mother had spoken to them in a friendly way about him or her, and less friendly in both the other circumstances. Babies with an 'easy' temperament were the most responsive to what has been called *social referencing*; that is, to influence by their mothers in their appraisal of an unknown person or event.

It remains to be shown how much social and intellectual development in the first year depend on a good fit between the social activities of care-giver and baby, a fit that is clearly threatened when there is too little time for play and sociability or too little opportunity for accurate and empathic parental observation and response; when too many care-givers have too many children to look after; or a mother is either ill or overburdened with responsibilities and anxieties. We shall look in the next chapter at the more long-term consequences of lack of closeness at this early stage. Here we have been concerned with the nature of this intimacy.

Developmental hazards and resilience in the first year

We have already indicated some of the possible dangers of being born after a difficult delivery; of being born blind; and especially of early separation from the mother. Some infants may be more resilient to such hazards than others. Werner and Smith, for example, in a longitudinal study of the children of Kauwai, found that the long-term effects on later educational progress and emotional adjustment of birth injury, varied greatly according to the care-giving environment (Werner and Smith 1982). When the child's family was stable, ill effects were minimal. How much this good outcome depended on the mother's calm responsiveness to her baby in the early months, and how much to later family or educational influences, is not known.

The effect of the child's temperament

The effect on young babies of a barren hospital environment varies with the child's temperament (Schaffer 1966). Lively, active babies show less of a drop in intelligence while in hospital than more passive, quiet infants. The possible explanations are that either active babies provide more interesting spectacles for themselves from which they can learn, or, under conditions of time-limited and impersonal group care, they attract more attention and care to themselves than their more passive companions.

Some evidence for the second explanation comes from the observations of two babies aged 6 and 20 weeks living in a residential nursery. During brief, daily training sessions these babies were rewarded with smiles whenever they stopped crying and looked or smiled at the experimenter. At other times they were presented with a non-responsive face. Although this was a study of the efficacy of operant conditioning, it was noticed that, back in the nursery, the care staff gave more time and social stimulation to these babies once they had become ready smilers than they had done before, clearly now finding them more attractive and rewarding to be with (Etzel and Gewirtz 1967).

A baby's difficult temperament can also tip the balance towards a post-natal depression in predisposed mothers without adequate social supports, by further reducing their self-confidence and self-esteem (Cutrona and Troutman 1986).

The implications of studies of infant-care-giver interactions are profound, especially since they help us to explain how transient difficulties can be perpetuated into the future.

Obstacles to maternal attachment

Some years ago it was suggested that mothers deprived of physical contact with their newborns, because of rigid hospital routines or illness in mother or baby, may be permanently impaired in their affectionate responses to the child. A 'sensitive period' for maternal attachment to the baby was postulated. This notion has had excellent effects, in humanizing maternity units and enabling parents to have ready access to their newborns even if these are in intensive medical care. More recent work (Lamb 1983) suggests, however, that lack of early contact with the baby affects only some, predisposed, mothers especially if they are having their first child, and that even in these mothers the effects tend to disappear in the long term.

Mother-infant separation: the 'separation reaction'

Once specific attachments have been formed, the baby not only protests at temporary, domestic separations, which in fact he learns to tolerate better and better as his ability to hold his mother in his mind improves, but, if completely separated from familiar care-givers, he passes through a dispiriting sequence of reactions first described by Bowlby and Robert-son some twenty years ago. A period of *protest* with acute distress, loud crying, searching for the mother at the place at which she was last seen, and refusal of attention from anyone else is the first stage. It lasts from a few hours to a week or more. Then comes a period of *despair*, when searching for the mother ends, the child is weepy, inactive and withdrawn, lacking in interest in his or her surroundings. After a variable period of weeks or months in which hope is revived episodically, *detachment* follows, the child now becoming responsive to attention and comfort from others. If the mother reappears during the first two stages, she may be greeted with initial anger and active avoidance, and has to woo back her child. If she reappears during the stage of detachment, he has clearly forgotten her and treats her like a stranger (Bowlby 1979). Mothers unprepared for such reactions may themselves now be disappointed and even angry at their hostile and unresponsive child, and this can be one reason for the emotional difficulties that often follow especially repeated hospitalizations in the first four years of life (Douglas 1975).

If instead of group care in which all attempts to form new bonds are constantly frustrated, the child is offered a familiar foster mother during the natural mother's absence, the separation reaction tends to be mild and the return to the mother less troubled by the child's anger (Robertson and Robertson 1967–72).

The mother as a secure base

Ainsworth observed the different types of attachment behaviour of fifty-six 1-year-old infants to their mothers in a standard playroom during a fixed sequence of changing circumstances: alone with mother; with mother and a stranger; alone; alone with a stranger; and on reunion with the mother. Most babies showed active interest in their new surroundings while alone with the mother. When the stranger arrived, they played less, drew closer to their mother and watched the stranger. Left alone with her, most babies cried and attempted to search for their mother, although a minority did not. When the mother came back, most babies greeted her, clung to her, and stopped crying. Repetition of the sequence evoked more intense reactions of the same kind. Half these children had previously been observed in interaction with their mothers at home throughout the first year. The amount of exploratory play in the playroom, as well as the children's reactions to their mother's departure and return, varied with the sensitivity of the mothers to their babies' signals during the previous home observations. Mothers who responded promptly and appropriately tended to have *securely attached* children who, at 1 year of age, played a lot while in her presence, looked at her frequently, brought her toys and went to her regularly. After the brief absence, they greeted her warmly. At the other extreme were *insecurely attached* children, whose mothers for reasons not at that time made explicit had been less sensitively responsive. In the experimental setting, these children *either* had little to do with their mother, were relatively unperturbed by her absence, less positive in their greeting and avoiding of her after her return, *or* showed extreme anxiety in her absence and yet ambivalence towards her on her return. Some of these anxious children were passive, with very little exploratory play (Ainsworth *et al*. 1974).

These findings, as we shall see, have been the impetus for important work of much relevance to our understanding of personality development. In one study 34 toddlers from united families were observed in the Ainsworth 'strange situation' at 12 and 18 months. They were rated as 'securely' and 'insecurely' attached. The children were followed into their nursery school when they were 4 years old and it was found that 16 children, previously rated as 'securely' attached, were now rated by their teachers as more self-reliant, more confident and more resourceful than those previously 'insecurely' attached. Actual observations in the nursery showed those rated as 'securely' attached also to be less dependent on their teachers and more actively involved with other children (Sroufe *et al*. 1983).

The meaning of clinging to the mother changes with age. In the second six months it spells developmental progress and eagerness for a relationship. Beyond the fourth year it signifies insecurity and may interfere with personality growth. This illustrates how the same behaviour can have a totally different meaning at different ages.

Among the determinants of 'security' or 'insecurity' in early childhood are the child's neurological status and temperament. Other factors are economic disadvantage and life stresses affecting the mother (Sroufe 1985). But perhaps the most important, as we shall see later, are the mother's own childhood experiences and personality.

Maternal depression

The impact of this common psychiatric illness on child care is being actively explored. Because most studies have been concerned with observations of depressed mothers and toddlers, we will describe these in the next chapter. Here two clinical examples will be used to illustrate the range of possible depressive disorders in the mother that can seriously interfere with infant care.

Two identical twin girls were repeatedly admitted to a children's hospital in their first 6 months of life with 'failure to thrive'. They were underweight, pale, apathetic and socially unresponsive. They were otherwise healthy and, in hospital, they always ate well and gained weight. The mother, under suspicion of deliberately withholding food and care, was then referred to the psychiatric department of the hospital.

Smilingly she at first denied all difficulties with her babies, although she was anxious about their poor progress. Only a detailed enquiry into how she herself was feeling elicited the account of a total change of mood. Ever since the twins were born, she had felt depressed, at times suicidal, and guilty about her lack of feeling for the children. She ate and slept poorly, felt she could communicate with no one and wished she could, but could not, cry. The transformation in her and her children, initiated by anti-depressant medication, was remarkable. But for some years afterwards she welcomed the emotional and practical support of the paediatric community nurse who visited her regularly. For a long time this mother lived in fear that her suicidal depression and almost total unresponsiveness to her children might return. The twins themselves remained physically, behaviourally, and linguistically stunted throughout their first two years but then caught up and, on school entry, functioned as normal 5-year-olds. Of course, the supportive interviews with this mother, in which the father too participated, focused on many aspects of her early and current life, although this had not been particularly traumatic. Treatment involved not only medication but active efforts to give validity to her own viewpoint and to strengthen her self-esteem.

Non-psychotic depressive illnesses in mothers are much commoner. They often reflect complex and highly individual strands of intergenerational life experiences that can lead to failure of early bonding, experiences to which research into groups of people can never do justice. The following example illustrates also that the causes of psychiatric problems tend to be multiple, involving both parents and children.

Mr and Mrs Brown and Ingrid were referred by a worried health visitor. Ingrid, at 2 years 7 months, was not yet talking and her relationship with her mother was poor.

As the family walked in, Ingrid wept and angrily pushed her mother away, while the mother turned her back on the child and said 'I'm totally fed up with her.' She complained that Ingrid hated her little brother, that she has to keep the children apart because Ingrid would 'kill him', and that she herself felt guilty because she had never got on with her daughter. The father then led Ingrid from the room, indicating his wife needed to talk.

The mother, only 22, now began to weep as she described the death of her own mother, aged 55, of cancer just 6 weeks after Ingrid's birth. Up to that time her feelings for the child had, she thought, been normal, but now they changed. She said 'I wasn't totally attached to her. I felt I could replace Ingrid but not my mother. There was far more of a bond between me and my mother than between me and the baby.' Mrs Brown slept and ate poorly and was irritable with her husband. After her mother's death she thought of suicide, and often she felt she could just walk out. 'Ingrid kept me ticking over. If I'd never had Ingrid, I'd have walked over a cliff.' She still cries at night, thinking of her mother. She said: 'I feel guilty about not liking Ingrid . . . I can enjoy my son.'

Ingrid, conceived after two miscarriages, was born at 35 weeks, weighing just 5 lb and was in an incubator for two weeks. The mother wanted to breast feed but failed. In the child's second year, the mother became pregnant with Jack, also premature, and born by Caesarian section. The mother was in hospital for two weeks, and readmitted briefly a week later, to Ingrid's distress. Jack then developed pyloric stenosis and was in hospital twice. The obvious concern of the parents for this second child may well have made Ingrid's natural jealousy of the baby the more frightening for her.

Ingrid herself stood and walked at the normal times, and understood language well. But only now, in her third year, was she beginning to express herself in words. A maternal uncle, least favoured by Mrs Brown's mother, began to talk only at 5, and had always been slow at school. Mrs Brown said: 'My mother couldn't stand my younger brother. She totally ignored him and he became an angry and difficult young man.'

The mother's family history came to life only during a joint interview she requested with her younger sister. Feelings in their family had always been 'swept under the carpet', and during their mother's terminal illness their father enjoined all the children to 'keep your pecker up; don't let your chin hit the floor'. The sisters thought he had totally blotted out his wife's memory; he had remarried and 'dropped all of us'. Ingrid's mother said: 'If I had cancer, I'd like to tell my children — and we couldn't talk to her.' Yet gradually the idealized picture of this grandmother changed. She had favoured the oldest brother and, even when the girls were working, they had to do the chores while this brother was waited on hand and foot. When they were small, their mother was strict with them: 'You ate what was put in front of you or did without.' Both sisters declared pride in being brought up strictly: 'I never called my mum an old bag.' Mrs Brown had hoped to show off Ingrid to her mother as the first grandchild but the mother, far from overjoyed, had said: 'You might get a son next time.'

Mrs Brown was treated with anti-depressants, supportive interviews, and help in finding a nursery for Ingrid. Within a week she was eating better, but her feelings had not changed: she referred to Ingrid as 'so aggressive', 'a little bitch', and said 'she's bad'. She longed to 'have a break' from her. The child herself now interacted more cheerfully with her mother and played well, with good concentration.

Three weeks later, the mother said 'the pressure's off me', but was not sure 'whether it's the pills or you'. A month later she no longer wanted 'a break'; and two months later still she remained well without her pills and reported positive feelings for Ingrid. She and her sister had become reconciled with their father and 'step-granny'.

It was important in this case to let the health visitor and the nursery staff know that the mother's hostility and unresponsiveness to the child were not the cause of her language delay, but that this had a constitutional, familial basis.

Ingrid was in temperament intense and active; and her father responsive to her needs, while supportive of his wife and fully involved in the care of both children. The twins, in contrast, had had a smoother birth history but were, like their father, somewhat lacking in energy and drive. Moreover, their mother was left with full responsibility for their care and, although the possibility remains that their twinship had contributed to their initial developmental retardation, it was my belief that this was mainly due to lack of parental responsiveness.

The biological implications of the child's tie to his mother: Bowlby's later work

Bowlby holds that the maintenance of proximity between mother and infant is universal in all human cultures and, although varying in duration, in birds and mammals too. He argues in the first volume of his trilogy *Attachment and Loss* (1982) that both the infant's behaviour patterns and those he or she evokes from care-givers, especially the mother, are biologically determined by evolution and that their aim in keeping mother and young together while the baby is immature is twofold: to safeguard the infant's survival by protecting him or her from physical dangers and, second, to help the baby, in close proximity to the parent, to learn certain vital social skills, including language, without which he or she is cut off not only from intimate human relationships but from the culture.

Baby monkeys reared in isolation cannot as adults take part in the normal hierarchical social structure of their group. They fail in their communication with others and become angry loners. They do not mate normally and, if artificially inseminated, female monkeys lack maternal attentiveness to their offspring. What is more, their babies in turn are more aggressive than those of mother-reared monkeys, play less and engage in less sexual behaviour with other young monkeys (Harlow and Zimmerman 1959; Ruppenthal *et al.* 1976). Rhesus monkeys can be effectively compensated for lack of mothering by brief daily contacts with other baby monkeys, but this is not so for the human baby. Yet infant monkeys separated from their mothers display separation reactions very similar to those of human babies, and they share some of the determinants of the strength and duration of clinging behaviour. A rejecting monkey mother, just like her human counterpart, tends to have an excessively clinging child (Hinde *et al.* 1978).

Bowlby goes further to suggest that despite the varieties of family life found in human cultures, the mother's role towards her young baby has a number of universal features. Certainly all efforts to reproduce for a baby what a mother normally achieves in the first year fail unless foster care, or at least part-time fostering by a particular care-giver, is laid on. Of course, there is much blurring of roles between fathers and mothers, and it remains to be established whether *on average* fathers are as good at bringing up a baby as mothers are. They seem as concerned about their offspring and as good at picking up the baby's cues. But they smile less and tend to play with their infants rather than take on nurturing tasks (Parke 1981). Bowlby suggests that males have more freedom of choice about their role as parents and that, from the narrow viewpoint of the preservation of the species, they are more expendable! What is more, recent work (Grossman *et al.* 1985) has shown that, while the quality of a young child's attachment to the mother and father may be quite different, it is the nature of attachment to the mother that has the greatest effect on future emotional development. We shall see in later chapters that, while perhaps unnecessary for the mere survival of the baby, the father's presence in the family has effects on the socialization of the young for which mothers cannot easily substitute.

The concept of sensitive periods

We have already discussed the notion that at some periods of life we are more ready to learn certain things than at others, and that children deprived of family life, especially of continuous mothering, between 6 months and 3 years are at risk of later deficits and distortions of personality, and of educational failure, not remedied by subsequent family care (Goldfarb 1945).

Bruner speaks of '*tutor proneness*' not only in human children, but among young chimpanzees (Bruner 1972). By this he means an eagerness to learn from adults. Children in middle childhood are more educable than grown-ups, more intrigued by novelty, alert to details in the world around them that escape the attention of adults, and better at detecting rules in novel situations. Language is certainly best learnt in very early life and a foreign accent is not accurately acquired beyond early adolescence. The same is true for athletic skills, dancing, and playing a musical instrument. But it is the stability of early learning that has proved most controversial, especially the idea that what is not learnt in very early life produces some immutable change within the child which cannot later be made good.

Stability of the effects of early childhood deprivation of maternal care can have causes other than fixed inner change. It is a fact that children deprived of adequate early parenting often suffer subsequent losses and privations also, and it is in practice not easy to arrange transfers to permanent substitute families. Moreover, as Tizard and Rees pointed out, when children are adopted or fostered after starting school, the amount of time for the kind of intimate parent-child contact in which early gaps of experience could be remedied, is strictly limited by the school day (Tizard and Rees 1976). The permanent ill effects of early childhood privations, as we saw in Chapter 1, can be due to at least three different interacting influences: the continuation of an adverse environment; mutually reinforcing negative interactions between a traumatized child and his later care-givers; and an inner, long-lasting change of personality whose emotional component will be the effects of the child's early memories on his or her interpretations of and reactions to later experiences.

The Clarkes have argued strongly against this last idea, citing case-reports of children totally isolated from normal human contact who recovered their intellectual and language skills in response to subsequent sensitive and concerned parenting (Clarke and Clarke 1976). Yet the inner lives of these children have not been documented, nor do we know about the quality of their later relationships. What is more, most of them had not, like many young children brought up in care, suffered repeated disruptions of bonds. Recovery from early deprivation may well be possible. But it is not easy to achieve and often it does not happen at all. The question is whether, when a child is brought up in his first 3 years not in what Bowlby has called 'the environment of human adaptedness', that is by the mother or an equally responsive and available substitute mother, and is unable to form long-lasting and strong bonds with specific parent figures, he or she is predisposed to more permanent impairments of the capacity for later human attachments and of intelligence. Sadly, the answer must be 'yes'. We must conclude that certain things are best learnt at certain times. They can, with the sort of effort many adopters and long-term foster parents are prepared to sustain, be acquired later, but it is not easy and recovery may not be complete. Fortunately, the lesson Bowlby has taught us has been well learnt, and every effort is now made by social workers to prevent very young children from ever entering institutions.

George Brown and his colleagues (Brown 1982), in their studies of depression in working-class mothers, have interpreted the later effects of childhood mother-loss as sensitizing the individual, through impairment of self-reliance and self-esteem, to loss events in adult life in the absence of an intimate and supportive relationship at that time. What has not yet been established is whether women who have suffered such early losses then find it difficult to sustain adult supportive relationships, for example in marriage, as a result of personality disorder, or whether the lack of adequate support in later life is merely yet another fortuitous disadvantage suffered by these vulnerable people.

The place of feelings and intentions

Bowlby holds that it is part of our genetic programme, and essential for
the survival of the species, to be responsive to the helpless young. The
appeal of human and animal babies comes in part from how they look.
They are small, have rounded foreheads, big eyes and tiny noses and
chins. The emotions aroused by a baby, which accompany our efforts
to provide responsive care, are likely to be mirrored by feelings the baby
has towards the care-givers, as his or her perceptions of them and the
baby's sociability mature. But about the feelings of a baby we can never
be sure.

Even when children can communicate their feelings, a problem
remains: how do feelings fit in with the evolving patterns of behavioural
interactions? Bowlby has offered us one solution. He urges us to think
of feelings as part of an individual's intuitive appraisal of his bodily state
including need for action, and of the external setting in which he finds
himself. Feelings provide a monitoring service and, because usually
accompanied by distinctive expressions and gestures, they also announce
our intentions to others. The questions of what causes feelings and
whether feelings can cause behaviour are solved by viewing feelings not
as separate but as integral accompaniments of behaviour. 'We must conclude', says Bowlby, 'that the processes of interpreting and appraising
sensory input must unquestionably be assigned a causal role in producing whatever behaviour emerges. . . . Whether the feelings experienced
as a phase of such appraising should also be assigned a causal role is
a much more difficult question' (Bowlby 1982: 117).

Bruner by-passes these arguments, observing that even infants clearly
have intentions. He says 'Intention viewed abstractly may be at issue
philosophically. But it is a necessity for the biology of complex behaviour,
by whatever label we wish to call it' (Bruner 1973).

Bowlby's *attachment theory* replaces a psychoanalytic model of the
first human relationship with an evolutionary biological one (Campos
et al. 1983). We are no longer dependent only on psychoanalytic data
and theories about the first, or 'primary', human relationship; we have
concrete observational data about the accompanying behaviour. Peter
Marris stresses the uniqueness of important human relationships and
agrees with Bowlby that the child's experiences within the family become
working models of how important people are likely to treat him, and
influence his expectations of others and his future plans: 'Unique relationships are crucial to the structure of meaning that each of us develops

to make sense of our experience and direct our lives' (Marris 1982: 191).

We shall now trace the development of this first relationship into later childhood and describe recent work confirming that new and very different capacities begin to mature in the second year: for self-appraisal and aspirations for achievement; for the emotional and behavioural skills needed in group interactions; and for morality.

Chapter five

From infancy to childhood: social relationships in the pre-school years

In the first part of this chapter we shall review what happens to the child's tie to the mother as he gets onto his feet and becomes an active participant in family life and in the nursery or playgroup. We enter a time of life which is at least partly remembered and has been shown to have a lasting impact on later personality. In the second part of the chapter we focus on an equally important but rather different developmental achievement in the second year of life: the beginnings of inner standards of competence and morality, which coincide in time with the child's ability to play his or her part, not just as a member of a pair, but within a social group.

Attachment in the second and third years of life

Specific attachments are at their height when they first appear (Schaffer 1971) and proximity-seeking declines as the infant gets onto his feet and begins to explore his environment more actively. In fact being able to walk so enthralls the toddler that he sometimes forgets his mother until he notices the distance between them.

Early ethological studies of toddlers were concerned with the gradual attenuation of proximity-seeking between mother and child, and with the child's increasing attention to the rest of his or her environment, human and inanimate. Anderson, for example, in a study of mothers and toddlers in London parks (Anderson 1974) found that children tended to keep within a radius of 200 feet from their mothers. If, without noticing, they exceeded that distance, the mothers would retrieve them. If the children noticed they had toddled too far they would return themselves. At that age (15–30 months) children can return only to a stationary mother. If she moves away the child freezes. Following is not yet possible, and when a mother precedes her young toddler she invariably pauses every few steps to allow him to catch up. In choosing his couples for observation, the experimenter knew which child belonged to which mother by watching at whom the child looked when astonished or startled by something he or she had seen or found.

In their second and third years children tolerate increasing periods of separation. Schaffer argues that if we widen the concept of attachment beyond proximity-seeking, which clearly declines with age, to include the internal representations of the mother object, and if internal representations are used increasingly by the child to regulate his or her behaviour, we can more easily explain these observations (Schaffer 1971). The 1-year-old has to return to his mother frequently to confirm his memory of her by checking it against reality. The older child does not need such frequent reminders but can carry the image of his mother forward with him for longer. He can even make allowances in his mind for his mother's independent movements so that he is not shocked, as is the younger child, when he fails to see her exactly where he left her.

McGrew studied a different aspect of attachment behaviour when he observed 3-year-olds entering a nursery school (McGrew 1974). A quarter of the children cried on the first day when their mothers said goodbye, or after they left. A mother's failure to take proper leave of her child initiated the worst disruption seen during a child's first day. We do not know whether the mother slipped out surreptitiously because she knew her child would cry or whether the child cried because he had not been prepared for her departure. Established nursery children treated the newcomers with neutrality or helpful attention, girls being particularly solicitous (e.g. 'When's my mummy coming back?' 'All the mummies come back after milk. When the bell rings'), sometimes trying to cheer up the new arrival, pointing out his distress to the teacher, holding hands, patting and kissing the newcomer in imitation of what they had seen mothers do. Several established nursery children appeared to be reminded of their own initial separation distress. As they watched the newcomers they regressed to thumb-sucking, scratching, rubbing or fingering their mouths, noses, ears or hair.

Observed vicissitudes of the first human relationship

Normal variations

Robert Hinde has for some years attempted to form a bridge between clinical and developmental psychology. Concerned about the fact that developmental psychologists attended mainly to 'the universal child' and clinical psychologists to individual differences, he took a realistically complex view of developing human relationships. One of his crucial discoveries was that in his Cambridge colony of monkeys, the strongest determinant of the nature of the infant's separation reaction was his or her previous relationship with the mother (Hinde and McGinnis 1977). The quality of relationships, Hinde holds, depends on the different personalities of the individuals concerned; the expectations that the one has of the other (in part determined by past experience); and the social group, with its specific structure, norms and myths, in which the relationship is embedded.

In a study already referred to (p.39) Hinde and his colleagues watched 40 children at home and at playschool, at 3½ years and again at 50 months, together with their mothers, peers and teachers (Stevenson-Hinde and Hinde 1986). They assessed the children's temperament; the family background; the mothers' mood states; and their expectations of their children. When mothers were low and irritable they were more physically affectionate towards their daughters, using them as comforters, than towards their sons, but were also more hostile to the girls than to the boys.

Definite differences were found between boys and girls in their relationships at home and at school. Boys were more involved with other children, initiating more peer-relationships. Boys played with more physical gusto but girls showed more physical friendliness. When the relationship with the mother lacked warmth, girls, but not boys, initiated much contact with teachers. Hostility towards other children reflected a hostile relationship with the mother, and friendly contact with peers occurred more in children, especially boys, who had frequent positive interactions with their mothers at home (Hinde *et al*. 1983; Hinde and Tamplin 1983).

These workers speculate that the new experiences within the nursery or playgroup, among strange adults and children, have profound effects on development; and also that the reciprocity involved in interactions between young children may be essential for learning the empathic skills necessary for close relationships in later life.

An important advance in exploring the effects of early upbringing on later personality, and especially on the capacity to provide sensitive child care, has come from the work of Mary Main and her colleagues (Main and Kaplan 1985). For the first time, mothers' and fathers' communications about their own childhood memories, and the styles in which they reported these, as well as their feelings, have been systematically related to observations of their children's behaviour in the Ainsworth 'strange situation' at the age of 1 year, and to aspects of later behaviour. Observations at one point in time were made blind to the assessments at another. Children 'securely' attached in infancy were for example found at the age of 6 to portray their families in drawings more realistically than those previously 'insecurely' attached.

When the children were 6, their parents were given a semi-structured 'Adult Attachment Interview' and it was found that parents of 'insecurely' attached infants either defensively dismissed or devalued their own past attachments to parents, or were still painfully preoccupied with these; while parents of securely attached babies either reported happy and satisfying early attachments or had come to terms with and presented frank, coherent and realistic accounts of poor childhood experiences.

This study is remarkable for making a bridge between observations of actual behaviour and systematically evaluated accounts of people's inner lives. It adds strength to the notion that the nature of our early attachments to our parents becomes translated into inner working models of these relationships, and that these in turn powerfully influence our intimate relationships in adult life. To this theme we shall return in the chapters on psychoanalytic theories of personality development.

Explorations of the causes and consequences of different styles of early mother-child relationships have now been extended from the study of families in the general population, as in the work of Hinde and Main, to the study of disadvantaged or disturbed mothers and their children. In particular, the effects on child care and on the development of children of depressive illness in the mother has been documented, as well as the high association of a depressive illness with both childhood deprivation and current personality disorder of the mother.

Maternal depression

Depressive states have been found in almost 40 per cent of working-class mothers of young children (Richman *et al*. 1982). George Brown identified provoking agents, or triggering experiences, as well as vulnerability factors in the causation of such illnesses and found that their excess among working-class women was due to greater exposure of such women to both sets of causes (Brown 1982). Vulnerability factors included the loss by death or separation of the mother's own mother before the age of 11; having three or more children under 14 at home;

not being employed; and lacking a close, confiding relationship with another adult, such as a husband.

Triggers for depressive illnesses, in the presence of one or more such vulnerability factors, were a loss or disappointment (involving another person, one's own achievement or an idea); and ongoing major difficulties such as domestic overcrowding or having an alcoholic husband. Early mother-loss can act through personality changes, especially chronic feelings of insecurity, which themselves can contribute to a poor choice of husband, to lack of intimacy with this husband, and possibly a failure to limit family size. Other studies (e.g. Pound *et al.* 1985) have confirmed the association of depression in mothers of young children with childhood loss events, especially the death of the maternal grandmother, but also with the mother's childhood experiences of family discord and disruption; and have further documented the association of such depressive states with current life stresses, especially poverty and poor housing, and with personality disorder of the mother herself, that is with pre-existing difficulties in interpersonal relationships.

A mother's low mood state in turn is often accompanied by high irritability followed by a deterioration of the marriage and of relationships with the children. Such depressions tend to be long-lasting or recurrent (Pound *et al.* 1985). In contrast to other mothers of young children, most depressed mothers had histories of many deprivations and life stresses, especially separation from their own parents who had often been harsh and unaffectionate. By the time of the survey, the mothers' relationships with their parents had usually improved. A full life history was then necessary to uncover the important past adversities. Depressed mothers had married earlier than the control group, and had less supportive relationships with their husbands, many themselves personality disordered, aggressive and antisocial. The families often lived in poverty and poor housing. Their children were significantly more disturbed as well as retarded in expressive language. Although the children's disturbance was highly related to personality disorder in the mother and to marital discord, the mother's depressive illness made its own contribution to the child's disorder. The picture that emerged of these depressed mothers included bleak material circumstances and little medical or social work care, even after suicide attempts.

The physical care of the children was usually good, but an observation study revealed significant differences between depressed and non-depressed mothers in their interaction with their children (Mills *et al.* 1985). Depressed mothers were less sensitively attuned to their children, more actively controlling, and with fewer pleasurable inter-changes with their offspring. They were unresponsive to the children and spent much time staring into space. Bored and miserable 2 year-olds often become challenging and provoking by the age of 3.

In a recent American study, depressed mothers in the community were compared with non-depressed mothers in Ainsworth's 'strange situation' (p. 65) together with their 2- and 3-year-old children. More of these were found to be insecurely or anxiously attached than among the con-trols, and this was especially so when the depressed mother was also a single parent (Radke-Yarrow *et al*. 1985). The effect of a mother's mental state on the quality of her child's attachment behaviour manifests only after 12-19 months of age, precisely at the time at which young children begin to show specific and overt responses to other people's distress. Children are now drawn into the feeling states of others so that a mother's tears bring the toddler to her side with efforts to comfort her.

Mothers themselves deprived of family care in childhood

Another group of mothers of young children thought to be at risk of pro-viding less than optimal child care, overlapping but not identical with mothers with recurrent depressions, are those who themselves have had long periods of institutional care in childhood, usually because of parent loss or severe discord in their own families of origin. Wolkind and Krug studied three groups of mothers having their first baby: a group separated from their parents either in very early childhood or for longer periods in later childhood because of family disharmony, but who subsequently rejoined their families (the 'disrupted' group); a group similarly separated who remained in local authority care (the 'in-care' group); and a group without such childhood separations (the 'intact' group) (Wolkind and Krug 1985).

Relationships and contacts with parents and other family members were best for the 'intact' group and worst for the 'in-care' group who had very little support when their first child was born. These mothers were economically deprived and often new to their neighbourhood. They looked forward to their pregnancy with less pleasure and gave birth to smaller infants. They enjoyed their babies less and were physically and emotionally less responsive to them. Throughout their child's first 3½ years, these mothers had significantly more psychiatric symptoms, mainly depression with anxiety, than mothers in both other groups. Only 20 per cent had managed to establish a good marital relationship by the time the child was 3½ compared with the 50 per cent of the 'disrupted' and 62 per cent of the 'intact' groups. The authors argue that it is not the 'in-care' experience itself but the traumatic childhood, for which reception into care is an index, that had left these women and their children so vulnerable; and that the important ameliorating factor, protecting against depression and anxiety, was the degree of support from spouse or mother. One might add that the 'in-care' group, because of their traumatic experiences, are likely to have developed personality difficulties, too, which would then impair their capacity both to elicit support from others and to provide good child care.

Linda Dowdney and her colleagues also studied mothers who had spent long periods of early childhood in children's homes, and compared them with mothers brought up by their own families (Dowdney *et al.* 1985). The focus here was on the actual mother-toddler interactions. It was found that the main characteristic of the in-care group of mothers was a lack of sensitive responsiveness. Mothers who had been in care were only slightly less 'warm' to their children and they smacked slightly more often, but their methods of controlling the child were significantly less effective and their rates of reconciliation with the child after disputes significantly lower.

In this study, too, a depression on top of other factors made matters worse. Fully one-half of the mothers who had either been in care as children or were currently depressed had poor parenting skills. But for both groups of mothers, a good marriage was related to better and more effective mothering. One of the important lessons from the studies of mothers who had been in care (Skuse and Cox 1985) is that, where the mothers had as children been returned to warring parents, their adult social competence tended to be worse than that of mothers who had stayed in care; while when mothers had been returned to more harmonious homes, their later life adjustment, including the care of their young children, was better.

The McKay family

Many of these research findings, and in particular all of Brown's contributors to depression in working-class mothers, are illustrated by a family I knew some time ago and was able to stay in touch with over a number of years.

Robert was referred by his headmaster because of anxiety, weepiness,

81

poor sleep, emotional withdrawal, temper tantrums, and stealing from his mother. At the time, his mother had a severe depressive illness following the spontaneous miscarriage of a baby girl at 6 months. This would have been her first daughter. There were three boys in the family already: Robert, 8; John, 5; and Michael, 3.

For Robert and John, this was their mother's second serious illness and hence the more threatening. Mrs McKay had had a previous depression after Michael's birth (when Robert was 4 and John 18 months), attempted suicide and was in hospital for six months for treatment which included ECT. Robert was then with foster parents; John and Michael in a children's home. On their return to the family Robert was unhappy, disobedient and began to steal.

When first seen, Robert was quiet and inhibited, concerned above all to be helpful. 'When your mum's ill you have to be very good because noise makes her worse and my wee brothers make a lot of noise.' The younger boys were indeed loud, overactive, disinhibited and impulsive. How much their early experience of group care had contributed to this cannot be known. In Michael's case there was another possible cause: he was born after a difficult delivery, was grossly lacking in concentration, and had serious specific learning difficulties, affecting his early language development and later his reading and spelling.

Recurrent depression was not this mother's only problem. Her parents had separated in infancy and she was brought up in a children's home. Throughout her marriage she suffered from her inability to show affection which she attributed to her impersonal upbringing. Thin and haggard in appearance, she wept as she told us that, although she loved her children, she could never bring herself to cuddle them. Sex had also been difficult for her and she was irritable both with her husband and her sons. Mr McKay in turn could not compensate them for his wife's disabilities. He, too, had had a disrupted childhood. His father had died when he was 6, his mother remarried, divorced and remarried again. Although a steady worker, he had become a heavy drinker, often violently aggressive to his wife and teasingly aggressive to the boys who feared him.

The mother had entered marriage when only 18, still in the children's home and pregnant with Robert. She did not respect her husband and he was fonder of her than she of him. Both suffered from poor self-esteem and there were frequent fights, witnessed by the children, in which the parents physically attacked each other.

Despite much social work support, welcomed by the mother, the violent marriage continued, as did the mother's recurrent depressions and hospitalizations. Finally, when Robert was 12, Mrs McKay left home and the three boys once more went into care. Robert, now an inhibited and solitary adolescent, became his mother's right-hand man and a go-between for his father in his repeated attempts to re-establish the marriage. While John's adjustment improved greatly once he had a base away from his turbulent family, the constitutionally impaired boy, Michael, remained educationally retarded and dangerously impulsive because fascinated by matches and fire.

When the boys were 19, 16 and 14, the mother was married a second time, to a man she had met in her psychiatric hospital. She was now less anxious, her depressive episodes were over and, plump and cheerful, she was working and content in her marriage. Her personality improvement occurred too late to protect her children from a violent family life with repeated admissions into care, much pressure for early maturity and, despite evident parental affection, a lack of sensitive parenting. Robert, on whom Mrs McKay had been so dependent when on her own, was now seen as a threat to the new marriage. He in turn repeated history by rushing into an early engagement.

Disruption of early attachments and lack of mothering

Mrs McKay's story illustrates the long-term personality difficulties that can follow prolonged institutional care from early childhood with lack of intimate and continuous mothering experiences. Fortunately children's homes are now no longer chosen for young children whose parents cannot look after them. Instead attempts are made to find them long-term substitute families.

In an important comparative study already referred to, of young women who as children had been in care for long periods and women brought up by their own families (p. 29), Quinton and Rutter documented how frequently the 'in care' group had rushed early into marriage with an equally deprived boy, not by deliberate choice but to 'get away' from their current unsatisfactory home or family (Quinton and Rutter 1988). Such marriages, like Mrs McKay's, tended to be stormy and unstable, with the young mothers sometimes being left to bring up their children on their own. Child care too was often poor. Yet not all deprived girls made unsatisfactory marriages and when they did not, their personal adjustment and mothering of their children was good. The main factor found to lead to marriage by choice to a boy the mother had known for more than six months was positive school experiences of some kind. The authors believe the effect of such experiences to be mediated by a sense of self-esteem and confidence in one's own control over one's destiny, which is then carried forward into later, adult relationships.

The childhood effects of early and prolonged institutional care

Although few children are now reared in children's homes throughout their first 4 years of life, we should not forget the serious and long-term consequences for both emotional and intellectual development that can follow (Bowlby 1951; Rutter 1981). Barbara Tizard and her colleagues found that in residential nurseries, the language development of 4-year-olds depended on the kind of intimate care and encouragement of language they received (Tizard *et al.* 1972). In nurseries where the people in immediate charge of the children had autonomy, with freedom to decide about day-to-day living arrangements, they interacted more, and more helpfully, with the children, and the children in turn had normal langu age skills. In more authoritarian establishments, fewer conversations were observed between children and care-givers, and the children's language development was below average for their age.

In a further study (Tizard 1977; Tizard and Hodges 1978; see also Rutter 1981) of children cared for in residential nurseries for 4½ months to 2 years of life and then or later adopted or restored to their own mothers, Tizard found considerable differences in behaviour and in intelligence and school functioning among the children, depending on the sort of family environment which followed their institutional experience and on the age of the child at the time of the move.

Adopted children on the whole did much better than children restored to their own mothers. But the family life in this second group was, not surprisingly, often turbulent with step-parents and many other children in the home, mothers under stress and with less time for the restored child than adoptive parents had, and often also with ambivalent feelings towards this child who had, after all, once been given up. The restored children in turn were more disturbed than the adopted and functioned less well intellectually and linguistically. The adopted children, too, when followed up both at 4 and 8 years of age, were still more attention seeking and slightly more disturbed than a control group of children who had throughout their lives been brought up by their families; and even at 16, while normally attached to their parents and much better adjusted than the restored group, the adopted children were judged at school to be more disturbed than the never separated controls, more dependent on their parents and with fewer close peer relationships (Hodges 1989). But the problems of the adopted group were manageable (many adoptive parents welcoming their child's dependency), while those of the restored group often were not. A further finding, not conclusive because of small numbers, was that children adopted late, that is, after the age of 4½ years, did not show the rapid increase in IQ after placement that had characterized those adopted between 2 and 4 years. And three out of five later-adopted children were also disturbed: fearful, worried, and solitary. Yet only one of these five late-adopted children failed to show attachment to the new parents.

The basis both for emotional and intellectual, especially language, development is created during intimate parent-child interactions in the earliest years of life. While the deficits which result from lack of sensitive and intimate parenting then can be remedied by really good later family care, this needs to take place as early as possible and certainly before the child is 4 years old, to avoid subsequent deficits of emotional and intellectual development. Language competence is essential for school success, and school failure, because inevitably leading to poor self-esteem, can, especially in an already emotionally deprived child, contribute in a major way to psychiatric problems both in childhood and later life.

From dyadic to group relationships: the child's entry into family life

The young infant is able to focus on only one thing at a time: an interesting object, or his mother, or another person. Only in the second half of the first year can he hold mother and object or mother and other person in his mind together and engage in truly shared activities, involving at first person and object, then more than one person. Until recently observations of young children focused primarily on the universal capacity to form attachments, that is, on the outer manifestations of the child's first or *primary emotional relationship*. Later stages of social-emotional development postulated by psychoanalysts — the second *'anal'* stage in which ideas of right and wrong begin; and the third *'genital'* stage in which emotions accompanying group relationships and adult role-modelling first arise, in which the child acquires sexual curiosity and a sexual role, and in which guilt and conscience first appear — remained as myths.

Recent studies of children within their own families, especially Judy Dunn's work on siblings (Dunn and Kendrick 1982), and of children interacting with other children in nursery or experimental playroom, have greatly added to our understanding and confirmed the reality as well as the timing of many psychoanalytic postulates about early emotional development. Perhaps more striking still has been Jerome Kagan's discovery of a second stage of biological maturation in which children suddenly become sensitive to flaws in the objects around them and acquire standards both of how things *should* be and of what they themselves *ought* to be able to do (Kagan 1981).

Cognitive and affective development proceed hand in hand, and it is now generally recognized that the baby's perception and responsiveness to people develop in parallel with his or her capacity for distinguishing the properties of an inanimate world. The two major developmental achievements during the second and third years of life which we shall now discuss in turn: the capacity for group participation and the earliest development of inner standards and of morality, also coincide in time. The sense of morality inevitably involves inner images of external others, that is of witnesses, absent in the first or 'primary' relationship between infant and parent in which the child can do no wrong.

One other preliminary point needs to be made. While participation in triads or groups requires the same cognitive and social skills whether the group is the family or a play or nursery group, the emotional significance, and especially the emotional charge, of family relationships are quite different from those of the more public and less intimate relationships in the outside world. Hartup (1980) emphasizes the distinctions between the two social systems of family and peer relationships and, like others, stresses that one of the functions of family life is to give the child a secure base from which to explore the outer world, indicating that if for any reason the family is disrupted, play and other activities outside the family tend also to be adversely affected. But the nature and significance of the very high levels of emotion associated with family life have not so far been adequately attended to.

Changes in the mother-child relationship in the second year

Schaffer sees the developmental process as one of sequential reorganizations that periodically overtake the child's mental life, initiated by the child's inherent maturational programme but accomplished by child and care-giver jointly (Schaffer 1984). He has documented the changes in the relationship between mother and child in the second year, but also under different circumstances. For example, requests and commands are made to the baby even in the first year but with no expectations of compliance. The baby picks up a toy and his or her mother *then* says 'pick it up'. She sits the baby up with the request 'sit up'. True commands and requests are made only in the second year, now with expectations of compliance. These are most successful if the child was already about to do what is asked of him or her, and if requests are made indirectly in the form of suggestions.

When, in an experiment in a day nursery, care-givers were observed in interaction with just one child at a time, and then with four children, considerable differences were noted. The amount the nurses spoke to the children was about the same, but the numbers of utterances to each child, not surprisingly, were much less in the group setting. Moreover, when with four toddlers, the nurses responded to fewer overtures of the child and ignored more; and in addition there was in that setting much more 'management talk', that is commands as to what and what not to do. The inference is that when mothers have to look after twins or a number of closely spaced children, their responsiveness to the children and their methods of control will also be different from when they bring up just one small child at a time.

Parents and siblings

In their careful observations of 40 families in the community, Judy Dunn and Carol Kendrick vividly portrayed the complex emotional family relationships in which 1½- to 4-year-olds are involved when a second baby is born (Dunn and Kendrick 1982). They followed up their families from before the birth of the second child, and were especially interested in the causes of difficulties. All first-borns showed signs of disturbance and unhappiness, as well as interest in and affection for the baby. Sibling rivalry is no myth. One 4-year-old asked his mother on the birth of his brother: 'Why have you ruined my life?' The authors stress that siblings are there 'for life'.

When, as often happened, the mother was tired and depressed after the birth, the older child cried more and sometimes evoked great irritability from the mother. An unexpected finding was that when the mother's relationship with her first-born had been especially close, the older child often reacted badly to the inevitable withdrawal of her time and attention. Not surprisingly, a close and intense relationship with the father had a protective effect. If the mother-child relationship had been very negative, the relationship between the siblings, perhaps to make up for what was lacking, was often positive. Younger first-borns tended to be more clinging after the birth of their sibling than older children. If the first child had a difficult temperament this increased the problems. In general, the more friendly the older child to the newcomer, the more positive the baby's response to the older child. Same-sex children tended to imitate one another more and often had more positive relationships with each other than opposite-sex pairs of siblings.

One finding of considerable practical relevance was that positive relationships between the children were associated with a particular style of maternal care: the mother treating the older child as a partner in the task of interpreting and meeting the needs of the baby. Dunn and Kendrick demonstrated that as early as the second year of life children are able to empathize with, comment on, and attempt to respond to the feelings and wishes of others, and are aware of the baby's limited understanding compared with their own.

Some of the 40 families in this study were followed up when the older children were 6, and a striking continuity was seen in the varying relationships between the sibling pairs over the intervening two to four years. Both emotional and cognitive aspects of development, as well as the children's temperament, and their relationships with both their parents had contributed to how they managed to get on with each other.

Of particular interest to this group of researchers were the manifestations and resolutions of conflict between the siblings and between mothers and children (Dunn and Munn 1985). Detailed and regular home observations were made during the second child's second year. Conflicts between older child and younger sibling and between older child and mother were recorded, as well as responses of the child to conflict between mother and younger sibling. The older children clearly understood the feelings and intentions of other family members: physical aggression and teasing increased after the younger sibling was 18 months old. Once the sibling was 2 years old, the older child assigned it responsibility in appeals to the mother. In the second year, but not before, children increasingly smiled teasingly at their mothers while doing forbidden things, clearly now aware of the rules; and mothers in turn no longer responded with just 'dos' and 'don'ts', but increasingly referred to rules of conduct. In all six families studied intensively, there was much discussion of what was not allowed, and the children themselves commented on their own and their siblings' breaking of the rules. If mothers referred to the older child's feelings in talking to the younger sibling when settling conflicts, then the older child would more often appeal to the mother for help during conflicts with the younger one. When older children witnessed mother-sibling conflict they would laugh if the sibling was teasing, but remain serious and often support the sibling if only anger was shown by mother and younger child.

The first signs of aspirations, values and morality

The discussions of Schaffer's work on children's compliance with mother's requests (p. 87), and of Judy Dunn's observations of conflict resolution and the use of rules by mothers and young children, have prepared us for our next topic.

Kagan's discoveries about the second year of life

Unlike Dunn and her colleagues, who were interested in the determinants of individual differences in the interactions between mothers and children, Kagan focused on maturational aspects of universal developmental changes (Kagan 1981). Although no admirer of Freudian theories, his observations led him to identify a second stage in the biological maturation of children, in which the *capacity for the development of inner standards* and of conscience is first seen. The changes Kagan regularly noted in children during their second year were associated with self-awareness and were recognized by him as the earliest manifestations of a built-in moral sense.

He observed children at monthly intervals in a variety of standard play settings. One was to present the child with three types of objects: ten small unflawed toys; ten flawed toys (e.g. a car with a wheel missing, a doll with a chipped face); and two unflawed meaningless objects. No 14-month-old behaved in any special way towards the flawed toys. But 57 per cent of 19-month-olds showed unambiguous signs of concern at one or more of these, saying 'fix it', 'broke', 'yuck', or merely pointing and vocalizing with concern or taking the broken object to the mother — and the proportion increased with age. In another experiment, the child was asked to watch an adult engage in difficult play with toys. All 13- to 14-month-olds were either bored or watched calmly. But at 15 months, and increasingly as the second birthday approached, children began to fret, protest, wish to leave the room or, clinging to mother, say 'It's Mummy's turn to play.' Clearly these older children felt obliged to copy what the adult did and, realizing they could not do it, became distressed. This change just preceded the beginning of *evaluative language*. Between 19 and 26 months the first references to 'broken', 'boo-boo', 'dirty', 'wash hands', 'can't', 'hard do', were heard; and by 20 months most children used words like 'bad', 'good', 'hard', 'dirty' and 'nice'.

Kagan repeated his experiments with children on the island of Fiji and found the same sequence of development there, indicating that the acquisition of inner standards and its timing are not culture-bound, but expressions of maturational change. Kagan concluded that between 18 months and 2 years children behave as if they are acquiring a new set of functions centred on their sensitivity to adult standards and their ability to meet them, as well as an awareness of their own effectiveness, that is of what they can and cannot do. They fret on noticing their ineptness and smile when they succeed, often at a self-imposed task. The standards now acquired related to cleanliness, integrity of property, harm to others and toileting. Kagan argued that these standards are biologically useful, helping the child, for example, to inhibit his or her aggressive impulses towards a younger brother or sister. Children can now imagine how others feel, on the basis of self-awareness of their own feelings, and offer comfort to people in pain.

Two observations in public places illustrate the importance for young children of this changed way of perceiving the world and of their new accomplishments at this time of life. In the beehive tombs of Mycenae in Greece, a 2-year-old was concerned only with their blackness: 'It's dirty,' she kept saying, pointing an accusing finger at the walls. At an art gallery where the spectators were distanced from the pictures by ropes which did not extend around the corners of the room, a young child, with little interest in the exhibits, complained loudly to her older brother that the ropes were 'missing' at the corners. The mother proudly confirmed that her daughter was approaching her second birthday.

Empathy, the basis for moral behaviour

Emotions are important, not only for reflecting a person's inner life, but for the effect they have in regulating social relationships (Campos *et al*. 1983). Pleasure, rage, and fear are evident in early infancy, but only when the child has a sense of self as distinct from the outside world, from around 9 months onwards (see Chapter 6), can true emotions, related to the people and events outside, be felt: affection, fear of strangers, fear of danger, sorrow at loss, anger at other people. Anxiety emerges at around 1 year, and shame at awareness of personal failure, as Kagan has shown, only by about 18 months.

Emotional responses to the feelings of others occur even in the neonate: when one baby in a nursery for newborns begins to cry, all the others cry too. Yet this 'reflexive emotional resonance' (Campos *et al.* 1983) is thought to express the infant's sharing of the emotions of others without realizing their difference from his or her own. Between 4 and 9 months, babies respond emotionally to facial and vocal displays of emotions; and at around 9 months they are thought capable of locating emotions in other people.

Martin Hoffman has analysed the development of empathy in young children (Hoffman 1984). He too notes that in the first year children respond to distress in others as if it were happening to themselves. But in the second year of life, as Radke-Yarrow also found, only when children have attained a sense of others as separate from themselves (dualism) are they capable of sympathy, that is of offering comfort to other people. Often such actions are inappropriate, suggesting that the child still perceives the emotions of others as its own. When another toddler cries, the child appeals to its own mother to comfort the other, even when the distressed child's mother is there; or will fetch its own comforter for the other child. By the third year, role-taking occurs in play and children are now clearly capable of realizing that other people's feelings can differ from their own. In the fourth year empathic distress results in offering appropriate help.

In middle childhood yet further changes in empathic responses are seen. Children now empathize more with others who are like themselves, offering less help to children perceived as outsiders. Also, when the distress of the other is overwhelming, they tend to withdraw. In addition, children now concern themselves with the long-lasting distress of other people, even if unknown, and with distressed groups of people far away, such as the Ethiopian famine victims or the victims of war. Moreover, only at about 9 to 10 years do children realize that other people can have two different emotions at the same time.

Hoffman believes that empathy forms the basis for morality; and that morality consists of a feeling of obligation to foster not only one's own but the welfare of others. This basic inner dictum, rather than actions for reward or to avoid punishment, determines true morality. Hoffman also believes that children are best socialized to act in accordance with this inner moral principle if, once capable of empathic understanding of others, their parents' disciplinary methods focus on pointing out the possible harm to others of antisocial behaviour.

Morality and convention

It has recently been found that from as early as the fourth year children distinguish between morality and convention. *Conventions* are behavioural uniformities which serve to harmonize social interactions and form part of, and are themselves determined by, the social system. For example, it is a convention in most schools and nursery classes to call the teacher by her second, not her first, name. In themselves such acts are arbitrary and could be altered by consensus. In his systematic questioning of children of different ages, Turiel asked 'would it have been wrong to call the teacher by her first name if there were no school rule about that?' (Turiel 1983). Even very young children thought not. *Morality*, in contrast, concerns prescriptive judgements of justice, rights, and welfare, about how people should behave to each other, irrespective of the social context. Such judgements are thought to emerge directly from social interactions, including harm done to others and violation of their rights.

> A 2-year-old, just after the birth of her sister, was seen comforting a make-believe baby by means of 'mommy's milk', apparently trying out how it might feel to be the mommy. On another occasion she was observed laboriously and repeatedly to walk between the two front legs of a large hall cabinet, distributing pieces of paper she had torn up, commenting 'one for you'; 'and one for you'. Clearly a notion of justice and fair shares had entered her mind.

Turiel cites the example of a child entering a playground and finding all the swings occupied. She proceeds to push another child off his swing and takes his place. The children Turiel questioned all thought this was wrong, even if there was no rule about such behaviour, 'because he could get hurt and start to cry' (Turiel 1983:49). When children were asked whether the rules governing certain forms of behaviour could be changed if everyone agreed, the majority of children thought this could be done for the rules of games and social conventions. But most children thought the rule that says stealing is wrong could not be changed, nor the rule that forbids hurting other people. Younger children on the whole regarded rules as more fixed, and older children had a better grasp of their underlying purposes. But all the children distinguished between rules of morality and rules of convention.

Even at this stage of life moral development, as indeed the development of the child's human relationships, involves both emotions and cognition. In the next chapter we describe the unfolding of the child's cognitive abilities with age.

Chapter six

The growth of intelligence and the birth of language

A little later (two and a half years) she was very much struck by the sight of the moon. She wanted to see it every evening . . . when she walked it seemed to her that it walked too, and this discovery charmed her. As the moon according to the hour appeared in different places, now in front of the house now behind it, she cried out 'Another moon, another moon!' One evening (three years) on enquiring for the moon and being told it had set (*qu'elle est allée se coucher*) she replies 'But where's the moon's *bonne*?' All this closely resembles the emotions and conjectures of primitive peoples, their lively and deep admiration for great natural objects, the power that analogy, language and metaphor exercise over them, leading them to solar and lunar myths. . . .

(M. Taine 1877)

Again, one hand is pressed down by the other flat upon the table until it hurts, as if the hand were a wholly foreign plaything, and it is still looked at wonderingly sometimes (62nd week).

The same child, who likes to hold a biscuit to the mouth of any member of the family to whom he is favourably disposed, offered the biscuit in the same way, entirely of his own accord, to his own foot — sitting on the floor, holding the biscuit in a waiting attitude to his toes — and this strange freak was repeated many times in the twenty-third month. The child amused himself with it.

Thus, at a time when the attention to what is around is already very far developed, one's own person may not be distinguished from the environment.

(Wilhelm Preyer 1888)

In the late nineteenth century a few eminent scientists who were also affectionate fathers discovered with evident astonishment the intensity with which young children explore the world, how hard they work at understanding it, and how different their logic is from that of adults. A generation before Jean Piaget began his monumental studies into the nature of the child's thinking, Darwin (1877), Taine (1877) and Preyer (1888) noticed that in their first two years children are constant and active experimenters, using for the purpose both themselves and the things about them. They are intrigued by chance observations, seek to reproduce what they have accidentally achieved, and do so repeatedly until the novelty wears off and a new range of phenomena and activities captures their attention. At first, an object encountered in different places is perceived as a series of different objects. Once he can speak, the child endows everything about him with his own feelings and life circumstances. Although Preyer may not have been correct when he thought his son, in offering a biscuit to his toes, did not realize the toes were part of himself (it is possible that what Preyer saw was the beginning of make-believe play: the toes being cast into the role of another person), he was probably right to interpret earlier, pain-inducing behaviour as indicating his child's confusion between what was part of him and what belonged to the outside world.

Why an understanding of cognitive development is important for the practitioner

In this chapter we shall explore the changes in thinking and reasoning that occur during different stages of childhood. Educators, parents and teachers need to know what children at different ages are able to grasp, and how best to foster their understanding and competence; and everyone concerned with children under stress should be aware of the particular misunderstandings and anxieties so regularly brought about by intellectual immaturity.

If we want to make sense of people, children and grown-ups, we need to know how our thinking changes as we grow up. The *subjective viewpoint* of personality development postulated by psychoanalysts can be understood only in the light of the synchronous transformations in childhood of social participation in family life on the one hand, and of language and a consistent but at first fallacious logic on the other.

In his second year the child gets onto his feet and becomes an active member of his family. His relationships with other people, as we saw in the last chapter, expand remarkably and become ever more complex. Language provides the tools for more efficient thinking about himself and the world; it frees the child from the concrete here and now, facilitating memories of the past and speculations about the future. From the start, words are used to classify and group the phenomena perceived and to commit them to memory. Instead of an inner life tied to pleasant and unpleasant but diffuse emotional states, to visual displays, to sound patterns, to his own motoric exploits and their practical results, the child can now remember significant events and meaningful emotions and can make connections between experiences over time.

These important developmental steps are taken precisely during that period of childhood, from about 18 months to 7 years, when the nature of logic is different from adult rationality and the child's explanations for the phenomena and events he or she encounters are potentially frightening.

The roots for irrational anxiety and irrational behaviour in later life can, in the absence of abnormal brain function or other major constitutional impairments, be regularly unearthed among the experiences of these early years, reinforced by subsequent traumatic life events. Unless we are familiar with the way the under-7s think and reason, we shall not be able to understand the misperceptions and misinterpretations to which everyone is prone in times of stress, and which pervade the lives of those otherwise healthy people who have personality disorders or neurotic illnesses. The particular, idiosyncratic, and often emotionally charged communications of people under stress require a knowledge of childhood logic, illustrated in the communications of the patient now described.

An exceptionally intelligent girl, Sylvia, the last by many years of a large, non-intellectual family, complained of panic attacks on going to school, although passionately keen to be educated. Her symptoms began on starting school, at which time a teenage aunt had died. Three years later, when she was 8, after the death of her maternal grandmother, the school attendance problem increased, and since then she was intermittently off school for months at a time and became socially isolated.

At 13 years 10 months she said 'My mum asks me what's wrong

and I say I don't know, but really it's the impression I make on other people as if I'm vain . . . at 5 I didn't care, I was happy and [then] I got quieter and quieter. I remember I was 6 or 7 when the change happened. . . I get on OK but you feel left out because there's nine years between me and my brother. . .

'I've asked how they decided to call me by my name. I never said how I felt. . . Other girls are called Carol and Anne, never Sylvia. I remember asking my mother how she thought of that and she gave me a version and my brother said something else. My father wanted to call me a Highland name because his dad's from up North — like Morag. You get three weeks to register a name and they went up on the twentieth or twenty-first day. . . [If she were a mother] I wouldn't just think up a name myself. There are books of names and I'd ask people. . . I like being called *after* someone. Not to be thought of as an original.'

And at a subsequent interview she said: 'My mother always says "leave your bag behind at dinner time" because the daughters of women she knows do that and she wants me to do the same. You should be like this or talk louder or wear that other jumper because all the other girls do. . . "You don't want to look out of place" . . . but she doesn't end up in making me do these things. She just says "Do what you like" and brings it up again and again. She's got it in her head that the reason I've been off school is that I've been like that: too conspicuous.'

Her father was working away from home on and off, and always, in anticipating his return, she felt tense. Then after a few days it's all right. It reminds her of when she was 7 and 8 and 9 when he also worked away from home. 'Dead quiet you had to be, like some Victorian household. It was the old story: his word was law. In the freedom we had when he used to go away we voiced our opinions to each other. There was anxiety when he came back. I always thought I'd done something wrong. Silly sort of things, as if I was in the wrong somehow, continually doing things. Guilty but at the same time he was picking on me as well. The same with James [her brother] but not so bad and we'd talk about this and I realized James wasn't doing anything and I wasn't either, to annoy him. When the school trouble started I realized what he was saying was not my fault. There must have been a reason but not to do with me. I don't know if he was very unhappy about something we were doing unconsciously, or he didn't like being away from home on these jobs.'

And about the school absences, 'He's incredulous that I'd been back and off again. As if I do it on purpose, out of spite.'

Frightening events happened in the life of this child: the death of a young aunt, and then of her grandmother. To these events Sylvia's mother responded with depressive illnesses, as she had to Sylvia's unexpected, and for her embarrassing birth, so long after the family had seemed complete. Sylvia herself, however, was faced with these stressful events and her mother's depressions just as she started her life outside the family and began to compare herself with other children. Her mother's eagerness to have her inconspicuous was mirrored by her own early anxieties about her name. This became the focus of her self-consciousness and of her doubt about her parents' affection for her. Her father's irritability made her guilty as if she must have done something wrong to deserve it. By the time she could work out for herself that this was not so, the basis for recurring irrational anxieties had been solidly laid.

From a more *objective viewpoint* also, when our aim is not the understanding of an individual's inner life history but the discovery of the causes of psychiatric disorders and how to minimize their effects, we find that certain adverse events are causally linked to later disturbances if they occur at particular stages of development. Hospitalization, for example, surgery, and grave illnesses have different effects on children according to their cognitive level (Wolff 1981).

The age of 7 had for centuries been regarded as a turning point in childhood, long before Piaget discovered the transformations in children's thinking that occur around that time. In historical eras not characterized by particular affection for children, the under-7s were treated differently from older people. In Tudor England boys and girls from the upper and middle classes were regularly sent away to be brought up and educated in other households, but only after the age of 7 (Pinchbeck and Hewitt 1969). Once schools were established, they too started at 7.

While the cognitive style of the under-7s is the most significant for later personality, it forms only one of a series of intellectual transformations between birth and maturity.

The contribution of Jean Piaget (1896–1979)

Like Sigmund Freud, Piaget gave us a new vision of child development. While Freud focused on emotional development and its relationship to neuroses and character disorders in later life. Piaget concerned himself with cognitive development and its implications for education and the philosophy of knowledge. Both were stage theorists, believing that qualitative transformations (not merely quantitative growth) take place as we grow up; both were influenced by Darwin's biological and evolutionary ideas (Dixon and Lerner 1984); and both have been much criticized for their methods of enquiry and for their errors. But they did their work in a different historical era and in a different scientific climate, and it is remarkable, not that they were often wrong, but how often they were right. For this reason, a fairly full outline of the work of Piaget will be presented here, and of Freudian theories about emotional development in the following two chapters.

Piaget's interest was not in levels but processes of intelligence; not in individual differences *between* children but in the evolution of such processes in children in general. He made meticulous observations of groups of children of different ages. He watched what they did; questioned them systematically about their thoughts and beliefs; and structured simple experiments for them to perform. His concern was with the quality of children's responses: how they arrived at correct solutions, and the nature and consistency of their errors. He charted the common trends seen at different ages, and from these he derived a sequence of developmental stages and a theory to account for the transformations involved, simple in outline, more complex in relation to specific intellectual accomplishments.

His methods have been challenged because he did not use a statistical approach to indicate how typical his observations were for the particular groups of Geneva children he studied. Yet a statistical approach involves the examination of large numbers of subjects with an inevitable loss of depth and detail of recorded observations. Such an approach also precludes the exploration at the time of chance observations which do not fit the previously conceived hypotheses to be tested. While replications of his work have revealed errors both of fact and interpretation, his findings have in general been confirmed, and much of his theory stands unchallenged.

Piaget's theory: schemata; assimilation and accommodation; the circular reaction; equilibration

'The essential functions of intelligence consist in understanding and in inventing' (Piaget 1971). Children do not just copy what they see and repeat what they hear; from the start they think up new ways of handling their environment, and from the beginning language is original.

Piaget postulated mental structures, *schemata*, which become increasingly more complex and which govern the child's intellectual activities. Two processes are assumed to mediate between the child's actions and thoughts, and his schemata. *Assimilation* is the incorporation of new objects, actions and ideas into pre-existing schemata. For example, the 7-month-old baby who can regard and reach out for an object and put it to his mouth performs these activities on every small object he encounters: his rattle, a piece of food, a pebble. Every object he sees he submits to the routine he knows. The corollary is that he attends only to those aspects of new objects that have their counterpart in the schemata already in his mind. He is selective in what he can notice and in what he can do. He structures his environment to fit in with his inner capacities and preconceptions.

The child assimilates new objects and ideas to the mental structures it already has. He handles new objects and ideas with old methods. At the same time he is open to novelty, provided the novel experience is not too discrepant from what he knows already. *Accommodation* is the postulated process whereby inner schemata are modified to fit in with new aspects of the environment. The 4-month-old baby, for example, reaches out for a rattle only when he sees it and his hand at the same time. If his hand is out of view the object seems unattainable. A little later he notices that a chance movement has brought his hidden hand into his visual field where the rattle already is. He now incorporates this movement of his unseen hand into the schema for reaching out for objects which previously had contained only movements of a visible hand. With this more sophisticated schema he now continues his experiments. Piaget considered these two functions: assimilation, that is the structuring of reality, and accommodation, building up of the child's inner structures, to be inseparable, and that to know an object is to act upon it and transform it. Intelligence, according to Piaget, derives from action.

Whenever a schema has been modified, practice follows and the new schema is exercised until well established. This Piaget has called the *circular reaction*. For example, a baby in her cot accidentally strikes the rattle strung up before her, sees the coloured balls jump and hears a pleasant tinkle. She now deliberately repeats the striking movement that evoked the 'interesting spectacle' and will do so over and over again until she is a proficient rattler. When some time later she notices that the toy rabbit she has accidentally dropped from her pram is obligingly restored to her by her human companion, she deliberately throws it overboard again to recapture the experience, and does so repeatedly until the novelty has worn off and an *equilibrium* has been reached. Piaget held that the cognitive system is equilibrated and adjusts itself constantly to cope with new demands and challenges from the outside world.

The stages of cognitive development

Piaget describes four main stages of intellectual development: the sensori-motor stage, the symbolic stage, and the stages of concrete and abstract operations. These occur within fairly well-defined but by no means rigid ages. Very intelligent children may attain intellectual sophistication earlier and mentally handicapped children later. The sequence of stages, however, is the same for everyone.

(1) The sensori-motor stage, from 0 to 1–2 years

During his first two years the child acquires inner representations of the practical world of objects and people and of himself within this world. We saw in Chapter 4 that although vision and hearing are intact, the newborn responds only to part-aspects of people and is able to differentiate one person from another only in the second half of his first year. Only then does he gain a sense of the uniqueness and permanence of others. His perception of himself in relation to his animate and inanimate world has been systematically described by Piaget on the basis of detailed observations of his own three children.

Like Preyer before him, Piaget noticed that at first children treat parts of their body as they do other things, apparently unable to distinguish between themselves and the world outside. They regard their hands and feet with intense interest and at times they hurt themselves. Their inability to distinguish between 'me' and 'not me' is called *adualism*. It provides a cognitive basis for psychoanalytic postulates about the infant's projection and introjection of emotions: if he feels distressed he is likely to think the world is bad and if his environment is frustrating he may well feel bad himself (see also Wolff 1981).

In Piaget's view the child at first conceives of outer objects only as part of his own actions upon them. He behaves as if the object he looks at is different from the one he touches and the one he sucks. Piaget believed the child inhabits a multilocular space. There is eye space, mouth space and hand space. This notion has some similarity with psychoanalytic postulates about the infant's ability to relate only to part-objects. At 3 months the baby looks at a little red brick and starts drooling. If the brick is brought to his hand he grasps it. If it touches his lips he sucks it, but he cannot yet reach out for what he clearly wants. This he cannot do until around 4 to 5 months, and even then he succeeds only if both object and hand appear in the same visual space.

Once the schemata for eye, hand and mouth activities have become co-ordinated at around 5 to 6 months and the child can grasp what he sees and bring it to his mouth wherever his hand may be, the object begins to be a thing in itself, 'out there', separate from the actions the child performs upon it and separate also from himself, the instigator of action. This important step Piaget viewed as the beginning of a complex process of *decentring*, whereby one no longer sees one's own body as just another object. Yet even when this step has been taken the child still behaves as if he or she lived in an evanescent world of 'shifting and insubstantial "tableaux" which appear and are then totally reabsorbed' (Piaget and Inhelder 1969).

Under about 7 to 8 months, when a baby in a high chair is presented with a little toy, she looks at it with interest, drools in anticipation, reaches for it and pops it in her mouth. If before her very eyes the toy is covered with a cloth, she goes on looking for a moment, does nothing and ceases to pay attention. At 9 or 10 months, faced with a similar sequence, she successfully lifts the cloth to reveal the toy, clearly expecting it to be there. While this was taken as evidence that only now does she have an image of a more permanent object in her mind which sustains her in her search for hidden, or absent, objects, the situation is now known to be more complex (Bower 1974). Even at 5 months babies reach out for toys they have seen if plunged into darkness. Their failure to uncover hidden toys is thought to depend less on poor memory than on their notion that objects are tied to their positions and no two objects can occupy the same place, and the failure to grasp that one thing can be inside or underneath another. Moreover, babies up to 7 months regard objects seen in different places as different objects. Whatever the precise mechanisms, only in the last quarter of the first year of life does the child begin to have notions of separate objects in the world outside, human and inanimate, that can move about in space, have some permanence over time and can be hidden and found again.

During the second year, the child's motor development is rapid. He can now stand, walk, feed himself, and make all sorts of things happen. He now actively explores spatio-temporal and cause-effect relationships. His behaviour illuminates his early errors of reasoning.

Piaget, describing a nephew, wrote:

> Gérard, at 13 months, knows how to walk, and is playing ball in a large room. He throws the ball, or rather lets it drop in front of him and, either on his feet or on all fours, hurries to pick it up. At a given moment the ball rolls under an armchair. Gérard sees it and, not without some difficulty, takes it out in order to resume the game. Then the ball rolls under a sofa at the other end of the room. Gérard has seen it pass under the fringe of the sofa; he bends down to recover it. But as the sofa is deeper than the armchair and the fringe does prevent a clear view, Gérard gives up after a moment; he gets up, crosses the room, goes right under the armchair and carefully explores the place where the ball was before.
>
> (Piaget 1967:59)

Piaget thought Gérard's mistake indicated that around the age of 1 year children cannot yet accurately locate moving invisible objects. They reach for objects where they see them or where they have just seen them, unable to trace their itinerary in their minds. The moving object is still in part attached to what the child does, and in retrieving lost objects he repeats those actions that were previously successful.

Describing his daughter Piaget wrote (1967:205):

> At 1;6 Jacqueline throws a ball under a sofa. But instead of bending down at once and searching for it on the floor she looks at the place, realises that the ball must have crossed under the sofa, and sets out to go behind it.

Piaget took this to signify that Jacqueline now had not only inner representations of spatial relationships between objects, but could imagine herself being *in* space and not 'a privileged centre' around which everything else revolved.

As an example of the child's initial misconceptions of causality he wrote (1967:303):

> At 1;10 Jacqueline plays in a room in which I have been in bed since morning, as I am ill. She does not see me and is behind the wood of the bed, my keys in her hand. She encounters the waste-paper basket and strikes its empty bottom with the keys. Then I cry out: 'Oh . . .'; she starts, then laughs, knowing it is I, and without turning around,

starts to strike again. I cry out again, and so on for six or seven times. Then I pause and look at her without her seeing me. She increases her blows and, noting failure, withdraws her keys with her right hand, and with her left slowly pushes the basket about 10 centimetres further away, as though to adjust it, and begins striking again. . . Jacqueline thus seems to believe that my cries depend on the way she strikes and the position of the basket, as though they were substantially governed by these factors and not solely by my wish to amuse her. Jacqueline does not try to look at me or to exchange a word with me.

The beginnings of language

At the end of her first two years the child has acquired a working knowledge about people and objects, about time and space and about some aspects of physical causality. Her first logico-mathematical concepts have been abstracted, not from the objects she perceived but from her actions upon them. She now has inner representations of herself and the things about her as permanent objects which she can manipulate in space and remember over time. Her hands and then her feet have been her allies in achieving these accomplishments, just as her face has in this same period been the main feature for establishing her first human relationships. Her look was followed by her smile and with her hands to help her she began, towards the end of the first year, deliberately to imitate human communications.

Bruner holds that the basis of grammar is to be found in expression and gesture between child and adult and that mutual regard by mother and child of an object constitutes the first sentence (Bruner 1978). Looking, pointing, giving and taking are the first verbs mediating between subject and object. Macnamarra suggested that infants learn language by first determining the meaning a speaker intends to convey, and then working out the relationship between meaning and language (Macnamarra 1972). From the start the child's pleasure in experimenting with the practical world (Piaget has called this the 'joy of being the cause') is accompanied by his satisfaction in producing babbling sounds and then labelling, that is attaching names to, the phenomena he encounters. His classification of objects, actions, events and wishes is at first idiosyncratic: 'dinner' for all food and associated activities; 'all gone' as commentary and wish; 'doggie' for most four-legged creatures (see also Clark 1983). Just as physical operations are repeated over and over until they are mastered (Piaget's circular reaction), so children practise language by rehearsing what they know. Ruth Weir, in tape-recording her 2-year-old alone at night in his crib, established the vigour and industry with which toddlers in the quiet of their bedrooms practise the words they have learnt and try out, quite systematically, the rules of grammar as they know them (Weir 1962).

(2) The symbolic (animistic) stage, from 2 to 7 years

Once on their feet and active, children acquire language at an astonishing pace and by the age of 7 they also have the rudiments of literacy and mathematical skills. Because they are now competent practically, talk well, and often conduct themselves responsibly and with poise, their misconceptions and faulty logic are easily overlooked. Unless we are watchful, we miss the signs of immaturity during this second stage of cognitive development.

> Alan, aged 9, whose main trouble was stealing biscuits and money repeatedly from home, came to the psychiatrist after a complete physical check-up. He described in detail his visit to the paediatrician and the blood test he had had 'because my mummy thought there was something wrong with me. And I did think there was something wrong with me and I kept on taking biscuits and that. That there was something wrong with that. And I thought they'd test my blood for that to see what sort of boy I'm like.' And when asked what sort of boy he thought he was, he said 'Well when I steal I think I'm bad, but when I don't I think I'm helpful.' This boy, although now 9, still animistically interpreted his blood test as assessing his moral worth.

In his numerous writings Piaget described four main features of the animistic stage: the child's egocentrism, his animism, his pre-operational logic and his authoritarian morality.

(i) Egocentrism

Piaget noticed that in a nursery class children stimulate each other to talk and, in fact, two children together take turns in talking. But records of such interchanges show that much of the time each child talks about his own concerns, not caring whether he has been heard or not, satisfied in the knowledge that someone is listening. Each child sticks to his own ideas and there are few shared topics. This form of interchange, typical for the under-7s, Piaget has called *the collective monologue*: the child's talk is egocentric and he does not put himself into the position of his listener. After about 7, socialized speech, that is true conversations between children about shared topics, become the most common types of interchange. Under 7, the child often talks to others as if he were alone. After that age, even when alone he talks and thinks to himself as if in conversation with another.

Vigotsky (1962), the brilliant Russian psychologist, saw egocentric speech as a transition between earliest multi-purpose speech and mature speech, consisting of socialized (or communicative) speech and inner speech. He believed that egocentric utterances do not disappear but become internalized as 'thinking for oneself'. He subjected nursery children to minor frustrations, such as setting up a painting class but not providing any brushes for some children. He found that this increased the proportion of egocentric speech from these children as they commented on their plight and gave themselves instructions about what to do next. With advancing age such commentaries would at first follow the action taken, then accompany it and finally precede it; just as very young children draw their picture first and then say what it represents, slightly older children label their product as it is produced, and older children still declare beforehand what they are going to draw.

In an experiment with pairs of children of different ages, Piaget sent one child out of the room while the other was read a story which he had to explain to the first child, who was asked to reproduce it for the adult. Younger children were unclear in retelling the tale, even when they themselves had grasped it, convinced that the listener would understand anyway, and the younger listeners thought they had understood everything. However obscure the story in the retelling, both children were satisfied. They filled gaps with inventions and when they misunderstood a point they changed the rest of the story to fit in with their errors. Older children also often failed to remember the whole tale but they asked questions when points were unclear and tried hard to get the listener to grasp the story, checking to make sure the other child had understood what they meant. If they forgot parts of the story, they were aware of this, and if they invented something they said so.

Piaget concluded that it is only from around 7 or 8 years that there is genuine understanding between children. Till then egocentrism of verbal expression and comprehension predominate. Children over 7 or 8 differ from younger children in their efforts to be objective. The younger ones cannot distinguish romancing from faithful rendering of a story, believing that what they had made up *was* the story (Piaget 1960).

Young children know how the world looks for them but cannot

readily put themselves into someone else's shoes. Whatever is of most concern to them obviously concerns others. This has profound implications for emotional development. Because children believe grown-ups know automatically what is in their minds, they don't bother to be explicit. They also believe that whatever happens, happens because of them.

Sylvia (p. 97) thought her father was irritable because of something she had done. Only later did she work out for herself that he must have had other reasons for feeling unhappy.

The child literally sees herself as the centre of the universe believing even that the heavenly bodies follow her. Conversations with children under 7 or 8 about the sun and moon regularly went like this: 'When you are out for a walk, what does the sun do? *It comes with me.* And when you go home? *It goes with someone else.* What does the moon do when you are out for a walk? *It goes with us.* Why? *Because the wind makes it go.*'

Later, when children have learnt that the sun does not move and yet they still perceive it apparently following them, they hold on to both ideas, although incompatible. 'What does the sun do when you are out for a walk? *It follows us.* Why? *To make it light for us.* Then it moves? *No, you'd think it did.* Then what does follow us? *It follows us but it stays in the same place!* but *sends out its rays*' (Piaget 1929:218).

(ii) Animism

The above examples indicate that young children endow the inanimate world with feelings, thoughts and wishes just like their own. All causes are psychological, that is due to motives. Physical, scientific explanation cannot yet be conceived and nothing happens by chance. At first all things are conscious and capable of feelings and all useful things are alive; then things that can move are conscious and alive; next consciousness and life are attributed to things that move on their own accord; and finally, at around 11 to 12 years, consciousness is restricted to animals and life to animals and plants.

Allied to animism is the young child's inability to distinguish between words and the objects they refer to; between thoughts and the things thought about; between dreams and reality. Under the age of about 7 the word 'table' is as much a part of the object it names as the fact that it has a top, four legs, and is made of wood. That language is a convention and that different languages have different words for the same things are notions that the under-7s cannot grasp, even if they are themselves bilingual.

Piaget questioned children systematically about their thoughts and their dreams. Five-, six- and seven-year-olds when asked what they think with, mention their ears or their mouths. A 6-year-old defined memory as 'when you remember something . . . it suddenly comes into the mind. When you've been told something it comes into your mind, then it goes out and then it comes back,' and when asked where it goes, he said 'into the sky'. At around 8 years, thoughts are located in the head or forehead, often in the form of 'a little voice'. One boy said he thought with his 'mind': 'It is someone who isn't like we are, who hasn't skin and hasn't bones and who is like air which we can't see. After we're dead, it goes away from our body' (Piaget 1929:45, 50, 53).

The under-7s locate dreams in their room and almost universally say they come from the night. They cannot explain how it is that they see dreams and yet are asleep, and no one else can see their dream. A 5-year-old, asked if a dream was inside the room or inside her, replied 'It isn't in me or I shouldn't see it.' Only at around 7 or 8, or even later, do children get the idea that dreams are thoughts inside their head connected with the brain and with intelligence (Piaget 1929:44); and that thoughts are distinct from the things thought about.

During the animistic stage, just as names are attached to the objects they denote and thoughts to the things and events thought about, wishes are an integral part of what is wished for and are endowed with magical properties. When children have hostile thoughts about someone they love and are dependent on, they are regularly afraid in case their thoughts might come true and the important person be hurt. When they sustain an accident they may blame their parents, believing that by will-power the parents could have saved them. During this stage a belief in magic is sometimes declared and often acted upon.

A 7-year-old whose younger, cleverer sister, June, had unexpectedly died following heart surgery, had had her adenoids removed and after a trivial reprimand from the teacher on rejoining her class, became so anxious she could not bring herself to enter school. She insisted she would return only 'if June comes back', and clearly believed this to be possible if only she used enough will power.

(iii) Pre-operational logic

A crucial feature of the child's reasoning between 2 and 7 is that it is not founded on observations but on belief. Children do not argue on the basis of evidence but on the basis of conviction, and despite their many questions they often provide and believe in their own wrong answers. They are happy to accept any idea as true and are not bothered by contradictions. A 7-year-old indicated that this year she no longer believed in Father Christmas 'because if he brought the presents down the chimney they would be all sooty'. She could not explain how it was that last year she failed to notice this.

Five- and six-year olds are perfectly satisfied with their drawings of human figures in which hair rises vertically upwards and legs emerge from either side of triangular skirts. When asked to draw a face in profile they always put in two eyes because they know there must be two.

Logic is tied to the child's own actions, not to formal operations, and he is incapable of deducing simple scientific laws from what he notices, or of understanding them if they are taught. Faced with two identical balls of plasticine and asked to roll one out into a sausage, he declares they are now different in size. The sausage is 'bigger because it's longer'. Asked to empty a jug of water into a long narrow beaker and then into a short wide one, he indicates there is 'more' in the narrow container because it is 'taller'. Although he may be muddled about the meaning of words, equating 'tall' and 'long' with 'big', his consistent inability to grasp physical laws, such as those of conservation of matter, suggest that the linguistic confusion is part and parcel of a more profound logical difficulty. When asked to draw the fluid level of an upright beaker of water, the under-7s correctly draw the line parallel to the bottom of the jar. But when asked to draw the level as the beaker is tilted to pour the water out, even when they can see what happens, they still draw the fluid level parallel to the now tilted bottom of the jar. Ten counters spaced close together in a row become 'more' as they are spread to cover a longer distance, and the child is not at all sure that when he counts them first from left to right and then from right to left he will get the same answer.

Family relationships are equally difficult for the child to grasp. She may know that she has a brother and a sister. But in her view her brother has only one sister and her sister only a brother. She cannot imagine herself as being a sister to the other two. Husbands tend to be viewed as fathers, and wives as mothers, not only to their children but to each other.

The magical world of the under-7s where anything could happen remains largely unnoticed by adults. Children can do simple sums but do not know, or provide false accounts of, how they arrived at their answers. Unless asked, children do not declare what they think, believing that everyone thinks the same. Most parents in this enlightened age respond to children's questions about where they come from with accurate information, and most young children now know they came from their mother's belly. But the question 'how did I get out?' is less often put, and parents may be unaware of the fanciful answers children give themselves and believe as if they were received knowledge: 'you have to have an operation to get a baby' (even though mother has no scar); or 'it comes out of your belly button'.

The growth of language

While towards the end of their first year children imitate gesture and vocalization, and in the second half of the sensori-motor stage they produce one-word sentences, the symbolic stage is marked by the arrival of word sequences and grammar. Noam Chomsky has revolutionized our notions of language learning in childhood, demonstrating that children do not copy the grammatical constructions of their elders but process the language they hear, invent their own grammatical rules, and produce their own grammatical speech (Chomsky 1976). By studying the errors children make it was possible to discover basic common trends in individual language development suggesting that here, as in the development of logic and mathematics, grammatical forms are determined by common neurological structures (Chomsky's *language acquisition device*) whose maturation is a prerequisite for language. Piaget held that language is not the source of logic but, on the contrary, is structured by it, and that the roots of logic and language are to be found in the general coordination of actions which include talking. The child models his utterances in part on what he hears and his speech is in turn encouraged by the proficient linguists around him. From 6 to 9 months, children's babble is the same the world over. From 9 to 10 months the range of babble sounds narrows and later on children produce the sounds and syllables of the language in which they are reared. Cazden pointed out that in the verbal interchanges between mother and child *language structure* is not emphasized by the mother, yet always learnt by the child (Cazden 1974). Mothers do not correct grammar but meaning. But they do tend to respond to grammatically wrong utterances by repeating what the child said in an elaborated form; and to grammatically accurate utterances by extending the topic of the interchange (Penner 1987).

Moreover, from the start mothers, and indeed everyone including children, universally and involuntarily adopt a special way of talking to infants and very young children. 'Motherese' is high-pitched, musical, and consists of short, slow and distinctly emphasized utterances with a limited content of meaning adapted to the child's level of comprehension.

In language *use* the child is helped by what he is encouraged to say rather than by what he hears others say and mothers, because they know their child intimately, respond accurately to the child's meaning since they grasp even his least clear utterances. Children's early telegraphic sentences can convey a wide range of meanings, and their grammatical structure is similar across different languages. Mothers interpret the specific meanings correctly, respond appropriately and, in their reply, often repeat the child's utterances in a linguistically more sophisticated and more specific form. For an excellent account of language development, see Howlin (1980).

(iv) Authoritarian morality

Among the most relevant contributions from a psychiatric point of view is Piaget's work on social rules and morality (Piaget 1932). His initial observations have been largely confirmed in a longitudinal cohort study (Kohlberg 1963; Colby *et al*. 1983) although there may be more overlap between the different age groups than he suggested, and children find it easier to adopt a more mature view of morality when general conduct and not their own behaviour is under discussion (Tapp and Levine 1972).

We saw in the last chapter that from their second year children can empathize with the feelings of others and are distressed when others are hurt; and that from at least 4 years onwards they can distinguish conventions and rules of games from the need to avoid causing pain to others. Piaget systematically examined children's perceptions both of the rules of games and of morality. The ancient game of marbles is played the world over. Piaget found that the under-7s grasp the rules imperfectly; they make mistakes and are content to play alongside others without participation; the game is most successful when no one loses and everyone wins. Yet for them rules are sacrosanct and belong to the game, just as names are parts of objects. Rules cannot be changed, and if asked who made them, young children either fail to understand the question, say 'It's always been played like that', or finally use 'God' as an explanation. Older children play competently, know the rules, and view these as conventions made by 'children long ago'. There is a common observance of rules according to which some win and others lose, but if everyone agrees, the rules can be altered and the game played in a different way. At around 7, 8 or 9 years, children change from an authoritarian to a democratic view of the rules of games and other social conventions, from a position of unilateral respect for sacred laws to a position of mutual respect and reciprocity (Piaget and Inhelder 1969). This is paralleled by a change from an authoritarian morality in which obedience is equated with goodness and all adults are unquestionably right, to a view of morality concerned with justice and a more detached evaluation of ethical standards. Piaget saw the social interactions between children as crucial in helping them move from a position in which obedience to their elders and avoidance of punishment are paramount, to one in which conformity to social rules, and later still participation in rule-making for the sake of universal, ethical principles, predominate.

The animistic child believes in the inherent virtues of rules; in absolute fairness; in matching the punishment to the crime (the *lex talionis*) irrespective of intention or consequence; and in 'immanent justice', i.e. that crime will inevitably be punished and that punishment must have been preceded by crime. When Sylvia's father was irritable with her, she thought that she must have done something wrong to deserve this.

(3) The stage of concrete operations, from 7 or 8 to 11 or 12 years

Once the child can distinguish between the psychological and the physical, between names and objects, between dreams and the events dreamt about, between thoughts and things thought about, he has completed *a second decentring process*. Towards the end of his second year he could see himself as an individual and other people and objects as permanent things in themselves which he could influence in a practical way. He saw himself as a doer. Now he can view himself as a thinker, and this degree of objectivity towards himself is matched by a new objectivity towards his inanimate and social environment.

He can now put himself into someone else's position and have an accurate view of reciprocal relationships. He argues on the basis of observations and can derive correct conclusions about the physical properties of the world. He has changed from operating on the basis of beliefs and what others tell him, to a more rational being who trusts his own observations, can compare one view with another, is aware of contradictions and has a degree of moral autonomy. Physical explanations have displaced magic and he can conceive of chance events. But he still needs concrete objects and concrete experiences in order to arrive at correct solutions. He has to see and manipulate the plasticine and the beakers of water before he can work out that substances can change their shape without change in volume.

A 5-year-old was told that his mother was really his stepmother and that his first mother had died. This idea he could not grasp properly until in his ninth year he 'saw a picture of my real mother and I saw a picture, no, I saw a photograph of the mother I've got just now, and I could see at once the difference — that I must have had another mother.' Even at this age he seemed to think that one can compare only like with like, that is photograph with photograph, and not, for example, his first mother in the photograph with his present mother in real life.

Piaget's discovery that under the age of 12 language is insufficient to transmit logic transformed our primary schools a generation or more ago. Active experimentation by the children themselves has displaced rote learning and purely verbal instruction.

(4) The stage of abstract (formal) operations, from 12 to 16 years

Between 12 and 16 psychological decentring becomes complete and at the end of this stage children can solve abstract problems in their heads with thought alone. They can now grasp notions of probability and can adopt a hypothetical viewpoint, that is they can consider propositions from which logical deductions follow, a form of reasoning impossible earlier; e.g. between 8 and 10 years children when asked 'If you could touch the sun, would he feel it?', replied 'You can't touch him,' and if urged, 'Yes, but if you could manage to, would he feel it?' they said, 'He is too high up' (Piaget 1951:68–9). Now they have shifted from the *real* to the *possible*.

The processes of intellectual development: maturation, practice and education

Piaget thought that *maturation of the nervous system*, complete at 15 or 16 years, was a necessary, but not sufficient, condition for the changing systems of intelligent action and thought outlined above. Such maturation determines the sequence of development and sets limits to its pace, opening up new possibilities for effective learning as the child grows up. The fulfilment of these possibilities depends on the opportunity for play or the *functional exercise* of the skills the child already has, and for new experiences, physical, logico-mathematical, and social, sought out by the child himself and provided for him in the course of his upbringing and education. The opportunities for functional exercise may be limited by handicap, for example, blindness, deafness or impaired mobility; but also by a barren environment in which practice of accomplishments is not possible, as when a baby is confined to a cot or a toddler to a room within an institution, and opportunities for handling materials and for interacting with people are limited. Moreover, children require a predictable and peaceful environment in which to practise their skills and make sequential observations. When everything around them shifts constantly they are unlikely to be able to distinguish between their own effectiveness and the changes imposed from without.

Anxiety and depression, too, can interfere with a child's exercise of skills. It is likely that the stunting of language development and other intellectual skills in children from disrupted and culturally impoverished homes or from institutions is due not only to the unstimulating and unpredictable environment but to the blocking effect on play of anxieties and miseries engendered by threatening and broken relationships. This is an as yet unexplored area of child psychology. We do not have systematic observations of young children's play and learning activities when in different emotional states.

The effect of *experience*, that is the input from the child's physical and social environment, becomes more and more important the further removed the child is from his sensori-motor stage; environmentally determined individual differences increase as he or she gets older.

It is sometimes argued that animistic thinking in children is induced by the fairy tales they are told and the misinformation they used to be, and sometimes still are, given, for example about childbirth. The fact remains however that parents who tell such tales do not suddenly change when their children are 7. On the contrary, it is their children who cease to be taken in. When parents and teachers take a different view and try to explain everything to help children towards a rational and logical approach, they are often surprised at the ineffectiveness of their teaching with the under-7s. Of course, the steps towards concrete and then abstract operational thought are encouraged by a scientific culture and may never emerge in the young of a culture based on magical beliefs and practices. Yet we know how rapidly young adults, for example from rural Africa, grasp the scientific viewpoint once they are exposed to an urban civilization or a Western style of education.

Intelligence and affectivity

Piaget saw intelligence and emotions as inseparably linked (Piaget and Inhelder 1969). Affectivity constitutes the energetics of behaviour, the motives from which intelligent action springs. Feeling states, on the other hand, depend on the individual's perceptions and comprehension and these form part of his or her intelligence. Affective and cognitive development proceed together. While psychoanalysts have almost totally neglected Piaget's work (see Sandler 1975), he himself was well informed about psychoanalytic teachings and respectful of their contribution. During the sensori-motor stage cognitive decentring is correlated with affective decentring and, as inanimate objects become permanent things in themselves, so the child's emotions become attached to recognizable permanent people, later perceived as sources of external causality.

In the symbolic stage the mental image, symbolic play, and language help the child to remember loved people even in their absence. Lasting sympathies and antipathies are now possible, together with an awareness of how the child himself feels towards others. Piaget considered social exchanges to parallel exactly the pre-operational logic of this age. The child cannot differentiate between his or her point of view and that of others.

True cooperation in play is not yet possible. The child's moral feelings consist of unilateral respect for his or her elders (respect being a mixture of affection and fear) accompanied by a sense of obligation and duty. Orders given are at first powerful only in the presence of the person who gives them, and rules are viewed as concrete and unshakable.

After 7, in the stage of concrete operations, moral relationship are based on mutual respect. During his or her pre-adolescent growth spurt, the child acquires a sense of justice, often at the expense of a less idealized and more ambivalent view of parents and teachers. Obedience is no longer the prime virtue, and social relationships are seen as reciprocal and cooperative.

The affective changes of adolescence were attributed by Piaget more to the social and intellectual transformations that occur at this time than to the awakening or reawakening of 'instincts'. He thought that the transformation of concrete thinking tied to reality, into *formal thought* about imagined or deduced events, created a profound change in the adolescent's perspective. For the first time the young person can now contemplate a variety of possible interpersonal and social relationships and his liberation from concrete operations allows him to orient himself towards the future and become receptive to new values of an ideal or supra-individual kind. Aesthetics, social reform and altruism become salient and the individual now sees himself not only in relation to his intimates but to his country, his culture, and mankind.

After Piaget

Piaget has been criticized on two main scores. First, because of his insistence on separate stages of cognitive development and second, because young children have subsequently been found capable of more mature reasoning than he led us to expect. A further criticism of his method is that he relied too much on verbal interchanges with young children and not enough on actions.

Certainly, not all aspects of each of Piaget's stages change together as children mature. And there are wide age differences between children in their intellectual development. But a number of studies which failed to confirm stage transformations with age (see Gelman and Baillargeon 1983) were cross-sectional rather than longitudinal and we know, for example from studies of physical growth, that cross-sectional approaches obscure growth spurts and qualitative changes with age, because of individual differences in the timing of their appearances. Longitudinal cohort studies are necessary to confirm or refute stage transformations with age.

It remains true that there is a sequence of qualitative change in thinking and reasoning as children grow up and, although the transitions may not be as abrupt as was once thought and individual children mature at different rates, the sequence is invariant.

More serious has been the challenge to Piaget's findings about children's egocentrism, animism and pre-logical thinking under the age of 7. Margaret Donaldson, in a most illuminating account of studies of young children, found their errors and misinterpretations due to limitations of memory and to linguistic and social misunderstandings rather than to faulty logic (Donaldson 1978). Children often answered an adult's question as if a different question had been asked. When the grown-up became more explicit or phrased the questions differently, children's performance improved. But we need to remember that, although in a child-centred world, children can operate with a logic more advanced than Piaget thought possible, children spend much of their time in an adult world among grown-ups speaking not to them but to each other, and this fosters childish errors and misperceptions, which then in turn have profound effects on how the child views and feels about his or her world.

Certainly children are capable of imagining how others feel much earlier than was once thought possible and, when given a concrete setting and simple tasks to perform, they are able to imagine what others might think and want. The egocentism Piaget described is less pervasive and more open to reason than he thought.

And there is one other error that needs stressing. Piaget held that each person builds up his own logical structures in his mind as a result of experiences and experimentation with the concrete practical world around him during the sensori-motor stage. Yet when children are prevented perhaps by illness and immobility from active physical exploration in their first two years, they are not handicapped intellectually, provided their environment is secure and stimulating. Everyone regularly develops logical thought, so that to think of this as dependent on experience and experimentation is less plausible than to postulate an inner biological programme for increasingly complex logical structures whose development is encouraged and fostered by observation and action. (For a fuller critical account of Piaget's work see Boden 1979, Gelman and Baillargeon 1983, and also Meadows 1986.)

Smallness of stature, immaturity and play

Tanner postulates evolutionary reasons for the time interval between weaning and the attainment of adult stature (Tanner 1984). This interval ensures that the young are relatively docile and sexually non-competitive during the years in which they are socialized. For humans whose growth is particularly slow, this takes a long time.

Bruner also adopted a biological view when he stressed the special burdens on human immaturity caused by living increasingly in a man-made world (Bruner 1972). Adapting to such an environment depends on the acquisition of knowledge and the learning of skills far beyond what is innately stored in the gene pool. Not everything that must be mastered is learnt by direct encounter; much is transmitted in the form of language, of written history and literature. Bruner described the human young as 'tutor-prone', eager not only to imitate but to learn from and be instructed by their elders. They are drawn to novelty and are very good at detecting rules in new situations. Although chimpanzee infants also learn from observation, their parents do not demonstrate what is to be learnt: 'among the primates there is very little intentional pedagogy of any kind' (Bruner 1972).

Bruner thought that play was essential for learning, for example, how to use tools. In play the goal is forgotten and activities are performed for their own sake. The consequences of actions are minimized, and as a result both social play and playful experimentation with objects are less risky. During play, words and tools are used and social interchanges modified and practised in as many different ways as children can think up. Actions and part-actions, involving both tools and words, of imagined social relationships are perfected, so that when in real life a new problem is encountered it can be solved by means of previously practised activities. Play equips children with a repertoire of possible responses so that they can adapt flexibly to the varying challenges of their world. Play leads to practical mastery, and group play involves symbols and conventions, that is agreement about procedures and roles.

Language, at first closely linked to action, frees itself from action and in turn influences both attention and performance. Alexander Luria has shown how the child's verbal self-instructions help him or her to learn and to solve problems (Luria 1957). Later, language is used to convey knowledge between people and, when written down, between people separated by space and time, forming a cultural link that is particularly strong between the generations.

In the following chapters we shall see what social and emotional encounters face children as they grow up, and what impact these make on their future personality, given their intellectual equipment at the time.

Chapter seven

Emotional development: psychoanalysis and the inner self

Two features distinguish the study of emotional from that of physical, intellectual, and social development and from considerations of temperament: the importance of *individual uniqueness* and the contribution of the *subjective viewpoint*.

The following case history is an example of the events and experiences which the theories of psychoanalysis help to explain.

The relationship between Jack and his mother illustrates the personal and idiosyncratic way in which early mother-child attachment can go wrong, on the basis of the kind of inner neurotic processes to be described in this chapter. Jack ran away from home repeatedly and dangerously, usually after some minor criticism from his mother, sometimes because he merely *felt* she was critical, and that he himself was bad. The mother in turn saw the running as a rejection of herself, so that her own response was 'I'll help you pack your bag' rather than 'But I need you here'.

The maternal grandparents had lived in strife, the mother's father, to whom she was particularly close, often leaving home for months at a time. When in later life these parents divorced, the father came to live with Jack's mother. The grandmother remarried and had a further son of exactly Jack's age. Jack's father was alcoholic and pathologically jealous, violent both to Jack and his mother. In his third year, mother and Jack went to live with a great aunt, and here the pattern for their later troubles was set: rivalry between the two women for Jack's affections, recapitulating perhaps for the mother her own experiences within the triangle of her family of origin. When he was 4, Jack became cheeky and destructive, played with fire and began to run. In later years, whenever he ran away from his mother, he ran to the aunt.

At 5, when asked about his daddy, he said 'His name's called Eddie. I've not got him now. My mummy sent him away. He ran away to Dundee . . . he just ran away from us for nothing. He stole my mum's fags and he ran away.'

His young mother was despondent, thinking Jack blamed her for the divorce. But she also saw his father in him and described her 'distrust' of him since he was 2 when, to use her words, 'he outgrew his babyhood'. She always saw him as more mature than he was, not needing her care. When he told her on his first day at school not to kiss him as she left, she took this not as a sign of shyness about his affectional needs in public, but as his no longer wanting physical closeness with her. Each had learnt to hide their affection from the other, and each felt frustrated when their cravings for affection were not met. From the first referral onwards, the mother wanted him 'taken away . . . He might feel that I'm pushing him further away, but it's a chance I must take.'

Jack, a particularly attractive 5-year-old, became inhibited and evasive with advancing years and lost his early cheeriness. He was too unassertive with other boys and remained unsure of his mother. The mother herself, coping well with other aspects of life, was less and less able to show her real fondness for Jack, presenting to him instead a critical, sullen, and withholding stance, about which she herself was unhappy. The only times in which the two could come together freely was when a partial separation was introduced into their lives by Jack's admission into a hospital unit and, later, a boarding school.

This mother had a second son, married a stable and supportive second husband with whom Jack got on well, and moved away from the neighbourhood of her aunt. But, because of his continuing, dangerous running away at the slightest perception of criticism whenever he was at home, Jack remained at residential school. He did well academically and socially, and he made friends. But by the age of 14, his private sense of failure had not left him.

To anticipate later sections of this chapter, my understanding of the problem was that, because of the mother's own unresolved guilt about replacing her mother in her father's affection, and her shaky identification with her own mother, her feelings of attachment to Jack and his for her were excessively eroticized and hence guilt-inducing for both. Jack's needs for unconditional love were not met, and she was frustrated in her wish to be a loving mother. But this understanding, while helpful in averting blame on the part of the professionals, was not in itself therapeutic. The mother's defensiveness was such that she could tolerate only emotional support, not exploration of her feelings; and Jack's behaviour called for active care beyond what his mother could supply.

Individual uniqueness

For the effective treatment of physical illnesses, it is enough that we know about growth and development in general and about disease processes as they can affect everyone. Appendicitis is occasionally ushered in by unusual, perhaps even unique symptoms, but as a rule its course runs true to type. Its treatment demands the application of strict rules of practice in the light of current knowledge. A less vital aspect of care is the personal consideration given by the surgical team before and after the operation to the patient as an individual.

When we consider the emotional component of personality, however, of the greatest importance in all human relationships and in most psychiatric disorders and social catastrophes, we enter a field where generalizations and rules, while at times crucial (as in the diagnosis and treatment of a depressive illness), cannot be relied upon as the sole basis for intervention. Here what is unique is at least as significant as what people have in common, and may be of overriding importance for good treatment and care. Some existential psychologists have taken this view to its extreme, maintaining that each life history must stand alone, that there is no valid way of grouping emotional experiences because these are never sufficiently alike in their essentials between people. This is not the position of more orthodox psychoanalysts and was certainly not Freud's.

Psychoanalysis has made its particular contribution by postulating universal psychological structures and mechanisms mediating between inner experiences and between experience and behaviour. These postulates help us to understand individual emotional development. The uniqueness of intimate childhood relationships crucially affects our assumptive world or, as Bowlby has called it, our 'working models' of other people which can then influence our expectations and plans for the rest of our life (Bowlby 1975). Yet the psychological mechanism mediating between inner experiences and between experiences and action are held to be at work in everyone and it should be, and in a small way has been, possible to confirm this.

Psychoanalysis, science and the subjective viewpoint

Freud modelled his theories on those of the physical sciences of his day, and his critics stress the naivety of nineteenth-century mechanistic physics and the errors of biological facts which so strikingly influenced the form in which he cast his ideas. One criticism is that Freudian theories were formulated in terms of causal relationships, yet not as hypotheses which could be refuted. The fact that the theory of the oedipal conflict holds whether a 3-year-old is hostile *or* placatory to his father, that is whether he openly expresses feelings of rivalry or represses these excessively because they make him uneasy, is not an insuperable obstacle to scientific enquiry. But it does make such enquiry more difficult. The exasperation of scientific psychologists with psychoanalysis may in part reflect the complexities of the issues, rather than an inherent impossibility of a scientific approach in this field.

Indeed such enterprises have taken place. Whiting and Child, in correlating specific child-rearing practices of different cultures with adult beliefs about the causes of sicknesses and their remedies, found evidence for the existence of the psychological mechanisms of fixation and regression (Whiting and Child 1953). Halla Beloff confirmed that the obsessional, or 'anal', character is no mere figment of psychoanalytic fancy (Beloff 1957). Among university students there were some in whom the predicted personality traits of obstinacy, parsimony, and orderliness, identified on questionnaire enquiry, cluster together, although logically they are independent. Moreover, students scoring highly on these clustered traits tended to have mothers with similar personality attributes. More recently, as we have seen, the work on attachment has validated aspects of the 'oral' stage of emotional development; and Kagan's work supports the development of standards and of conscience during later 'anal' and 'genital' stages (Kagan 1981).

Three fundamental ambiguities in psychoanalytic activity cannot however be passed over: *first*, the frequent confusion between the two levels of argument, the scientific and the subjective (p. 3): psychoanalysts often discuss their individual patients' subjective, experiential connections and reasons as if they were causal and could form the basis for prediction; *second*, the unchallengeable fact that no attempt has been made, especially by Freud's followers, to separate observation from interpretation; and *third*, the closed social organization of psychoanalytic practice.

Scientific and subjective psychology

A major source of confusion is to equate a scientific approach to psychoanalytic theories with the processes of psychoanalytic treatment. What happens within the unique relationship between individual patient and analyst is not 'science'. Kräupl Taylor reminds us that Freud was concerned with the psychology of particular meaningful connections, not with causal explanations (Kräupl Taylor 1987). Yet this does not mean that psychoanalytic theories, as they apply to groups of people, cannot be validated by scientific observations.

Freud's basic tenet is that the seeds for later psychoneurosis and character disorders are to be found in early childhood experiences associated with anxiety-laden erotic and aggressive urges, and that the onset of symptoms or repetitive maladaptive behaviour patterns is triggered by later experiences which revive memories of these early traumata. His first and perhaps most significant demonstration was that symptoms of neurotic illness are connected with *ideas*, and that if these are communicated freely to another person the symptoms can disappear. In *Studies on Hysteria*, written with his colleague Josef Breuer (Freud and Breuer 1893; 1893–1895), Freud showed that patients with hysterical paralyses can be helped to discover in their minds uncomfortable thoughts and feelings which they do not usually think about, and which relate both to their present predicament and to memories of events significant to them as children. Freud and Breuer observed that patients who were helped to unburden themselves of these experiences lost their hysterical symptoms.

These studies contain the kernels of subsequent developments in psychoanalysis: they pointed to childhood as an essential part of adult experience. Some of our behaviour, not only symptoms of neurotic illness, but actions and communications of all kinds, are unpleasant at times for others, often for ourselves. They are, like Jack's running and his mother's critical stance, not what we intend, and they are repetitive. Although we strive to be different, old unwanted patterns recur, and we act not from choice but from compulsion. Our behaviour is contrary to our beliefs and out of step with how we wish to be. Everyone can identify such patterns in his or her personality. They are minimal in the fortunate majority; more intrusive in people with personality difficulties or symptoms of neurotic illness.

The external biography can point to possible causes of such irrational and maladaptive patterns and, as we have already seen, there is now much objective work, for example that of Brown and Harris (1978), to validate these ideas. But for one person to come to understand another or to increase his or her own self-knowledge, a study of the inner life story is indispensable. And in treatment, just as environmental manipulation can lead to learning of more adaptive behaviour and to changes in self-perception, a transformed understanding of our life history by changing our self-perceptions can help us take a new control of our destiny.

Outer events and inner experiences are not equivalent. The transformations in children's thinking and reasoning discussed in the last chapter modify the impressions made by similar events on children of different ages. This introduces an element of distortion, particularly in children under 7 or 8, between the external events and attitudes of other people, and how these are perceived. Children react in the light of such distortions, and in turn evoke responses from others who may or may not be able to recognize and compensate for these manifestations of immaturity.

A 2-year-old, for example, whose mother is suddenly admitted to hospital, is not only anxious and miserable but may, depending on the intervening care she gets and the duration of the separation, react to her mother with anger and rejection when reunited, believing that the mother had abandoned her and blaming the mother for her miseries. There is now a risk that the mother in turn will be disappointed and, depending on her own physical and emotional state, even irritable with her daughter so that what might have been a brief traumatic episode becomes a prolonged series of negative interactions between mother and child, each reinforcing the disappointments and frustrations of the other. The child finds her misinterpretation of the initial event confirmed repeatedly: her cross mother really does not love her; that is why she abandoned her in the first place. This memory she now carries forward into her later years. It influences her presentation of herself to others to whom she is drawn, and contributes to the actual course of these subsequent relationships.

Anna Freud thought a major disadvantage of subjective enquiry was that it can only be retrospective (A. Freud 1966). She stressed the distinction between reconstructing a patient's formative life experiences from revelations in the present and spotting adverse events in childhood *before* they have had their effect. Psychoanalysis, she said, can identify harmful influences retrospectively, but it cannot predict what interventions in the upbringing of normal children will prevent future pathology. This difficulty is a general one: retrospective information is not predictive. When we know that multiple hospital admissions are more than twice as common in disturbed than in other children (Wolff 1981), it does not help us to estimate how many hospitalized children are likely to be disturbed.

A greater obstacle to scientific exploration of how childhood events and later personality are related is their sheer complexity, and the difficulty of making explicit both the intricate translations between outer events and inner experiences and the innumerable mutually influencing interactions between individuals and other people in the course of their lives.

Finally, and this may be the one real obstacle to scientific enquiry in this field: our views of inner connections are fluid. Apparently contradictory interpretations can both be true. We have many equally valid reasons for feeling and acting as we do, and we can choose from moment to moment which affords us most relief. Keith Oatley clarified these issues by stressing the difference between private theories of interpersonal action and the theories of natural scientists which aim at objective knowledge (Oatley 1985). At the same time, the study of objective, causal connections does not preclude the use of subjective data.

In scientific enquiry, observation and interpretation must be kept apart

While in therapeutic encounters, the therapist must act in the patient's best interest, scientific observations must be uncontaminated by such interventions. This is why research can only occur outside the psychoanalytic hour, while the ideas to be explored by research are generated within it.

The organization of psychoanalytic training and practice

A major difficulty is the professional barrier that divides psychoanalysis from other disciplines and is perpetuated by the geographical, financial, and organizational aspects of psychoanalytic training. With few exceptions, psychoanalysts are not open to the discoveries made in other fields even if, like those of Piaget and his followers, these are of the greatest relevance to their own work. But the barrier operates in two directions. Although psychoanalytic discoveries and theories have permeated our culture, including our vocabulary and our public life, this professional barrier has made it possible for many practising psychologists, social workers and doctors, not themselves analysts, to describe their treatments as if these owed nothing to psychoanalytic insights and theories, but were based entirely on scientific enquiry, on a wish for social reform, or on humane common sense. Yet in their interactions with their patients and clients, the clinically helpful therapists are fully sensitive to the fluctuating meanings of their patients' communications and to the interactions between themselves and their clients. While covertly these professionals make full use of psychotherapeutic skills and of the psychoanalytic formulations about personality on which these rest, they often do not acknowledge this.

The family therapy movements, too, have largely failed to declare their dependence on psychoanalytic ideas. (See Will and Wrate 1985 for an excellent account of psychodynamic contributions to family therapy.)

No further explanation will be offered here for the theoretical postulates and descriptions of emotional development which follow. They are written in the belief that it is important to expose the processes of clinical appraisal, even when these extend beyond the confines of scientific enquiry.

Normality and abnormality

It is often claimed that we must study what is normal before we can understand the abnormal. Of course we should know the range of normal variation, for example, in height and intelligent behaviour when faced with parents concerned about these aspects of their child's development. But in order to be personally helpful to people, the concepts of normality and abnormality are not useful. If a basically healthy person is anxious, she is not comforted when told that other people in her predicament would feel the same. Paradoxically it is the more deviant individuals who get relief from knowing that their reactions and mental processes are not unique.

Moreover, discoveries about normal development are more likely to come from a study of errors and aberrations than from observations of perfectly functioning organisms. Language acquisition in childhood has been illuminated by the grammatical errors children make; the misinterpretations and faulty logic of children have shed light on intellectual development; and studies of brain injured patients have contributed more to our knowledge of normal brain function than studies of healthy people. Normal variability is great and often we do not know where to start looking. It is the exceptions to the rule which stand out and from which we are likely to learn most about what usually happens. The criticism that Freud's conclusions about normal development are based on his encounters with neurotic patients is therefore not valid.

The structure and processes of the subjective self

Many of Freud's ideas had their parallels in the writings of others (e.g. Macdougall 1924), but no one before him had used theoretical constructs, such as instincts or layers of consciousness, to clarify and organize a wealth of clinical observations. Freud saw patients all day long. Ideas derived from one case were open to confirmation by another, and were modified when they seemed not to fit. A highly simplified outline of some of his basic postulates follows.

The anatomy of mental personality (Freud 1923)

The subjective self has three components: id, ego, and super-ego. Our primitive self, the *id*, present from birth, is thought of as the reservoir of instinctual needs, drives or impulses. These were held to be fired by mental energy and to generate mental activity from within, in contrast to responses evoked by external stimuli (Freud 1905 and 1923). Freud described two kinds of drive: Libido, the erotic drive towards survival and sexual fulfilment, biologically attached to specific parts of the body (the 'erotogenic zones') and Thanatos, the death instinct or *drive towards aggression* without a physical basis.

Id processes are not open to awareness. We can only guess at them on the basis of the thoughts and actions into which they are transformed by our *ego*, or learned self. Freud saw the ego not as inborn but as an achievement of living: 'the precipitate of the learning process of the individual in his encounter with the external world of people and things' (Munroe 1957:86). It arises by differentiation from the id. Its function is to preserve the organism's equilibrium in the face of demands from the environment, the id, and the super-ego by means of integrating conflicting demands and shielding the individual from excessive anxiety. This defensive function is carried out by the ego's *defence mechanisms* to be described below.

Subsequently 'ego-psychologists' have viewed the ego not only as a product of the id and with functions limited to the resolution of conflict. They have used the concept to include intelligent, creative and conflict-free behaviour, recognizing, as did Piaget, that this brings subjective satisfactions and contributes in an important way to our adaptation in the outer world (Hartmann 1951).

In the sequential development of the subjective self, the *super-ego* is the last arrival. We enter the world with ready-made biological urges or drives. Our ego is formed as consciousness dawns in interactions with inanimate objects and people. But the super-ego is thought to appear only as we recognize ourselves to be distinct from other people and are able to imitate and later to identify with their social standards which finally we incorporate and make our own. Its main functions are conscience, moral self-scrutiny, and the formation of ideals. With the advent of the super-ego an important new source of conflict exists, between our wishes and actions and what we believe to be right.

The layers of awareness

Three levels of consciousness are associated with the components of the inner self: at any given moment we are aware of our *conscious* experience and perceptions arising from within and from without. Consciousness extends into the *preconscious* which contains perceptions and memories immediately available for conscious attention if the need arises. Many everyday activities, like walking or driving a car, become habits. We are unaware of how, and often precisely why, we perform them. But if we try, we can attend to ourselves in action. Our vast memory store, too, is in large measure available, but only on demand. Similarly, we screen out perceptions irrelevant to our immediate purpose, such as street noises. Yet we notice them if we want to.

The term *unconscious* Freud reserved for those experiences which we cannot bring into awareness at will because protective barriers, *defence mechanisms*, intervene. The unconscious is formed from childhood onwards as a result of anxieties, and consists of repressed thoughts and instinctual wishes which the child perceived as dangerous or forbidden and against which his ego erected defensive barriers to minimize anxiety. Such repressed, unconscious thoughts and wishes cannot be matched against reality, and hence the individual never discovers from *reality testing* whether his childhood fears were justified or not. Moreover, material repressed in childhood no longer shares in the developmental transformations as the capacity for reasoning matures. The result is that relegation of experience to the unconscious is often justified only in terms of the child's view of his or her world rather than the reality as it was, and that much unconscious experience is immature. Freud called this *primary process thinking* (in contrast to rational adult, *secondary process thinking*) and the writings of psychoanalysts make clear that this has much in common with the type of thinking Piaget discovered regularly in children during their animistic stage of development.

We have no direct entry to the unconscious. It surfaces in dreams and is revealed during psychotic illnesses. Hypnosis and psychoanalysis give access to it. Under stress it is translated into psychoneurotic symptoms and it contributes to many minor everyday errors such as slips of the tongue or the forgetting of emotionally charged events or duties. It is also recognizable as the source of some of the repetitive and maladaptive choices we make in our lives, apparently against our will or better judgement. Such distortions of personality derive from thoughts, fears, and wishes of which we are not aware. It is one of the aims of psychoanalytic and psychotherapeutic treatment to put the patient in better touch with this part of himself: to make what is unconscious, conscious.

Anxiety, repression and the mechanisms of defence

Anxiety is an emotion with many measurable physical accompaniments, such as increased heart rate, sweating, and dilated pupils. It signals possible future danger and first manifests as an inborn emotional response to *actual* dangers in the present, such as pain, hunger, and abandonment.

Anna Freud described the activation of six contributory sources of anxiety as the child grows up (A. Freud 1966). (1) *Separation anxiety* derives from inborn reactions to life-threatening stimuli once the infant is capable of some anticipation of future events. Its source is fear of annihilation and later, when the child has become attached to familiar people, fear of losing them. Once object constancy is achieved (towards the end of the first year) anxiety springs also from (2) *fear of loss of love*. It is at this time that mothers begin to express pleasure or displeasure to their children at what they do. During the second year (3) *fear of criticism and punishment* contributes to anxiety. (4) *Castration fear* is activated by oedipal experiences beginning in the third year (to be described more fully below), followed very closely by (5) *guilt*. This is disapproval from one's own conscience (the super-ego), formed in identification with parents, and incorporating their authority. A further possible origin of anxiety is (6) a *wholly internal conflict* between id impulses and wishes, incompatible not with the outer world nor with the remembered wishes and prohibitions of parents, but with the child's own ego. Such conflicts arise from incompatible emotions or wishes, for example, love and hatred towards the same person, or a wish to be both active and passive.

Freud gave varying descriptions of the concept of *repression* and its relationship to *psychological defence mechanism* (Laplanche and Pontalis 1973). It is a device used by the ego to banish thoughts and wishes in conflict with the outer world, the super-ego, or parts of the ego itself, for the sake of mental comfort. While a modicum of anxiety spurs us to greater effort and achievement, too much disorganizes our behaviour: we cannot attend to our surroundings; we cannot do our work; our sleep and even our appetite are interfered with. Children often know when they cast uncomfortable thoughts from their minds. Adults in retrospect do not remember such childish manoeuvres.

> Alan, eager to tell his mother of a secret he had discovered (that she was not his real but his step-mother) was concerned that she might be angry if she knew. He imagined in bed each night what he would say to her in the morning. When faced with his mother by day he felt 'a bit shy. And I didn't know what to say. So I said something else and then I forgot. But at night I remembered and then it was too late.'

Repressed thoughts and impulses are not lost. They continue to strive for expression and are thought to require constant vigilance to prevent them from disrupting conscious experience. Present experiences resembling those repressed in the past can activate them, and when this happens, defences are increased and may manifest as psychoneurotic symptoms or irrational behaviour.

Excessive repression in childhood leads to stunting of personality. The individual cannot freely express his or her thoughts and needs. Because not within awareness, they take no part in later maturation and are not gratified in real life. Much of later life remains in the realm of childhood fantasy, increasingly out of keeping with actual work and human relationships.

> Alan, having read stories about step-mothers, became wary of his mother and was never naughty just in case she might be cross. He never found out (through 'reality testing') what she would do if, for example, he interrupted her on the telephone, or helped himself to the last cake on the teatray. He repressed quite normal feelings of childish impatience, greed, and anger. When finally he began to steal, his

mother, not surprisingly, did get cross. This confirmed for Alan his distorted inner image of her, strengthening yet further his psychological defences. The therapist saw the stealing as a neurotic symptom by which Alan gave vent to repressed feelings of greed and anger.

Anna Freud has clarified these issues (A. Freud 1961). The ego of the young child uses defence mechanisms to keep mental content charged with anxiety from conscious awareness. Such mental content includes drives, emotions, memories of events, and dictates of conscience. Later in life both the content and the ego's activities are unconscious. Even during childhood we have access to repressed material largely via the behavioural products of the defence mechanism which guard it, and these vary with the particular mode or style of the child's ego.

For example, a child's failure to show normal and expected emotional reactions such as sibling rivalry, childish greed, aggression, or sexual curiosity points to *repression*. Apart from this basic defence there are many others. They include *reaction formation*, expressed for example by excessive concern for parental safety in a child who never permits him or herself to be normally rebellious and hostile towards the parents, or by a display of exaggerated bravery in a situation in which other children would be fearful.

Dominic, aged 6½, was worried about his mother's many illnesses. He himself had had a series of operations on his ears. 'I get into a big state because I always think they [the parents] were going to die and I never get that out of my head and she says "I'm ill" and she doesn't mean it. If I can't say things, I can't get the thoughts out of my mind and it pushes other things out.' He doesn't like grazed knees 'and my mummy doesn't like it streaming blood and she doesn't like it a bit' because it messes up his clothes. But he insisted he was *not* afraid of getting hurt. To make his point he demonstrated how he can bump his nose hard with his fist without flinching. The shallowness of this assertion, a *reaction formation* clearly designed to give him courage, became evident as he commented: 'that's where the most important parts of me are: heart and nose and eye because the nose and heart can kill if it gets damaged. Bones protect special parts.'

When asked what he was going to be when he grew up, Michael, aged 4, said 'Dead. A skeleton. When I'm 13. All the beasties eat you under the ground.' Asked whether he knew someone who had died he said 'Blackie died. My granny's doggie.' His parents reported that after the dog's death Michael quite cheerfully said that *he* wanted to die to see what it would be like to be a skeleton.

Projection is another defence. Here one's own unwanted feelings, such as anger, are attributed to others to whom one now reacts as a victim of *their* anger.

Dominic was reported to be very aggressive to other boys at school. His complaint was different: 'I have problems in the playground. When I do nothing they come and chase me and I don't know what on earth they're doing when I'm doing nothing . . . I'm not very strong and I hate fighting because all the fighting boys keep coming on the gentle boys . . . They get cross because I don't hit them. I just stay out of harm's way.'

Other mechanisms of defence are *denial of reality*, when children do not remember that they stole or when, in response to a sudden death, the bereaved at first acts as if nothing had happened; and *displacement*, when feelings meant for one person are expressed towards another, as when a child is in active rivalry with a school friend but endlessly encouraging of his little brother, or a girl complaining that her teacher shouts a lot, never grumbles about her own mother's irritability.

Sublimation is one defence which allows instinctual drives to find expression by redirecting them into socially acceptable patterns. Childhood sexual interest becomes scientific curiosity; childhood aggression is turned into leadership. Many career choices may in part be based on such processes: an operation in childhood reinforcing oedipal guilt can call forth an early resolve to be a doctor. When this is in fact a realistic choice it allows repressed feelings to be expressed as ego achievements.

Other ego mechanisms enhancing social maturity are imitation of and identification with loved and respected adults to form one's ideal self, and finally *introjection* or incorporation of the standards of such adults to form one's conscience.

Freud's view of emotional development

One of Freud's earliest discoveries which shocked his Victorian readers was childhood sexuality. Not only do children have sexual feelings and interests, according to him the psychoneurotic illnesses of adults as well as the sexual perversions have their roots in faulty development of the sexual drive in childhood. Although he considered both constitutional and 'accidental' factors to contribute to this, psychoanalysts, he held, could deal only with the latter, that is with life events (Freud 1905). The notion that a first experience colours later similar experiences was a profound insight with which Freud credited Binet: one always returns to one's first love.

Fixation and regression

Freud carried this idea much further with his concepts of *fixation* and *regression*. Great pleasure as well as pain and anxiety in childhood indelibly mark future personality. The choice of love object, the modes of adult satisfactions, and relationships retain the characteristics of childhood patterns. Under situations of stress even individuals usually coping well revert, or regress, to these earlier modes. These may have been associated with a particular stage of childhood or with particular childhood events and relationships.

One of Freud's briefest and less well-known case histories (1913), reported prospectively, although the childhood experiences were clearly revealed retrospectively in adult life, vividly exemplifies these mechanisms, in this case fixation and regression to anal eroticism. This history illustrates Freud's capacity for sympathy and understanding and, incidentally also, how often even affectionate parents are blind to their children's feelings and needs.

The story as told begins when the patient was 7. She asked her father for money to buy colouring for Easter eggs. He refused, saying he had no money (a lie Freud did not comment on). Yet later he gave her a large bank note with which to contribute to a school fund. She returned less than the full change to him, having secretly bought the paints she wanted. On being confronted with the fact that money was missing, she lied. Her brother, however, betrayed her, the paints were discovered, and the father asked her mother to punish her. This, presumably physical, punishment she retrospectively saw as the turning point in her life. From being an outgoing lively child, she became withdrawn and inhibited. As a young adult she had irrationally strong feelings about money, being too shy to ask her husband for what she needed, and rigidly distinguishing between his money and hers.

The analysis revealed an even earlier childhood experience that had sensitized her to the events that occurred at 7 and had turned these into the crucially inhibiting experience they became.

At 3½ she had often accompanied her nursemaid, whom she loved, on visits to this nursemaid's lover, a doctor. To ensure secrecy, the nurse would give her money for sweets on the way. But on one occasion the future patient, jealous of the nurse as Freud thought, played so ostentatiously with the money that her mother questioned its origins and the nursemaid was dismissed. Freud saw the money (accepted by the nurse from the doctor, by the child from the nurse, and later taken by the child from her father) as representing for the patient the gifts of erotic love. The experience of her father's refusal and subsequent punishment Freud interpreted as 'a rejection of the tenderness she was offering him — a humiliation — and so it broke her spirit' (Freud 1913:307). When, during the analysis, Freud asked her to call on him for money should she ever be in need, she could not bring herself to do so.

The characteristics of early childhood

Although he spent his time with adult patients, Freud was well aware of many crucial characteristics of young children, some of which we now know to be determined by their cognitive immaturity (Chapter 6). He referred to the cruelty of young children, which he attributed to their lack of empathy, a quality which he thought (wrongly as it turned out) to develop late. But he also described the 'natural assumption' of children that everyone is alike.

> The foster parents of a 4-year-old, still uncertain whether his natural mother would consent to adoption although he had been with them since he was 4 weeks old, deliberately kept the idea of his 'other mummy' alive for him. In play with his 7-year-old foster sister he often had 'two mummies' and his sister would organize the drama by saying 'you go to your mummy there, and I'll be your mummy here'. One day in a family conversation it emerged that both children thought everyone had 'two mummies'.

Small boys may believe that everyone has a penis and be shocked when they notice that girls are without this body part. Freud still thought that children's stereotyped but erroneous sexual theories (that babies are cut out of their mother's stomach; are born through the anus; that eating starts them off growing inside the body; and, if intercourse is seen, that this is an act of aggression) were due to parental secrecy and lack of opportunity to make observations (they cannot know the role of the seed and they do not know of the girl's genital opening). Anna Freud however is quite clear that despite enlightenment, young children cling tenaciously to their own sexual theories and it is impossible to rid them of sexual anxiety (A. Freud 1966).

> When he was 5, his big sister had told Alan 'they come out of their mother's stomachs . . . but I didn't believe her then'. Now at 9 he does, but has no idea how the babies get out. When invited to guess, he said 'I'd say, they cut a hole in your stomach.'

The more open and less punitive the parents, the harsher the child's own conscience. The more permissive his conscience, the more the child fears the consequences of his own aggressive and sexual impulses (A. Freud 1966).

The stages of emotional development

Freud, like Piaget, saw child development not as an even progression towards increasing maturity but as a sequence of qualitatively different stages. He too assumed that personality has biological roots and these he located in what he called *erotogenic zones*: the lips, the urethra, the anus, and the genitalia. For him the crucial experiences of early stages of childhood were the pleasures derived from each of these body parts in turn.

(1) *The oral stage*

Until ethologists showed that early attachment is mediated in humans through social stimulation, and not eating (Chapter 4), the *secondary drive theory* held sway: that because the mother satisfies the child's most basic need for food, she becomes the object of the baby's first love and the mouth the *source* of libidinal drive. The *aim*, or mode of expression of this drive, is incorporation which symbolically extends to other aspects of the child's first love relationship: e.g. he 'drinks in' his mother with his eyes. Thumb- and finger-sucking recapture the pleasures previously obtained from a life-preserving function. In the second half of the first year, when teeth appear and weaning starts, aggressive drives find expression in biting and eating up.

(2) *The anal stage*

In the anal stage which Freud placed rather later in time than subsequent workers, at from 2 to 4, the urethra and anus were thought to take over as the primary sources of gratification. Holding on and letting go, obstinacy and generosity are the main modes of libidinal expression: the child is now open to shame, disgust, and cruelty and a very primitive morality begins. The symbolic function of faeces as agents of destruction (or sadism), and also as the child's first gifts, impinge on the possible new modes which now appear of relating to others: opposition and submission.

(3) *The genital stage*

In the next stage, children focus on their genitalia, derive pleasure from masturbation, become sexually curious and erotically attached to the parent of the opposite sex. Jealousy of the same-sex parent evokes fears of punishment, and the observed sex differences between boys and girls reinforce these anxieties: boys fear castration, and girls believe they have already been punished, having once had a penis and finding it gone. Masturbation and erotic fantasies, fostered by seductive behaviour on the part of adults, now engender guilt, especially when these same adults react fiercely (as parents in Freud's day certainly did) to any signs of childhood sex interest or activity. The *Oedipus complex* (or *Electra complex* in girls) is normally resolved by identification with the same-sex parent and incorporating his or her standards to form the super-ego. The following example illustrates how young children express feelings of guilt.

> Michael, who at 4 so blandly reported on the death of his granny's dog, recalled the experience when he was 7. It died 'because my grandad died and the dog looked for my grandad and then it got put down. It got a jag . . . My dad told me when I was 4 . . . , she [the granny] is getting another dog because Blackie died. When I was a baby I was in a cot and I used to torment it.'

Now in the animistic stage, Michael linked the dog's death clearly but erroneously to his own early misdeeds. He probably *had* teased Blackie and been reprimanded for it. As he remembered the dog's death, he recalled his teasing. The one followed the other. Causal links are made and guilt is fostered.

The child's erotic love for the opposite-sex parent is in part a longing for maturity, an anticipation of the future: to be big and do everything that the same-sex parent does, to bake cakes, mow the lawn, drive the car, be married — and to whom else but the partner of the parent who is the role model? The child's erotic love for the parent is not an invitation for an actual sexual relationship, however attractively small boys and girls may display themselves.

(4) *Latency*

At about 5 or 6 years, according to Freud, the child recognizes the uselessness of his sexual strivings and represses these, but never completely. *Latency* is the name Freud gave to this stage which extends to puberty. The child now enters a period of 'socialization' and sublimation. Erotic drives are transformed into eagerness to learn his culture. What Bruner called 'tutor proneness' was certainly known to Freud. He noticed also that no memories are retained of the first year of life, and that most people have partial amnesia for the subsequent five to seven years. This 'forgetting' he attributed to active repression.

Although Freud's ideas continue to arouse disbelief despite what children tell us about themselves if asked (like Piaget, Freud noticed that children do not tend to reveal spontaneously what they think and feel), his theories and observations fall into place when we put Freudian and Piagetian developmental sequences side by side. The first three stages of emotional development coincide with prerational thinking. The child's gross misperceptions, egocentric viewpoint, and extraordinarily punitive view of morality, the belief in magic, and the acceptance of everything as possible, should no longer surprise us.

Latency begins as rational logic develops, and it is quite possible that this contributes to the 'repression' of infantile sexuality, the child putting aside foolish beliefs and hopeless longings, now recognizing the impossibility of their fulfilment.

(5) *Puberty and adolescence*

Freud makes much of the 'chemical' changes at puberty reviving sexual longings which strive for expression towards a love object. The baby has such an actual object: parts of the mother and then the mother as a person. In the genital stage, object choice is made anew and differently but sexual gratification is auto-erotic. At puberty, erotic longings are transferred to a new love object which can now in reality be gratifying. The nature and mode of the erotic attachments which follow puberty carry within them remnants from the individual's genital stage which can be seen as a sort of practice period, a non-functional forerunner of later behaviour and experience, reminiscent of the newborn's non-functional walking and non-social smiles.

While Freud was certainly aware of the impact of events and circumstances on the emotional development of children (he mentions father loss as a possible predisposition to homosexuality, parental overprotection as fostering psychoneurosis, and the possibility that neurotic parents can transfer their ailments to their children other than through the genes), he emphasized far more the role of instinctual drives, psychological mechanisms and constitutional predisposition in shaping adult personality and contributing to emotional disorder.

Concepts of Melanie Klein

Melanie Klein (see Segal 1979 and Mitchell 1986), who contemporaneously with Anna Freud began to apply psychoanalysis to children, modified Freud's system of ideas and added her own explanatory concepts which appeal to some but less to others.

She, and here she was certainly in error, saw a number of developmental steps as occurring much earlier in the child's life than Freud or his followers had suggested. She thought infants in their first few months were able to conceive of body organs like their mother's breast and their father's penis, and she located the oedipus conflict and the birth of conscience in the first year of life, before the child is cognitively capable of such complex experiences.

On the other hand, her concept of developmental *positions*, as contrasted with stages, requires attention. She made explicit the notion, implicit in Freudian writings, that experiences and modes of reacting that characteristically appear for the first time at certain stages of childhood are not confined to these but persist as potential patterns of emotional experience and behaviour throughout life. More specifically, at each stage particular configurations of object relations arise: anxieties and defences which contribute to later personality, and to the manifestations of psychiatric illness.

Melanie Klein, however, more than other child psychoanalysts, confounded causal with subjective explanations. It may be enlightening to describe the infant in his first 3 to 4 months as existing in a *paranoid-*

schizoid position, because, like some schizophrenic patients, he is capable of relating only to part-objects, and is unable to differentiate between himself and the world outside. It is also reasonable and perhaps helpful to postulate that the mental mechanisms of projection and introjection, which feature prominently in schizophrenia, derive from these early months. It is certainly not warranted to draw conclusions from such analogies about the causes of schizophrenia, nor to claim, as she did, that the precursors of this serious psychosis can be identified and possibly remedied in early infancy.

During the second half of Freud's oral stage, from 6 to 12 months, the child is in Klein's view in a *depressive position*. He now relates to his mother as a whole and separate person and is capable of experiencing mixed positive and negative, that is *ambivalent*, feelings towards her according to whether or not she meets his needs. Certainly this is the time when the child's behaviour shows that he can feel profound sorrow and anxiety, emotions which are the hallmark of depressive illnesses in adult life. What seems less likely is that in these early months babies are capable of guilt, a state also prominent in the depressions of adulthood. While the affect of patients with depressive illnesses, and indeed all adult sorrow and anxiety, may well recapture for each individual the precise feelings he or she first had in infancy, there are no grounds for assuming that these somehow cause the later illness, nor is there evidence (and indeed there never can be) that, despite the validity of the retrospective view, such infantile feelings influence even the content of later experiences.

From Freud to a psychoanalytic view of man in society

Freud's theories have entered the vernacular but their application to our own experiences, professional and personal, requires even today a leap from accustomed to new and at times uncongenial forms of thought and language. The care of psychiatric patients, especially those with neurotic illnesses and sexual perversions, demands that we undertake this acrobatic feat. Even when the main cause of a psychiatric disorder is physical (as in the dementias of old age) or the best treatment educational (e.g. a behavioural approach for a street phobia), we cannot respect and enter into the feelings of other people, nor help them to preserve their self-esteem, without the insights Freud has given us. Psychiatric disorders, unlike physical ailments, are never only something a person *has*. To a large extent he *is* his illness since, even if its cause is a brain disease, it affects his personality.

Freud demonstrated how a perversion (exhibitionism or shoe fetishism, for example), or a psychoneurosis (such as an obsessional state with compulsive hand-washing and elaborate rituals to avoid the possibility of contamination by germs), conditions of which people are often painfully ashamed, can be traced back to perfectly normal emotions and mental activities in childhood whose residues exist in us all, and also how particular childhood experiences can be related to these later symptoms. Such insight reduces a patient's horror and fear about himself and is a necessary step before he can face his difficulties and their often arduous treatment. Unless professionals themselves have overcome their astonishment at the strangeness of some human behaviours and can see these as understandable developments, they cannot convey this to their patients.

People with neurotic illnesses require medical treatment. Few would argue with that. But there are very many more people with personality disorders, disastrously disrupting their family and working lives and often the surrounding community, whom doctors claim less confidently as valid patients and for whom a range of other professionals assume some kind of responsibility from time to time (see also Wolff 1987). Patterns of delinquency, of domestic and street violence, of addiction and disrupted family relationships, vary of course with social milieu and with accidents of fortune. Yet there are common threads in the lives of individuals and of human groups which persist despite changed circumstances and which can be traced to personal and shared childhood experiences. To understand these personality patterns and to empathize with people who have such difficulties a simpler and at the same time more comprehensive view is needed. This, as we shall now see, Erik Erikson has given us.

Chapter eight

Emotional development: psychoanalysis and the social self

The 'life cycle': Erik Erikson's cultural approach to personality

Psychoanalysis had at first often been blind to the social environment. Even those child analysts who, like Anna Freud, concerned themselves with parentless children, with the physically handicapped and the socially deprived, gave quite insufficient weight to the actual catastrophes that befall some children, dramatically change their behaviour and that of others towards them, and can carry over their effects to the next generation through the long-term personality distortions they usher in. Charles Rycroft wrote: 'Many of our patients are the offspring of tragedy, not of faulty child rearing' (Rycroft 1968: 17).

Erikson accepts many of Freud's biological assumptions and postulated mental structures and mechanisms. But he places the individual firmly in a social, cultural, and historic setting, stressing the particular ways in which the child and society impinge on each other at each stage of life, and the consequences of these encounters for what he calls 'identity'.

Like many later psychoanalysts, he turns a blind eye to Freud's theory of instincts. These notions we can do without when we view the person not as a solitary being facing the world that awaits his actions, but as interrelating constantly with others. Yet the origins of human motivation remain mysterious whether they are explained in terms of biological instincts or 'control systems' (Bowlby 1982), or of 'social forces'.

For Erikson as for Freud, first experiences are crucial. Like Freud he views emotional development as a succession of stages tied in early life to the child's discovery of and attention to the bodily orifices and their functions: eating, urination, defecation, and genital pleasure. Like other analysts, he knows that children think and reason differently from adults and often totally misunderstand what they see and hear, and that this gives a special colouring to their early experiences. His particular contribution is to point out that each stage opens up a new range of social encounters associated with new types of emotional experiences. In part these depend on the child's own physical and intellectual growth; in part on the expectations others have of the child. The coincidence in time of these different developmental and social processes is thought to determine the clustering of later personality characteristics.

Erikson sees the individual in society as both absorbing and making history. Parents and teachers express in their behaviour to children not only their idiosyncrasies but the traditions of their culture. In part they do this unconsciously and in part they deliberately pass on to children their own version of what their parents had taught them. The way parents bring up their children also reflects their status and acceptance within their community as perceived by themselves and others. Moreover, we choose our marriage partners in our parents' image, or at least with our parents in mind, and this strengthens the continuity between the generations and the preservation of family and cultural traditions.

Erikson's description of the 'life cycle' (1965; 1968) gives us an outline into which highly individual and also more general life experiences can be fitted. Each stage reflects the social roles and tasks demanded of the growing person and his or her abilities to fulfil them. Each stage of childhood brings with it a new set of alternative patterns for social interaction, together with the capacity for new emotions. Which of the alternatives predominate determines the patterns of feelings, attitudes, and possible responses the child stores up for the future. Every period of life has its particular conflicts, and from the way each child resolves these he or she learns what to do in future: first solutions become enduring solutions.

Let us pause here to examine a basic principle of most theories of personality development: that some permanence attaches to the emotional experiences of early childhood not matched by subsequent encounters. By setting child-rearing practices into their cultural background Erikson has opened the way towards a biological explanation for the observations on which this principle rests. As we saw earlier, Bowlby holds that inborn behaviour patterns foster early mother-child attachment, and that these patterns have come about as a result of natural selection. Equally, one might argue that cultural continuity of specific behaviour patterns both protects individuals against ostracism from their groups, ensuring that they can earn their living and establish families in the society in which they live, but also preserves cultural and subcultural differences.

Such continuity of different cultural styles depends on the stability over time of what one generation learns from another, and on the survival of personality characteristics acquired in childhood.

If certain social and emotional patterns were not learnt once and for all, we would be learning and relearning these patterns throughout life from the people around us. Theoretically this would lead to a loss of specialization of styles and roles. We would all in time come to resemble each other: social and cultural differences would disappear.

While most aspects of personality transmitted across the generations are perfectly adaptive, there is now observational evidence, from the Berkeley longitudinal studies, for the reproduction through marital tension and ineffective parenting of problem behaviour and unstable family relationships in the next generation (Capsi and Elder 1988).

Every child is influenced by life events and by the people who look after him or her. While at each period a certain type of experience occurs for the first time, it is not limited to that stage but continues for many years. Mothers feed and nurture their babies, and for the infant this is the first experience of being looked after. Although mothers, and indeed fathers, continue their caring functions in their own particular style until their children are grown up, for the child the earliest experience of being looked after, according to Erikson, has the biggest effect. This view is less puzzling if we remember the powerful mutual influences between parents and children. A person's capacity for specific types of social interaction is more vulnerable when it first appears than later in life, in part at least for the very reason that one's initial responses alter the behaviour of other people towards oneself and this can reinforce these initial responses.

Erikson accepts Freud's concepts of *fixation* and *regression*. If there is excessive anxiety during a particular stage, the emotions and social patterns of that time are revived when in later life we find ourselves in a similar setting. On the other hand, if a stage has been especially happy we may in later life, when under stress, regress to modes of being characteristic of this former time. The life events and circumstances that matter are always specific and individual. Nothing, Erikson says, is gained from stereotypes such as that the patient had a domineering mother (Erikson 1968).

Erikson abandons the language of science for that of literature. He is not out to prove theories to us, as was Freud; merely to provide us with helpful reflections. For him each stage of life, and he takes us from the cradle to the grave, is associated with a specific symbolism the individual henceforth retains and expresses in his or her actions. It is here that Erikson exerts his greatest appeal. The scheme that follows derives largely from his ideas.

Stage I: The first year (the 'oral' stage of primary attachments): 'Infancy and the mutuality of recognition' — trust versus mistrust

Unknowing, helpless dependency characterizes infancy. Babies feel hungry and enjoy eating. They become interested in their surroundings and then amused by their companions, developing bonds of affection for parents in their second 6 months. Helpless rage is aroused when basic needs are not met and suffering when human bonds are interrupted. Erikson views the first approach to the world as 'incorporative' and 'receptive'. The child learns to get what is given; to get others to give to him and finally, in identification with others, to be a giver. At first passive, the child becomes actively grasping. His first attitudes concern 'trust'. When the baby's needs are well met he learns to be realistically optimistic with a sense of security and resourcefulness which sustains him in later situations of dependency. He trusts himself, others, and his fate. *Excessive anxiety* in infancy, whether aroused by absence of nurturing care, or later by separation from parent figures, predisposes to pessimism and distrust. Infantile dependency and 'oral, incorporative' experiences are of course not confined to the first year. We depend on our parents throughout childhood and on society until we die. But the particular way in which we manage this type of human association and the feelings it will henceforth arouse go back to our infancy.

The parts of our person we like are always with us and we use them flexibly and to good effect. They form a continuity with our happy past. More troublesome aspects of our personality we tend to keep hidden. They can be traced back to early experiences of excessive anxiety. They surface under later situations of stress as stereotyped patterns of behaviour and emotions, often very difficult to control and change.

The child's own temperament contributes to the anxieties he or she experiences even in infancy. Mothers adapt less readily to hypersensitive, irritable babies. Small misjudgements about the timing or intensity of stimulation can lead to distress in the baby and mutually unrewarding interactions between mother and child, while a more placid infant hardly notices the error and maintains his cheerful relationship with his mother.

All kinds of adversities, such as illness, can disrupt maternal care. In later childhood the ability of parents to remain sources of trust depends also on their own trustworthiness. If they are identified with the life style of their community and its traditional systems of child care they feel secure as parents and are perceived by their children as providing what should be given. When mothers have a sense of not belonging, perhaps because they were themselves abandoned as children, their capacities for basic emotional care are reduced.

Personality traits associated with adversity in infancy are excessive craving for dependency, a sense of emptiness, unworthiness, and mistrust. In times of crisis resourcefulness can degenerate into gambling; nostalgia for the past into addiction. Risks are now taken with what little security remains for the sake of uncertain and temporary gains: wealth or withdrawal into a blissful fantasy world.

Marilyn Brown, aged 9, the oldest of three children living with her mother, had for three years suffered from aches and pains, fainting turns, and episodes of 'falling asleep'. Her symptoms began after her father left the family and her mother could no longer provide basic care. She relied on Marilyn for emotional support and help about the house, adding to the child's worries by her own ill health and hospital admissions.

Mrs. Brown was 29. With an embarrassed laugh she said she was the thirteenth of fifteen children. As the youngest girl she thought she had been favoured. Although she described all her brothers and sisters as having been 'mums and dads' to her, 'I was attached to my mum and dad and after they died I had nobody really — everything split up.'

When she was 15 she had an illegitimate son, looked after from birth by her parents and later by an older sister. Her marriage was happy until she was sterilized following a fourth pregnancy. Mr Brown then became promiscuous, stole to provide money for his girl friend and was imprisoned. These humiliations impelled Mrs Brown to start divorce proceedings. At this stage her mother died. Mrs Brown now became depressed and began to drink 'day and night'. While drunk, she made a number of suicide attempts. She developed serious kidney disease; her father died; she was evicted on account of rent arrears and finally entered hospital for treatment of her depression. The children were then admitted into care. She continued to drink after coming out of hospital until the local authority threatened to remove her children permanently if she did not stop.

Mrs Brown now began to put on weight. She continued to feel

lonely, getting no comfort from the many hours spent by her sympathetic social worker in her home. She found the social worker 'too young'. She never went out, fearing that she might start to drink again. She lacked all confidence in herself and said she felt 'hopeless'.

Her explanation of Marilyn's troubles was, 'She's no friends because the others have roller skates.'

This mother's chief personality characteristics were oral cravings (for drink and now food), and feelings of dependency and ambivalence in relation to having children. Clearly humiliated by her own grotesquely large childhood family which failed to meet her needs for individual care, she added to her humiliations by her early pregnancy and then got for her son the attention her parents were never able to give to her. Unlike her mother she did not want a huge family, yet her sterilization totally disrupted what had been a stable marriage and led to the loss of her one consistently supporting relationship.

Marilyn herself recalled that her latest faint occurred in an English lesson when the teacher told a story about 'David the Donkey'. He was left on a farm. Every Thursday he had to go to market and the farmer's wife put two baskets on him and then sat on top of him herself. His legs were thin and he kept falling over. The farmer's wife then hit him. When it was suggested to Marilyn that perhaps *she* sometimes felt like that donkey but did not like to complain, kept her feelings inside, and instead fell down and fainted, she said 'I worry in case my mum got ill.' She then *did* begin to complain: that her mother would not allow her to play with her friend in case she got into trouble; that the only girl she could play with was her cousin who, she thought, was not really her cousin; that her mother sometimes told her 'wrong things', for example that she had no money when she did, but needed it for other things.

The mother's miseries lay as a heavy burden on this child, like the farmer's wife who sat on her laden donkey. Although the mother was Marilyn's only security she could not be trusted: what she said was not always true. She was also a source of great anxiety because threatening, and threatened by, illness. As a result Marilyn had to repress her resentments. Instead *she* now developed symptoms of illness and enjoyed the hospital admissions that followed, especially 'helping' the ward orderly. The link between the succession of traumatic life events — the mother's sterilization, the father's imprisonment, the deaths of the maternal grandparents — and the mother's particular mode of decompensation — depression, alcohol addiction, and obesity — was Mrs Brown's oral-dependent personality, a legacy from the specific privations and humiliations of her childhood past.

The nature of experiences of infancy and early attachments can explain the type of later personality difficulties, but also some of the variability of normal life styles. Within limits there is room for differences even in the care of babies. Swaddling, rocking, and demand feeding are examples of different socio-cultural traditions of infant care (Pinchbeck and Hewitt 1969). They modify the child's personality in conformity with the norms of his or her society. When adult initiative is prized, parents enjoy seeing their infants' vigorous motor activities and reward early signs of enterprise, for example by letting babies decide their own feeding times. The evidence for cultural differences in child-rearing and their effects on personality will be reviewed in our next chapter.

For Erikson each early stage is linked to a more universal social institution. 'Trust . . . becomes the capacity for faith' (Erikson 1968). Religious beliefs and rituals he sees as suprapersonal, socially unifying expressions of dependency and its associated modes of being. Everyone brings to religion the residues from his infancy. The religious orders in turn can be a public safety net for spiritual and practical care.

Stage II: The second year (the 'anal' stage of initial socialization): 'Early childhood and the will to be oneself' — autonomy versus shame and doubt

As the child begins to have formed stools and gains control over his musculature he gets from elimination the satisfactions of 'a major job well done'. In more ways than one, he learns to contain himself at the expense of discomfort, for the sake of social approval. The capacity for self-discipline now begins. He is on his feet and his arms are free for action. He can hold tight but also throw things about wilfully. He needs his parents behind him, to back him up when success is near; to run after him and literally hold on to him when disaster threatens. In infancy the symbolism of mouth activities and the face becomes associated with relationships of dependency and attitudes of trust or mistrust. Now the symbolism of excretory functions and one's back (exposed to others with the attainment of the upright posture yet invisible to oneself) comes to

147

be linked with co-operative relationships and with attitudes of autonomy or doubt. Expressions like 'get off my back', 'a chip on his shoulder', 'things are going on behind my back' point to such symbolic associations.

All parents now instruct their children in what must and must not be done, even in cultures not focused like our own on cleanliness and punctuality. For the first time, the child experiences a co-operative relationship with a powerful other person and the choices and emotions attached to this. He can willingly do what is required, successfully express his own wishes or obstinately oppose his elders. He can be proud of achievement or ashamed of failure. A sense of trust in others and oneself is the basis for confident choices and for having one's own way. Parental firmness is needed to protect children against their own impulses. No toddler has impulse control; what he does is often intentionally or unintentionally destructive and, unless grown-ups are felt to be in control, he is terrified of breaking things and damaging himself and others. Parents provide a sense of security and safety. Yet they also instil confidence by encouraging their toddler to stand on his own feet and protecting him from too great a sense of shame when he falls over, for example, or 'accidentally' soils his pants.

If the child's stage of initial socialization and his parents' teaching of social conventions are successful, he emerges with a sense of autonomy, freewill and pride in his competence. He has gained the rudiments of self-discipline and the capacity to set and follow goals. When upsetting events occur in his second or third year, or *excessive tensions and anxieties* attach to these particular parent-child interactions, a sense of shame and doubt is born. Over-sensitive or over-controlled children may later develop a precocious and inhibiting conscience, with obsessional and ritualistic patterns. Others regress to infantile clinging, thumb-sucking and baby talk. Yet others become wilful and hostile. When young parents themselves are uncontrolled and uncontrolling, their toddlers' ever more impulsive behaviour — temper tantrums, smearing of food and faeces, tearing of wallpaper and running dangerously across main roads — can evoke from them outbursts of rage terrifying for them and their children.

Loss of self-control or parental over-restriction engender a sense of shame and doubt in the child which can be revived in later years by social encounters calling for co-operation with authority figures. The individual may then react with legalistic precision, obsequious over-compliance or pugnacity, quite inappropriate in adult relationships although understandable in terms of his or her childhood self.

In the second and third year the child experiences his first emancipation (he can walk and could run away), anticipating his real emancipation at adolescence. Just as the adolescent relives his oral modes in terms of his hopes for the future, so he recaptures his anal mode of being in his sense of worth, his intentions and the contributions he feels he can make to society.

Erikson believes that parents are helped in their training of young children if they themselves have a sense of control over their destiny. This is clearly not so for large groups of parents, uneducated, unskilled, and now often unemployed, depending on an uncertain labour market for limited occupational autonomy, and on dwindling public services for housing and security. Such parents may manage their children's infancy supremely well but are bewildered by impulsive toddlers and often have unrealistic ideas about small children's capacities for self-control.

The social institutions preserving the personality gains of this second stage are the principles of law and order in everyday life and the judicial system. These form a safety net for youngsters whose family life has failed to provide and instil controls over their immature and often destructive urges. Erikson suggests that parents can avoid a sense of shame and doubt in their children by teaching in impersonal terms — 'this is how things are done' or 'this is how we do it' — rather than by enforcing obedience 'because I say so'. Many parents of low social status, powerless over their own destinies, also feel powerless to control their children. They perceive the social institutions, not as reinforcing what they themselves believe to be right, but as a threat to themselves and their children. If they fail conspicuously as parents, their children may be taken away. For them childish misbehaviour *is* dangerous because it can publicly show up their own short-comings. Instead of taking over controls for the child, such parents give all they can to their children ('he gets everything he wants'), remembering how often they themselves in poorer times went short. When the children run wild, the parents punish or use the social institutions as a threat. They literally take their child to the police station 'to give him a fright' or threaten him with being 'taken away and put into a home'. They fail to realize that, without external protective controls, the child is already over-anxious and that what he needs above all is the opportunity, in a safe world and without threat, to watch and copy how his parents control themselves and him.

Stage III: from 2 to 5 (the 'genital' stage of primary identification): 'the play age' and 'the anticipation of roles' — initiative versus guilt

As children detach themselves from the immediate vicinity of their mothers and acquire a sense not only of the past but of the future, an enormous range of new experiences and modes of being open up. Language transforms their social interactions as well as their inner experiences. They listen eagerly to stories and learn about what Erikson calls their parents' 'heroic past'. An ethos of action, heroes and achievements accompanies their entry into the romantic period of childhood. But they misunderstand much of what they hear, and often frighten themselves with what they can imagine. A 'consuming curiosity' colours their thoughts and actions as they make comparisons between people according to size, age, and social role. Children now enter their first social circles: the family, the playgroup, the nursery class. No longer one of a pair, demanding individual attention from the parent, the child is now one of a family group with two parents whose attentions must often be shared with others.

Rivalries and jealousies are experienced for the first time. They can be mastered because the child has greater self-control and because he can compensate in imagination, in play, and in aspirations for the future, for what he fails to achieve in the present.

Erikson noticed that the manifestations of infantile sexuality are rarely prominent unless parents are seductive, prudish or threatening (for example to 'cut it off'), or unless groups of children engage in sex play.

Like Freud, Erikson considers the emotional development of girls to be more hazardous than that of boys at this stage. As they imagine their future roles as wife and mother, girls become erotically attached to their father, perceiving their mother as a rival. Their jealousy of her is the more frightening because in their fantasies of retribution from her, they lose their haven of security and source of comfort. Any criticism from her is now magically viewed as dangerous, particularly because, as in Freud's case described in the last chapter, it is secretly felt to be deserved. Boys during the oedipal stage, in contrast, merely change the nature of their affection for their mother. When magically they see their father as a hostile rival, they can still turn to their mother for comfort.

Yet clinical observation suggests that small boys are often more openly anxious at this stage than girls, especially when their social training in the previous stage was stressful. Many fathers in unskilled working-class families lack social esteem and work success, while the social status of mothers is less precariously tied to class and culture. Mothers can always fulfil their domestic roles, but if the social status of the family is low the father's esteem within it suffers. We shall see in the next chapter that the Great Depression in the USA affected the behaviour of fathers more than that of mothers. It also influenced the life adjustment of their sons more than that of their daughters (Elder *et al.* 1984). When mothers in unskilled working-class families are disparaging of all men, their fathers, their husbands and their sons, it is impossible for boys to resolve their oedipal conflict optimally, by identifying with an admired father and developing a firm male self.

Erikson recognizes the difficulties for boys in mother-dominated homes in which women, frustrated in their own masculine strivings, are 'disgusted' by men and aim to 'get even' with them. In Britain, class-related cultural attitudes towards sex and work roles are at least as powerful as more individually determined attitudes. Their transmission from generation to generation is an everyday clinical phenomenon which at the present time puts boys at special risk. This risk is increased further when, more and more, children are reared in families with no father at all.

The vigorous exploration by the now inquisitive and intrusive 'genital'-stage child brings with it rivalry feelings and fears for life and limb. 'Castration anxiety' ceases to be a surprising phenomenon if we remember the child's animistic logic (that thoughts can turn into actions and the crime beget the punishment) and his or her authoritarian ('an eye for an eye; a tooth for a tooth') morality. As children identify with and incorporate their parents' standards, *a powerful new source of anxiety in the form of guilt* arises. *Conscience* is born and with it a division between the self in action and the moral self: ego and super-ego. The latter is often harsh and cruel at this early stage, leading to self-restriction or lasting resentments, especially when parents themselves fail to live up to the standards they set for their children.

But children learn not only what is forbidden but what is possible. This is the time of *primary identifications*: a rehearsal for adolescence. Children now acquire a sexual identity, and hopes for their future family and working life. They look for new identifications outside the rivalries of the family in play acting and role taking. All options are still open. In their own imagination, and in their parents' eyes, they can become anything at all. In anticipation of adolescence they establish a life for themselves independent of the parents, and they begin to have secrets.

The social institutions supporting this period of childhood are marriage customs and traditional family structures backed by belief systems and legal codes. According to the individual's life experiences at this stage he or she emerges with a capacity for initiative strengthened, and with a view of him or herself as a future lover and parent, as a worker and member of society; or alternatively constricted, shy and inhibited in work, social and sexual activities. Excessive anxiety due to unresolved conflicts at this stage often lies buried, to emerge later in life as deviant sexual identifications, as sexual inhibition, lack of initiative, and excessive guilt, or as their opposites: a premature assumption of adult sexual roles, of independence from parents, promiscuity, and delinquency.

Brian Jones, just 16, appeared at Court on a series of charges for housebreaking. He was a handsome, physically mature boy, and for nearly a year he had lived in London working steadily, sharing a flat with an older boy, and having a number of homosexual relationships. He had had no difficulty at 15 in convincing employers that he was 16, and at 16 in getting a provisional driving licence. With his earnings he equipped himself with new clothes, and he surprised himself by his extraordinary competence in coping independently in a world of rather older people. He was proud of the fact that none of his sexual relationships had been for money and that he had 'never been to bed with anyone over 21'.

Despite his apparent self-confidence and lighthearted cheeriness when not in trouble, after each theft Brian was terrified to the point of suicidal thoughts by the possible consequences. His main pre-occupation was his mother, whom he had left behind in a Midland town. He worried about her depressions and her unfulfilled second marriage, finding it easy to put himself in her position, and share her point of view. Every time he was in trouble he feared that if she found out she would have nothing more to do with him. When, inevitably, she did find out, she always tried to protect him from the consequences of his acts, while at the same time never failing to berate him.

Brian was the oldest of three, born when his mother was only 16. Her parents were unhappily married and her pregnancy coincided with their separation. When she married Brian's father, her own father moved in with her. Her relationship with her mother had been stormy, the mother blaming her for the tensions between herself and the father 'because I was cheeky and out of hand, but my father never thought so'. She also remembered stealing from her mother, 'but never like Brian'.

Mr Jones was discharged from Borstal to marry Brian's mother.

He continued to be in and out of prison on account of house-breaking and, when at home, he was violent to Brian and his mother. Brian's relationship with his mother was exceptionally close ('I clung to Brian') and he helped her look after the younger children.

When he was 6 his mother divorced Mr Jones and in the same year the grandfather died. Brian's closeness to his mother was now interrupted by her new relationship to the future step-father. At this stage Brian began to steal from her. At once she feared a criminal future for him. She thought it was 'history repeating itself'. She punished and threatened him, not understanding the thefts as a protest aimed to recreate his former closeness to her. She in turn felt unable to 'get through to him'. He became excessively demanding, and she indulged him endlessly with toys and clothes. Whatever he wanted, he got. 'He's been spoilt. He's had it all his own way from a baby. Even now he gets everything he wants. He's lucky; he's had a good life.' His stealing from her and his grandmother, who doted on him, continued.

The step-father, exceptionally quiet and almost totally preoccupied with his pigeons, played a subsidiary role in the family. The mother, now a supervisor in a food store, earned more than he did, paid for his hobby, and took sole responsibility for the children: 'I wear the trousers in the house'.

Brian's puberty was early and, previously an outgoing and competent school boy, he now became shy and solitary, and his work declined. His only friend was a smaller, fatherless boy known at school as a 'sissy'. The two were inseparable, truanted together and then, afraid to face their teachers, truanted even more. On several occasions they ran away from home, always because they feared punishment for their school absences. The mother now saw Brian as a future homosexual; tensions between him and both parents increased, and the threat of 'being sent away' on account of school absence and stealing was ever present.

With increasing sexual maturity, Brian recognized his homosexual possibilities and gave up the struggle for male acceptance by other boys and teachers. He was now more outgoing, dyed his hair, wore an earring, and acquired a new set of rather older friends.

Finally, to escape a further Court appearance, he stole a large sum of money from his grandmother and went to London, having hinted to his mother that he had a homosexual friend. Once again she failed to recognize this as a bid for acceptance, and although she had suspected it all along, she expressed 'disgust' to Brian, indicating that she could have nothing to do with homosexuals. After he left she was distressed about the missing money but felt he had done right to evade the Court. She was in fact not shocked by the homosexuality either, only concerned for Brian. This she failed to convey to him.

As Brian came to look more and more mature for his age, his mother grew ever more youthful in appearance. She had recently 'fallen in love' with her husband's cousin. She had never met anyone like him before, nor been in love like this before. Yet of the man she said 'he has no conscience'. Trapped in a confusion of human relationships, she now became depressed and began to drink heavily.

Brian's sixth year was crucial for his future personality. It marked a turning point between an early childhood of exceptional closeness with a very young mother, uninterrupted by a father's presence, and a middle childhood filled with anxieties. During his first six years he had been his mother's real source of pride; she had allowed him to assume responsibilities beyond his age and his oedipal longings were in part fulfilled. Then, as the step-father moved into the family, Brian's longings for his mother were frustrated. When he stole to regain some symbolic closeness with her, she failed to understand the message and increased the obstacles in the way of a normal resolution of his oedipal conflict: identification with a father. Instead of helping him understand his own father and himself, she warned him that if he tried to be like his father he too would end in prison. Brian missed out totally on adequate father identifications, since the step-father had little to do with the children and his status within the home was low. Brian's conscience-development was impaired by his mother's indulgence on the one hand and her collusion with him in evading responsibility for his actions on the other. All he had to help him control his impulses was a sense of terror that he would lose her affection. He arrived at adolescence quite unclear of how he wanted to live his life, still in love with his mother, capable of sexual encounters with both men and girls, but without really close ties to anyone except his mother. Once more he assumed responsibilities for himself far beyond his age and every now and then he risked all he had through impulsive acts in states of mild frustration.

The recurring themes in three generations of this family were confused sexual relationships, allied to inadequate conscience structure, but also to emotional warmth, independence, and great practical competence. Twice this mother, much identified with her father, chose husbands she could not respect who left her free to run the family on her own. Her main loves were her father, her son, and then an unattainable boyfriend. While she was a mother when only a child, she endowed her small son with capacities for self-direction which he did not have. She had chosen a Borstal boy as her first boyfriend, and was then excessively shocked at her son's stealing. She indulged him materially, then made him feel he was exploiting her, and she failed to help him develop inner standards by siding with him against authority whenever he had to face either his teachers or the law. As a result he feared and could not identify with male authority, adopting instead a mother identification. He too had boyfriends; and he always tried to look after his family, his mother, and the younger children.

Stage IV: from 6 to 11 ('latency'): 'school age and task identification' — industry versus inferiority

Although between 2 and 6 children have profound emotions which they recapture repeatedly in later human relationships, their activities and aspirations are characterized by a quality of make-believe. But at around 7 years, when animistic thinking gives way to rationality, true commitments begin. Children bring from the previous stage much eagerness to learn from their elders. But they now enjoy direction, even mild coercion to do things they would not have thought of doing themselves. Self-esteem comes from 'real' as well as 'play' activities, and pleasure from things they can make, from shared obligations, conformity to rules, and collaboration with other children.

A *work identity* is acquired as children choose which aspects of the work styles of teachers, parents, and other children to copy. *Real friendships* are formed between children who discover similarities of age, sex, style, and aspirations in each other. This new mode of social encounter contributes to a *new social identity*.

Middle childhood is also the time in which *stigma* first appears. Children are now acutely sensitive to small differences from what is usual in appearance and achievements, in social background, and family circumstances. This is the age of playground games and rituals, of in-groups, gangs, and teams. Ostracism, for whatever reason, can have profound effects.

A rebellious 9-year-old who ran away repeatedly from boarding school was brought up by elderly, immigrant grandparents because her own parents had divorced and her mother had recurrent psychiatric illnesses. In later life she recalled that what had troubled her most was not, as I had thought at the time, the loss of her parents, but embarrassment when her friends met her dominating Italian grandmother and the crippled uncle who shared the household. Her greatest fear, on reading *Jane Eyre* at school, had been that she herself might go mad.

As she enters the wider world, the latency child discovers for the first time how people outside her family judge her personal attributes: her looks, her name, the clothes her mother gets her, the way she talks, where she lives and how her family compares with that of others. Most important for her self-esteem is whether or not she is good at things. During the previous stage the future held endless possibilities. Now children can suddenly find themselves constricted and excluded if their own attributes fail to match general expectations. The danger is loss of self-esteem and a lasting sense of inferiority in relation to work and the society of one's peers.

Work and peer group relationships are usually stressed as the new experiences of this stage. But there is a third important feature: *artistic creativity and athletic gifts*. Children become poets and painters. They sing and make music. Future writers and artists retain their creativity throughout their lives; most children lose these gifts as adolescence approaches. But for all children their products or athletic skills are a rich source of satisfaction which can compensate for the inevitable failures in other spheres.

In theory, the earlier a child is confronted with real success or failure in the world, the more likely she is to have distorted and unrealistic perceptions of her work and social self, and the more indelible the sense of inferiority if she seems to fail. Later success may actually be missed because unexpected. When so much has to be learnt, the temptation is to start formal education ever earlier. We shall discuss later the possible hazards of such a policy.

Societies vary in the range and complexity of adult work roles. In simple societies, only the seriously handicapped will fail to fulfil adult expectations. In our technological age work roles are almost infinitely varied, largely invisible to children because carried out in special work settings, and some are so complex that only a minority of gifted people can understand and master them after years of training. Instead of enjoying work and getting pride from achievement, the less clever child, unable to identify with more gifted peers and the teacher, is left with a sense of inferiority and fear of being no good. His anxiety impairs motivation and his work capacity drops further. The implications are the more serious because in relation to his work the child is no longer merely 'practising' for the future. Educational progress contributes almost from the start to actual opportunities for the rest of one's life. Unemployment has of course made matters worse. Instead of confidently expecting to bring home a wage in return for physical labour, once the pains of academic school failure are left behind, latency children, especially boys, are robbed of hope by the spectacle of their unemployed fathers.

Self-esteem in early childhood depends less on actual achievement than on how well this matches the expectations of parents and teachers, which in turn become one's own. Realistic goals for each child must be set if he is to preserve his pride and emerge from this period with his work capacities intact, whatever the level of his abilities. We have already pointed to the evidence we now have for the protective effects of positive school influences of all kinds on the later personality adjustment of even seriously deprived children (Quinton *et al.* 1984).

The *new anxieties of this stage* spring from feelings of social ostracism as well as from a sense of being no good. Competence can make up for social disadvantage, and social advantage or esteem can compensate for limited ability. When both are lacking, children are in serious danger. Moreover, some children are held back not by current failure but by past, unresolved family conflicts. Dependency and separation anxiety can literally stop a child from going to school and making friends. Poor impulse control can be totally disruptive of classroom activities; in lesser degree it interferes with children's attention to assigned tasks. Excessive inhibition and shyness impair curiosity and participation in joint learning ventures as well as sociability.

The social institutions linked to latency are the work ethos, the technology of the culture, and the arts.

Stage V: adolescence, from 12 to young adult life: identity versus identity confusion

The physical growth spurt and sexual maturity of adolescence heighten self-awareness, and the shift to abstract intelligence allows each person to review his or her past and envisage the future with a new perspective. Adolescence is the time at which from the strands of past experience we form more or less permanent selves as we assume responsibility for our future lives in the wider world.

Erikson uses the word identity to describe a conscious feeling of individual uniqueness, a generally unconscious striving for continuity of experience, and a sense of solidarity with the ideals of one's social group and culture. The last, ensured by the incorporation of parental standards and aspirations, becomes a vehicle for tradition and promotes historical and cultural continuities.

The adolescent years are, to use Erikson's word, a 'moratorium' during which youngsters can rehearse a variety of life patterns before finally committing themselves to those which fit best with what has gone before and will henceforth become part of their adult identity. Like the genital stage, adolescence is a period of experimentation, but with real consequences and real goals.

Erikson describes four adolescent tasks, each necessitating a range of trials and errors:

Separation from parents. Practice activities include joining the Forces, moving into a bed-sitter, hitch hiking to distant parts, becoming a resident student, and work. Without full commitment at first, the youngster finds out whether and how he can survive without his family.

Choosing a work role. This often follows a variety of work experiences and the discovery of what one can do in the light of what there is to be done.

The formation of a sexual identity. This depends on learning from a succession of erotic relationships how others react to one's self, what in others best matches one's own life patterns and self-perceptions, and what forms of sexual intimacy make for the greatest happiness.

Ideological commitments. These derive, for example, from looking for heroes to confirm one's ego ideal, joining groups identified by common belief systems or political ideas, and discovering religious experiences.

In adolescence specific memories from the past are revived and influence present choices. Previous stages contribute to the actual tasks of identity formation. Infantile and later experiences of primary attachments determine our faith in ourselves and society. Brian, for example (p. 152), who had always felt well provided for by his mother, left home exceptionally early, full of hope about the future and what he would find in London, trusting in other people's friendliness and with considerable confidence in his own ability to manage. In contrast, some youngsters approach adolescence with cynical mistrust and a feeling that everything is unpredictable and nothing worth while. Experiences during the stage of initial socialization are a basis for the exercise of will power and choice about our duties to society. Alternatively they can lay the foundation for a sense of shame and of being coerced. The primary identifications of the third stage are revived in adolescent patterns of imaginative life and erotic experience. A sense of initiative and purposefulness in intimate relationships, and in experimenting with different sexual partners and working roles, can be replaced, if the legacy of guilt from this stage is excessive, by role fixation and constriction of all ambitions or, alternatively, by a denial of guilt, with guilt-free delinquency.

The threat, at the height of his oedipal longings, that his father's fate would be his own as a consequence of his childish crimes, was more than Brian could tolerate. He did not feel guilty. He was merely afraid of punishment, and this fear of external forces was insufficient to control his delinquent impulses, especially since he knew his mother would always intercede on his behalf.

Latency contributes feelings of competence in the world of work, creativity and adult sociability. These Brian had up to a point, always ready to try a new job and confident in his relationships with women and homosexual men. He saw himself as capable like his mother who in turn, rather more than his male teachers, admired his abilities to cope in sexually neutral spheres. When school experiences impair self-esteem, work paralysis and social withdrawal can prove serious handicaps.

Erikson sees the alternatives in adolescence as a firm sense of personal identity and commitment on the one hand, and on the other what he calls 'identity confusion', that is, an indefinitely prolonged uncommitted state in which options are left open, no choices seem inevitable, and the individual fails to acquire a firm sense of who he is, of what he can do, where he is going, with whom, and to what purpose. Such feelings when transient are common in all youngsters. Sometimes they are defended against by excessive loyalty to readily distinguished groups intolerant and hostile towards outsiders, by acquiring provocative and shocking clothes and equipment, and at times by aggressive gang warfare. Stressful early experiences as well as traumatic events and circumstances in adolescence itself can hinder emotional development at this stage.

The special hazards of adolescence

Experimental activities can have real consequences

One of the hazards of adolescence is that activities meant to be experimental may have real consequences, limiting future choices, and sealing for ever some aspect of one's fate. Many maternally neglected girls seek comfort rather than intimacy from their boyfriends but neglect to look after themselves as their mothers had neglected to look after them earlier, and give birth to an illegitimate baby. Dependent boys deprived of proper care find refuge in the army and sometimes commit themselves to many years of a life they cannot know will suit them. Others, lacking all sense of purpose, join violent youth gangs, injure themselves or other people, and incur lasting physical or emotional scars and social degradation.

The danger of stigma

A further danger is that others may apply labels to the youngster which stigmatize him inescapably and, because he comes to see himself as others see him, perpetuate behaviour on his part — homosexuality, for example, or delinquency — which was merely experimental and might have been quite transient. West and Farrington showed that adolescent delinquents convicted of offences were significantly more likely to commit further offences than comparable youngsters who had engaged in the same amount of crime but had not been apprehended (West and Farrington 1973).

Growing up in a technological age

Our technological age imposes its own special difficulties. Not all youngsters can choose their occupation for the sake of work satisfaction, status, and security. Many miss out on the self-esteem that comes from competence and, because they cannot understand the complexities of the surrounding culture, on a sense of identity with their society. Schools took over education from parents when work was separated from family life in the era of early industrialization. In our present second industrial revolution, with rapid scientific progress, schools do not always effectively transmit to children the work ethos and technology of adults.

Another current obstacle to identity formation for adolescents is the increasing discontinuity during earlier childhood which impedes the integration of past experiences into the present self. When families are mobile geographically and socio-economically, children must adapt to material, social and educational changes as they grow up. Adolescence can then revive excessive nostalgia for former times and places, together with a sense of lost possibilities and longings for some other self one might have become.

Discontinuous parenting

More serious are the discontinuities in parenting as separation and divorce increase. To this theme we shall return. Here it needs to be stressed that children imitate, incorporate, and to some extent *become* their parents. When parent figures change, the sense of inner dislocation and uncertainty is profound, quite apart from the conflicts of loyalties which children in their animistic stage are incapable of resolving. Once again a permanent sense of loss, nostalgia for past parents, real or fantasized, and for that other self one might have been, contribute to identity confusion or, alternatively, inhibit adolescent experimentation and then restrict the range of activities and experiences during the years of maturity.

Adolescent identity is built on childhood experiences. But adolescence in turn contributes to the later stages of adult life, and during adolescence earlier deficiencies and distortions of experience can be made good.

I recently encountered again a young man about whom I had greatly worried when he was 11.

He was referred at that time for open aggression and opposition to his mother which frightened her, especially when he locked himself into the bathroom during their frequent rows. The reason for my concern then was that he was an only child with a mother already 49; that at 7 his father had died, aged 78; and that in the household lived his father's daughter by an earlier marriage, now also in her late 40s.

Yet at 34 this young man was happily married, had a rewarding profession, many outside interests, and was on excellent terms with his elderly mother and half-sister.

The turning point in his life had been going to a far-off boarding school when he was 13. He recalled how within a week he had run off home but how this event, far from causing opprobrium, had evoked his teachers' concern and made him a hero among the boys. Moreover, he now found he had 'surrogate siblings'. Because his mother could visit only rarely, other boys' parents took him out and also home for holidays. From these experiences he learnt how other children treated their parents, and he made many life-long friends.

What is more, he had retained in adult life quite vivid memories of a loving father; and he described his mother in her old age as still a most vigorous and forthright person. Certainly when he was a child, his mother, while full of self-doubt and guilt about her maternal capacities, had been frank and courageous in facing her own inner conflicts and even the feelings surrounding her unusual marriage: she herself had been raised by an elderly father as the child of a second marriage.

Stage VI: maturity: 'beyond identity'

Unlike other developmental psychologists, Erikson has given thought to the personality changes that occur in young adult life, in middle age, and in the declining years. Each of these periods, like each childhood stage, presents us with certain critical choices. The way we settle these, however, no longer depends on our parents and the culture in which we grew up, but on ourselves and the culture to which we and the next generation contribute. For success in the tasks of maturity a firm identity is necessary. Erikson sees each component of identity as expressed in and determining specific aspects of each stage of adult life. The stages he describes are as follows:

(1) *Young adult life: 'intimacy versus isolation'*

The new experiences now open to us are love, fidelity, and a shared privacy. Basic trust and a secure sexual identity are prerequisites for emotional, sexual and domestic intimacy, for mutual satisfactions, responsibilities and decisions, and for the shared anticipation of the birth and rearing of children. When sexual identity is shaky commitment to another person is postponed, erotic relationships are partial and often brief, and the individual remains isolated, now cut off from his parents and not fully attached to anyone else.

(2) *Parenthood: 'generativity versus stagnation'*

The following stage brings opportunities for investment in the next generation, for childbirth, child-rearing, and educating the young. Creative altruism characterizes this period of life when one has confidence in one's own authority and faith in the species. Boredom, self-indulgence, and a perception of children as burdensome are the alternatives when one's sense of autonomy is shaky.

(3) *Middle age: 'integrity versus disgust and despair'*

Adaptation to the achievements and disappointments of one's life is now called for and a sense of meaning, order, and acceptance of one's life style follow. Opportunities for confirming one's own responsibility for the choices one has made are linked to a new affection for one's parents, now no longer seen as having determined one's fate, and a new comradeship with other people. The alternatives are a critical contempt of others, of human institutions, and of oneself, together with a feeling that time is running out and opportunities for a new way of life are now lost forever.

(4) *Old age: 'wisdom and renunciation'*

The way we face our mortality reflects our personality as much as other challenges of life. Erikson suggests that a meaningful old age brings a more detached concern with life to which one's own experience and judgement contribute. As we prepare ourselves for our own death we maintain our concern for the welfare of the world we leave behind.

Erikson has given us a new view of human personality. A psychoanalyst and anthropologist, he takes account of sociology, history, religion, and the arts in describing human development. He is no scientist, but some of his ideas about culture, child-rearing, and personality, as we shall see in the next chapter, have been fruitfully explored by psychologists and social scientists. Others still await scientific attention.

Psychiatrists, social workers, and psychologists in clinical practice owe much to Erikson. More than anyone else, he has given us the means for accurate empathy with people who are caught up in a destiny they had not intended for themselves but which for inner reasons they cannot change. In our appraisal of human beings who repeatedly fail in one or other of their adult roles we can now be more specific and accurate than before. But to exercise our diagnostic skills, we need to know not only about the present but the past. We can then see whether the patterns of people's current social behaviour and emotional experiences match the events and circumstances of their childhood and their participation in past encounters. When this is clearly so, as in the two children, Jack and Brian, and their mothers described above, we cease to be puzzled and exasperated by current failures. With what Erikson has called 'a new kind of common sense' (Erikson 1968:106) we get a better appreciation of other people's needs, and also of their specific modes of relating to ourselves. We can have more realistic expectations of what is possible in the future, what kind of help might be most effective, and what situations are likely to make matters worse. We may not be able to help in any fundamental way — serious personality distortions are not readily fixed up — but at least we can prevent the other person from being cut off from human understanding, and we can avoid doing harm.

Part III

The social environment

Chapter nine

Culture and social learning

Erikson who, like other psychoanalysts, approached personality development from a subjective viewpoint, stressed the importance of the child's early identifications. The observational counterparts of these inner experiences are the behavioural processes studied by psychologists concerned with social learning. In this chapter we shall review different types of learning, especially social learning in and outside the family, and its particular contribution to the development of aggression. We shall then consider the influences of social class and the wider culture on personality, and the historic shifts in family life and culture that have taken place over time.

Social conformity, learning and the importance of role models

Experimental psychologists who study learning have given us an altogether different view from any we have considered so far. Their concern has been with processes of behavioural change rather than with age-related developments, and their work has greatly increased our understanding of how intra-familial and wider socio-cultural differences of personality are transmitted from one generation to the next. While conditioning or simple stimulus-response learning can occur from infancy, imitation learning or modelling, and the cognitive processes involved, begin only in the second year, coincidentally with the development of inner standards.

The Russian physiologist turned psychologist, Pavlov, discovered *conditioned reflex learning* in dogs. He found that when shown their food, dogs regularly salivate. If, just before the meal (the unconditioned, that is physiological, stimulus), a bell (the conditioned stimulus) is regularly rung, the dog will begin to salivate at the sound of the bell, clearly having learnt that this is the signal for the arrival of food. Dogs can be taught to respond to all kinds of stimuli by pairing these with others to which the animal has already been conditioned.

J.B. Watson, the father of behaviourism, first applied concepts of learning theory to human behaviour in his study of the experimentally induced phobia of an infant. Albert, aged 1 year, was shown a white rat and, as he was about to pat it, a loud noise was made behind his head. After several repetitions of this paired experience, Albert screamed with terror whenever he was shown the rat, even in the absence of noise. Moreover, his fear generalized to all furry and fluffy objects. Albert was gradually taught to overcome his fear by being soothed and fed as he was repeatedly exposed, quite briefly, to a distant view of the animal. Gradually, as his anxiety diminished, he was able to tolerate greater proximity to the rat, was finally able to touch it, and eventually lost his fear.

B.F. Skinner experimented with a different kind of learning in animals and held that the developmental changes in childhood behaviour are explicable on the basis of the learning principles he discovered. He observed how rats learnt, for example, to press a lever or run a maze in order to get a reward of food or avoid a noxious stimulus such as a mild electric shock. In each situation the animal at first displays a wide range of behaviour. The behaviour immediately rewarded or reinforced is then selected by the animal for repetition. A hungry rat in a box, for example, will do all kinds of things (he engages in *trial and error* behaviour) but only when he presses a certain lever does food appear. He now learns (from contingent reinforcement) to press the lever to get food and will do so repeatedly and at once when hungry. The rat in a maze at first runs this way and that, but if hungry, he soon learns to take the shortest route, when every time he does so he experiences the relief of hunger at the end of his journey.

Koehler found that trial and error learning occurred also in apes. But these animals have an additional method for learning, that is acquiring new behaviour patterns. Given a set of boxes and a banana dangling out of reach above his head, a monkey may engage in trial and error; he may jump as high as he can, move a box and climb on it, pile one up upon the other etc. until he reaches his goal. On the other hand he may scrutinize the novel situation, pause, and then at once build the boxes up into a high enough platform to enable him easily to grasp the fruit. This Koehler called *insight learning*. Faced with a problem never met before, the monkey need not waste his energies in trial and error; he can think, experience a sudden 'aha' reaction or 'insight', and at once adopt the successful strategy. Bruner holds that childhood play, in which activities and skills are systematically practised for their own sake without real life consequences, enables the individual, in a new situation in later life, to have a whole range of practised behaviours available from which to choose those likely to succeed.

An even more advanced mode of learning is *modelling or observation learning*. This occurs only in certain species, and is of special importance for understanding those changes in social behaviour that involve identification with others. It consists of watching what others do under given circumstances and what happens to them as a result, and then copying those aspects of the observed behaviour that seem to be rewarding. In chimpanzees and gorillas, for example, adolescent males spend much time watching adult males in aggressive display behaviour. Rudimentary patterns of aggression can be seen in male infants of these species and, less obviously, also in females. A biological predisposition to aggression seems to interact with exposure to specific social learning to produce later aggressive behaviour.

Bandura has made important contributions to our knowledge of child development through his experimental investigations of modelling in young children (Bandura and Walters 1963). He found, for example, that children who watched a film in which another child played aggressively with toys were subsequently more aggressive in their own play with similar toys than children who had watched a different film or none at all. The effect was enhanced by previous frustration. He also found that children with a dog phobia could be helped to give up their fears by repeatedly watching other children, at first approach, and then pat small and quiet, and then larger and more ferocious dogs.

More recently, psychologists have concerned themselves increasingly with the thoughts, expectations, attributions, and self-perceptions, especially of one's own ability to succeed, that mediate between observation and learning. And behaviour therapists have moved to a *cognitive approach* for psychiatric conditions held to be brought about or maintained by faulty strategies of thinking (Bandura 1977; see also p. 132).

Learning theorists have much to teach us about the processes whereby children acquire and can be helped to give up specific types of behaviour; and the principles involved underlie the behavioural treatment methods often so successful in overcoming the behaviour disorders, phobias, and compulsions of childhood and the phobias, compulsions, and perversions of adult life.

Childhood aggression and social learning

Aggression and delinquency are the most worrying psychiatric disorders of children. In a sizeable minority they persist into later life and almost always then attract disapproval and rejection from other people. If the social causes of childhood aggression could be identified and remedied, there would almost certainly be less pathological aggression too on the part of predisposed children and adults. Studies of how and under what conditions children develop aggressive behaviour and of the styles of aggressive interaction between children are therefore of special importance.

A classic study by Patterson and his colleagues showed that in the setting of a permissive nursery school with little adult intervention, 3- and 4-year-old boys from middle- and upper-class backgrounds became more assertive and aggressive as a result of their interactions with each other (Patterson *et al*. 1967). Among normal children, assertive and aggressive behaviour on the part of one child always evokes a response of some kind from the victim, and this reinforces the aggressivity of the attacker. An initially unassertive child learns, in imitation of the models provided by more assertive children, to defend himself when attacked, and every successful counter-attack reinforces his new-fledged aggressivity. In such a group setting, highly assertive and aggressive children remain so, while the majority of initially unaggressive children become aggressive in time. Only the most passive children with low rates of interaction with others failed to become aggressive.

These observations refer to boys, and we know that boys are more vigorous and physically active and also display and elicit from others more aggressive behaviour in a nursery school setting than girls. In part, these sex differences reflect constitutional differences of muscularity and motor activity (see Chapter 3), in part the children's imitation of adult role models, and in part differential expectations and responses of parents and teachers.

Patterson and his colleagues speculated that aggressive adult role models and emotional frustration (as when the child's aggression evokes authoritarian counter-aggression from adults) enhance the effect, and that a structured (rather than permissive) nursery routine and an actively diverting teacher, concerned to focus the children's attention on other matters of interest, can counteract the development of high levels of aggression in a nursery group (Patterson *et al*. 1967). This work provides some clues to explain why children reared in large and closely spaced families, especially boys, tend to be more aggressive (Rutter *et al*. 1970).

Patterson's later work has been unique both in analysing the processes by which children are brought up by their parents to become aggressive and delinquent, and in devising family-based treatment interventions for aggressive and antisocial children, successful even in the long term (Patterson 1982 and 1986). He starts out from three well-documented premises: first, that aggression in childhood is as stable over time as intelligence and that children do not tend to outgrow it; second, that antisocial behaviour co-varies with many other problems such as academic failure, rejection by peers and, possibly, low self-esteem; and third, that antisocial children have parents who lack family management skills.

Poor family management skills consist primarily of *failure to monitor the children's behaviour* adequately and, perhaps even more important, *a coercive approach to child training* which evokes counter-aggression from the child, so that a mutually reinforcing coercive process between parents and children is initiated, with ever increasing levels of violence. The process starts with relatively trivial non-compliance, whining, and teasing on the part of the child to which the parent responds with unnecessary punitiveness; the child's reactive behaviour ceases temporarily, reinforcing the parents' aggression; only to be followed by further child misbehaviour, evoking more parental punishment. An alternative sequence is when the parents' aggressive intrusion evokes counter-aggression from the child; this in turn leads to parental withdrawal, and the child's aggression is reinforced. Children show a regular progression from non-compliance to physical violence. The parents' behaviour is characterized by threats rarely carried out, by nagging, scolding, blustering, and episodic physical attacks on the child.

Children with a difficult temperament are most at risk of evoking parental coercion; and parents, particularly if socio-economically disadvantaged, are especially prone to act coercively when depressed, exposed to external stresses, or under the influence of alcohol or drugs. Perhaps even more important, faulty parenting practices are transmitted from one generation to the next so that coercive parents have often been brought up themselves by coercive grandparents. In these families expressions of parental warmth and positive, enjoyable parent-child interactions are rare, and the scene is set for incidents of child abuse. Children who in such a family system have learnt to be aggressive, lack social skills on starting school, and find themselves rejected not only by their parents at home but also by their peers: they fail academically, and their self-esteem is low.

Patterson holds that stealing too is often a form of non-compliance to unskilled parents, but that parents of children who steal tend themselves to be delinquent and, in contrast to the hostile parents of aggressive children, inadequately attached to their offspring (Patterson 1982).

The behaviour patterns learnt in interactions with parents in childhood become, as we saw in the last chapter, part of enduring personality patterns in adult life, and these in turn profoundly affect the upbringing of the next generation.

Role modelling and identification within the family

The behavioural counterparts of childhood identifications within the family have as yet been incompletely studied. One area in which research is more firmly based is the role of the father in child development (Lamb 1981; 1986a). While fathers and mothers take part in early nurturing and infants become attached to both parents, in many circumstances, such as threat or illness, the relationship with the mother is the more salient. Beyond infancy, fathers are, and are culturally assumed to be, more active in play than mothers, especially with their sons. Warm fathers who carry authority have been shown to foster 'masculinity' in boys and 'femininity' in girls and, of great importance clinically, father-absence has negative effects on the development of moral standards in boys but not in girls. Delinquents have repeatedly been found to include an excess of fatherless boys. Father-absence also affects sex role identification in boys and girls. When there is no close relationship with a father or father substitute, boys tend to be insecure in their masculine roles and girls predisposed to later difficulties in their heterosexual adjustment. Yet we now also know that the relationship between father absence and adverse child development depends very much on both the emotional and the material circumstances of the family (Lamb 1986b).

Culture and the wider social environment

The work of sociologists on class differences in child-rearing, parent attitudes, and child behaviour, and the discoveries of anthropologists about the varieties of social organization and family life in distant cultures have given perspective to our view of the values and social arrangements of the society in which we live. More astonishing has been the documentation of social historians of the profound historical shifts in family life and attitudes which have occurred in the western world. I believe that a wider view of human nature is important both when we evaluate social and political changes in our own society and when we try to understand and remedy deviant behaviour.

Social class differences in child-rearing

Even in one of the first studies of parents' child rearing attitudes and the behaviour of their children (Baldwin *et al*. 1949), different patterns of child-rearing were found to be associated with the socio-economic status of the parents. The behavioural differences between children are likely therefore to have reflected not only their parents' child-rearing practices but other features of their lives, and socio-economic factors may well have added directly to the constraints on parent behaviour. In this study child-rearing patterns assessed as 'democratic' were most common in college-educated parents, while 'parental rejection' occurred most often in economically deprived families. 'Casual' child-rearing attitudes and 'autocratic' behaviour characterized farming families who were the least well-educated and the least intelligent. Children reared by 'democratic' methods lacked sociability in the nursery years but became sociable, good humoured, and independent at school. Children 'indulged' by parents at home were friendly at nursery but shy and less sociable at school. Actively 'rejected' children were poorly controlled, excitable, and lacking in cheerfulness at nursery; they were resistant to their teachers; and at school they were both shy and quarrelsome.

In a later study (Sears *et al*. 1957) 400 mothers of 5-year-olds in Iowa were questioned about their child-rearing while their children were observed in nursery groups. Statistically significant subcultural differences in attitudes and practices were found among the mothers. Unskilled working-class mothers were less openly affectionate than middle-class mothers, used more aggressive methods of punishment and more tangible rewards, were more restrictive about sexual curiosity and behaviour, and more concerned about table manners. Middle-class mothers were more accepting of dependent behaviour, were less physically punitive, and used deprivation of love as a socializing techique in preference to tangible rewards and punishments. At nursery school, their children were less dependent and less aggressive than children from economically less privileged homes.

Doubt has since been cast on the relationships between low socio-economic status and coercive child-rearing practices on the one hand, and between the more punitive and less nurturing approach of unskilled working-class mothers and the more aggressive and dependent behaviour of their young children on the other (Zigler 1971). The social class differences found by Sears and his colleagues, while statistically significant, were numerically small (Sears *et al*. 1957). It has been suggested that what mothers say in an interview may be more a measure of what they consider to be acceptable behaviour than of what they actually do. A more important consideration is that the children of unskilled working-class parents are exposed to a host of other adverse family influences — birth injury, large family size, more frequent family disruption, maternal depression, and paternal delinquency — and these too will help to determine their behaviour. Intellectual and learning problems are also much commoner in economically deprived children, and teachers tend to evaluate such children's abilities and behaviour negatively, thereby reinforcing both their learning difficulties and the less attractive features of their conduct. Such school influences are likely to maximize the effects of differences in child-rearing experienced at home by children from different social classes, but are unlikely to be solely responsible for them.

Much evidence about a more familiar population came from John and Elizabeth Newson's longitudinal studies some years ago of 700 Nottingham families (Newson and Newson 1976). When the children were 7 years old, many social class trends noted previously were confirmed. Lower-class children were more aggressive and destructive than upper- and middle-class children (and boys more than girls), while lower-class mothers more readily resorted to physical punishments than middle-class mothers (and boys were more often physically punished than girls).

The Nottingham study revealed many other class-linked differences in behaviour and attitudes among families whose young children were born in the late 1950s. Compared with middle-class mothers, unskilled working-class mothers were younger and had more children; fewer had attended ante-natal classes or taken part in relaxation exercises during pregnancy; they breast-fed their babies less long; weaned them off the bottle later and provided a dummy more often; they allowed their 1-year-olds to stay up later at night; started toilet-training later, but were more concerned about early genital play. When their children were 4, lower-class mothers allowed more independence over going shopping, toileting, and settling quarrels between children; they more often encouraged children to hit back; they were more concerned about tidiness, and about modesty and genital play, and gave less, and more often erroneous, sexual information; they read fewer stories to their children, and the fathers in this group participated less actively in the child's care. At the age of 7, educational resources (such as books and cultural outings) as well as help with reading and increasing general knowledge were all greater in professional and white-collar families. While girls tended to get on better with their teachers than boys, there was no social-class difference in this at that age (Newson and Newson 1977).

The Newsons made it clear that parents from different social backgrounds not only act differently towards their children, but have different beliefs about the correct methods of child-rearing and about what is and is not acceptable behaviour in childhood, beliefs that are often based on what their own parents held to be right. Children in turn differ in their behaviour, in part at least in response to different types of upbringing.

These various patterns of child-rearing and childhood behaviour were all 'normal' or typical for the cultural sub-groups in society. Most parents bring up their children according to their inner convictions and beliefs, and they view the children's lack of early conformity as a sign of immaturity rather than as cause for concern. Nevertheless, the patterns of child-rearing and of childhood behaviour in unskilled working-class families, although 'normal', make their contribution to the educational failure and social deviance of children, and in this way they increase the risks for vulnerable children. While the emotional disorders of childhood, anxiety and misery for example, are not related to social-class background, antisocial behaviour, both aggression and delinquency, as well as school failure, are commoner among the socio-economically deprived. Lee Robins in her long-term follow-up of clinic attenders showed that seriously antisocial children had a high risk of becoming sociopathic in adult life, as their fathers had been before them, and that sociopathy and childhood delinquency are both associated with low socio-economic status. Robins held social class *per se* to be unimportant as a cause for such personal developments, but the adversities known to cause delinquency and adult sociopathy are regularly found more often among the socio-economically deprived (Robins 1966).

One other point must be made. Most disturbed children referred to helping agencies with family-engendered difficulties have parents who do not act from conviction, but instead find themselves repeatedly treating their children quite differently from how they think they should. 'I know I shouldn't give in to him'; 'I'm afraid of what I might do to her'; 'I can't show my affection', are common complaints of parents of disturbed children. It is likely that class-linked features of parents' attitudes and behaviour, if held with conviction, are less harmful than ambivalent and inconsistent child-rearing patterns.

Culture and personality: the discoveries of anthropologists

Human cultures, while surviving over many centuries, differ markedly from each other in their language, basic values, modes of human inter-action, and artistic expression. Real personality differences are likely to underlie and preserve these distinctions (Keesing 1981), to which genetic differences may contribute.

When Caudhill and Weinstein (1969) found that mother-child inter-actions were different for Japanese and American mothers and their 3 to 12-month-old offspring, Japanese mothers and babies interacting less often, less vigorously and less vocally with each other, their interpreta-tion was that the mothers' behaviour brought about the differences in the babies' responses. Freedman (1975), as we saw earlier (p. 40), suggested that because some cultural differences are apparent from birth onwards, heredity also plays a part. He speculated that the gene pool of a culture may have been achieved through cultural pressures such as sexual selection or infanticide. Twinning, for example, is more common in African cultures like the Yoruba who prize twinship, than in others. Here only a few examples will be given to illustrate how parents in different parts of the world, and with different life styles, bring up their children in their own image.

The members of a small Japanese village in Okinawa led a largely co-operative life with equal division of labour and economy between the sexes, a co-operative store in which everyone had a stake, and sharing out of communal tasks like road-mending between the able-bodied members of the community. Time was struck publicly twice a day. There were clubs and evening group entertainments as well as a democratic system for expressing political views. Families lived in nuclear households, women had high status, personal relationships were close, and happiness and sociability were prized. As the placenta was cut, each baby was welcomed into the world with the ceremonial wish: 'May this baby always laugh and be pleasant' (Maretzki and Maretzki 1963:458). Children were encouraged not to play alone so that they might not seem to be unpopular. From the time they were weaned at around 2 years of age until they went to school at 6, they walked or were carried by older children to their village kindergarten. Although regarded as lacking in understanding and deserving of indulgence for misbehaviour until 6 years of age, the Okinawa child was taught to be friendly from the start, to participate in group games and regard mutual obligation and duty as all important. In contrast, in Nyansongo, a community in Kenya (Levine and Levine 1963), anxiety about shortage of food and other resources was all pervasive; the rich bribed and dominated the poor; men often had several wives living in separate houses but competing and quarrelling with each other; marriages occurred only between hostile clans; women made a show of protest about intercourse both before and after marriage, and rape was common. Here mothers showed little open affection towards their children; weaning was severe and sudden; child training involved physical punishment, threats and warnings. At 8 or 9 years boys were circumcised and girls at puberty underwent clitoridectomy.

An enquiry into how the Utku Eskimo foster the most valued personality trait in their culture — autonomy — was undertaken some years ago (Briggs 1973). Utku children do have a holding-on and letting-go crisis at about 3 years of age, as Erikson's developmental scheme would predict, but this is not related to toilet-training. Instead the child, who up to then has been carried naked, back-packed by his mother, the centre of attention, requiring comfort when he or she cried, sleeping between the parents at night, and thought of as mindless and unable to learn anything, is gradually weaned during the mother's next pregnancy. But, once the new baby is born, the 3-year-old is suddenly put down, dressed, shamed about nakedness, taught to go out to play, and vigorously encouraged to be generous, patient, and helpful to the new arrival. If he is demanding he is threatened with imaginary dangers from which his mother will protect him only if he is good. He is told that his anger could kill his mother, that his screams make the sky dark at night, that his eyes bleed when he cries and that his tears will wet his feet and make them freeze. Nightmares and depression are common in the Eskimo child at this stage in which dependency must be relinquished, autonomy acquired, and jealousy controlled. Toilet-training is never an issue, the child being held out since infancy; genitals and anus are fondled, and there is little disgust except in relation to faeces. Shame is associated not with lapses of sphincter control but with excessive dependency, and fear with expressions of anger. How exactly this alternative mode of upbringing is reflected in childhood behaviour patterns, and whether and how it contributes to adult personality, is uncertain.

Schaffer has pointed out that the intimate, face to face, language stimulation of young babies ('motherese'), thought to be essential for adequate language learning (see Chapters 4 and 6), is by no means universal (Schaffer 1989). The Kaluli, a small, isolated, non-literate society of Papua New Guinea, who lay great stress on learning to talk as a social skill, set about helping their children to acquire language in a way surprising to westerners. In their early months babies are regarded as having no understanding and are rarely involved in one-to-one communications. Later in the first year, mothers do address their children. But, unlike western mothers, they never base their remarks on what the child has just uttered, nor do they try to evoke verbal responses. Intimate, mother-infant interactions are minimal and little conversational experience is provided. Instead, babies are held on mothers' laps facing outwards towards the social group and, when a third person addresses the baby, the mother responds on its behalf. Infants overhear much conversation between other people and, despite the absence of personal involvement in intimate interchanges currently thought to be essential for language learning, Kaluli children acquire language at the normal time and are well-equipped when older to participate in the communal living which takes the place of family life in that society. What we do not know is whether the Kaluli in adult life lack some specific linguistic skills that may accompany the emotional intimacy between people in other cultures.

A historical perspective

While societies in different parts of the world differ markedly from each other in customs, skills, social organization, and personality, there is a continuity of human attributes over time that often surprises us. The plays of Shakespeare and even of the Greek dramatists seem as fresh to western ears and eyes as they ever were, suggesting that the emotions associated with erotic love, with family affections, with the individual's place in society, and our view of personal destiny may have changed little over the centuries. Shakespeare's humour is on the whole our own and the personalities of his characters are all familiar to us. This is true also of the great early works of art and literature in other highly developed cultures: the Chinese or the Indian for example.

As remarkable as the persistence over time of certain aspects of human nature is the rapidity with which whole communities can change their outlook and radically reorganize their public life. Hitler won over the German nation and in less than a decade people professed beliefs and attitudes and engaged in actions they would have abhorred before and subsequently came to regard with shame.

Jonsson in a study of parents and grandparents of delinquent boys, developed the notion of 'social inheritance' (Jonsson 1975). He maintained that the attitudes of people towards their conditions of life are handed on from grandparents to parents and from parents to children, even when these attitudes are no longer strictly applicable. In the Berkeley Longitudinal Guidance Study (Elder *et al.* 1984) it was found that the great American Depression of the 1930s affected fathers in particular, making them explosive and irritable. Unlike their wives, these men, whatever their social background, in losing their job had also lost their sense of social significance. Difficult behaviour in the children, especially temper tantrums, correlated with undercontrolled behaviour of these fathers, and children with temper tantrums had in later life more erratic work records, lower work status, and more unstable marriages, the women also reporting more ill temper in themselves as parents.

Most cultural changes documented by social historians have been slow and piecemeal, affecting different sections of society at different times. Such historic shifts, of the greatest interest, are well-documented and illustrated as they affect marriage and family life, aspects of child-rearing, education, and the law in relation to children (Ariès 1973; Pinchbeck and Hewitt 1969 and 1973; Burke 1976; Marshall 1976), and we have some evidence about concomitant changes of adult personality (Stone 1977). But we know very little about the behaviour of the children themselves in other times.

Ariès in his history of European, predominantly French, perceptions of childhood, traced modifications of dress, games, education, and work participation of children over the centuries and also of adult attitudes towards children, for example in relation to sex and morality (Ariès 1973). Before the seventeenth century children under 7 were thought of as lacking in reason, while those over 7 were treated like adults. They had no special dress or bedtime; everyone shared games and entertainments; children took part in adult work which was largely home based or out of doors; they became maids and pages in the houses of noblemen or apprentices to craftsmen and traders, while poor children worked on the land. Child marriages were arranged among the upper classes to preserve property and family status at a time when mortality rates were high and parents could not confidently expect to survive to see their children grown up. While social-class barriers were firm and sex roles distinct, functional distinctions between living and working rooms, family and public life, and between age groups were small. The under-7s were exposed to sexual talk and activities and often teased provocatively by their elders. Sexual reserve was thought necessary only with children between 7 years and puberty. People of mixed ages were educated together and the principle that the difficulty of subject matter should match the child's developing understanding was not recognized.

Perhaps it was the entry of the physical sciences into the curriculum that made age segregation at school, which began in the seventeenth century, so essential. This was also the period when children's special mode of dress, games, toys, and books made their appearance. Change was by no means sudden and took place at different rates among different social classes. Then as now, new trends usually started among the upper classes, to be followed later by the less privileged (Burke 1976). Stone indicates that in England the spread of new ideas in the seventeenth century was largely through books and periodicals, coinciding with the spread of literacy (Stone 1977). The bourgeoisie of professionals, wealthy merchants, and landed gentry were the first to take up new ideas; for example, those of Locke that the child, far from embodying original sin, is entirely open to environmental influences. The aristocracy adopted new ways later, and the poor very much later still.

In his remarkable account of family life in England from 1500 to 1800, Stone relates the changes that occurred in political and economic developments and evolving belief systems (Stone 1977). His work brings home to us the horrifying effects on people's lives of squalor, disease, and death. Mortality rates among young adults were so high that second and third marriages were as common then as they are today as a result of divorce; only a minority of adolescents had two living parents, and many children had step-parents. But, while at present in nine cases out of ten it is the father who leaves home, and custody is most often awarded to the mother, in those days the mortality of women was three times that of men as a result of death in child birth and, perhaps with some reason, it was fathers, not mothers, who had legal rights over their children. We can also understand that life in those days might have been intolerable without a firm belief in the hereafter.

But not only adults were subject to early death. Infant mortality was enormous; almost half the children in each family died before reaching maturity. The pattern, ubiquitous among the middle and upper classes, of fostering out infants to wet nurses for the first one to two years of their lives is often seen as a sign of cruelty and lack of parental affection. It can also be interpreted as a protective device used by parents to shield themselves from intense emotional attachments to their young children and from the recurrent grief that would follow when these children died. Such parental self-protection has its equivalent among modern parents, many of whom need support and encouragement to visit their young children in hospital because they cannot bear to see the children cry when visiting ends; or among parents of children in care who cease visiting because of the pain of seeing their children looked after by others. Sadly, the practice of fostering out increased the mortality of young children even more.

Yet a further pattern of pre-seventeenth-century childhood, was that between 7 and 14 years, usually around 10, most children left home once more, for education in boarding schools and universities (for the children of the rich) and to become apprentices, domestic servants, or labourers in the homes of the wealthy (for the children of the poor). 'The reason for this mass exchange of adolescent children', writes Stone, 'which seems to have been peculiar to England, is far from clear' (Stone 1979:84). It may possibly have protected both the children and parents, exposed as they were to disrupted early attachments, from excessive emotional turbulence at adolescence.

Stone describes an 'open lineage, outer directed' family as the norm in England between 1450 and 1630, with little domestic privacy, much patronage of people of lesser status among the nobility and squirearchy in the great houses, and reliance for aid and direction from kin in these upper-class families and from the neighbouring community among artisans and the poor. Marriages were arranged to preserve property and family status, not mutual affection and individual happiness, and women were subordinate to their husbands. Stone believes that the remote and formal relationships between marriage partners and between parents and children in those days were related to the absence of early mother-child bonding and to the later disruptions of parent-child relationships. Certainly there was much physical cruelty between adults, and in the treatment by adults of children. This was justified by belief in the doctrine of original sin and the necessity to 'break the will' of young children. Whether childhood aggression, now known to be an outcome of disruption of early attachments, helped to evoke such parental cruelty is not known. Stone describes the common personality traits of pre-seventeenth-century English adults as consisting of suspiciousness, physical violence, and lack of strong affectionate ties to any one person; and the prevailing society as hierarchical, authoritarian, inquisitorial, and collectivist.

Stone records a decline of the power of kinship and an increase in the power of the state in the late sixteenth and early seventeenth century, with isolation of the nuclear family. The rise of protestantism and religious fervour, including the burning of witches and hanging of traitors, and a fierce domestic authoritarianism, were thought to have arisen from the insecurity engendered by political and social changes. The devil was everywhere.

Major changes of family life, however, mirrored by changes in domestic architecture, occurred during the age of enlightenment from the late seventeenth century onwards. A new family type which Stone calls 'affective individualism' emerged, with greater emotional commitment and affection between parents and between parents and children, with less responsibility for the socially disadvantaged (now a charge on the parish), with greater sexual freedom, and with more open concern for the welfare of children. Mothers began to breast-feed their infants and fostering out was no longer a universal practice among the well-to-do (although it persisted until the introduction of baby formulae and the modern feeding bottle in the nineteenth century). Child care, especially in England, was now often very permissive.

The greater family privacy was marked by the appearance of the corridor in domestic architecture so that rooms did not have to be entered when traversing the house. Different rooms now served different functions, and servants were banished to basements or attics, no longer part of an open family life in a great hall, formerly the arena for a variety of family and professional pursuits.

Yet, paradoxically, the brutality of public boarding school life, to which many, although not all, the children from wealthy families were still exposed, continued unabated. Stone describes the changes in seventeenth-century family life not as a total shift, but as an increase in the range of patterns of intimate relationships. He holds that historical change is not linear but oscillatory, instancing the return of a strongly paternalistic and morally repressive family atmosphere in Victorian times.

Even critics of Stone's emphasis on the changed approach to children in the seventeenth century record that from that time onwards individual diaries and biographies, in contrast to sixteenth-century writings, contain expressions of concern with the nature of childhood and the duties of parents, and a real interest in child-rearing methods (Pollock 1983).

After the Industrial Revolution lower-class children continued to work in order to help their families, now no longer on the land but under harsh and unhealthy conditions in mines and factories. Burke points out that early machinery had so simplified manufacturing processes that children not yet capable of a trade could work machines (Burke 1976). When the steam engine generated power in the nineteenth century, children were free to play with others of their age, and had time for education. The era of compulsory schooling began.

Adolescence has been viewed as a by-product of the Industrial Revolution, but we now know that it was as much a feature of pre-seventeenth-century life, when children were sent away from home to be educated or trained for work before a marriage which usually took place rather late (Stone 1979). More characteristic of an earlier European view of childhood was the idea that *the age of reason* began at 7 years. In a pre-scientific era the change from animism to rationality was the most important developmental milestone, while in our own technological age *the capacity for abstract thought* at adolescence marks the child's entry into the working world.

In medieval times the picture of childish innocence was as prevalent as the notion of original sin, yet whatever the view of childhood and its duration, the discipline to which children were exposed was often harsh. Indeed an American text set out to demonstrate how systematically children were ill-treated through the ages (de Mause 1976). Childhood suffering on a major scale, however, was a special feature of school life from the seventeenth century onwards, and of factory life and the mining industry after the Industrial Revolution. Street fights and student rebellions were apparent counterparts. Of street life, Ariès (1973) writes, 'Bowls and skittles, nowadays quiet pastimes, used to inspire so many brawls that in the sixteenth and seventeenth centuries the police magistrates sometimes banned them completely' (1973:85–6); and of school life, 'In England . . . Mutinies far from . . . finally disappearing, became increasingly frequent and violent in the late eighteenth and nineteenth centuries. There was indiscipline and rebellion everywhere' (1973:305).

Many moving documents and paintings exist (Marshall 1976), reflecting not only the history of common practices and beliefs concerning children, but the personal feelings, hopes, and sorrows of parents in former times for their offspring. Yet our evidence is greatly biased because it relates more often to the upper classes than the population as a whole. Even more serious, if we wish to chart the relationship between child-rearing practices and personality development, is the lack of descriptions of children's behaviour through the ages to match the varying adult views of childhood.

Some important features of present day family life

Here some features of current family life will be mentioned to set beside the varieties of family relationships in different parts of the world and in different historical epochs described in this chapter.

Health and longevity characterize western cultures. Newborns are confidently expected to survive to maturity and the life span of parents is now such that the potential duration of marriages is greater than it has ever been. Our increasing rates of divorce and separation must be seen in this context. We need to remember also, especially in relation to the current concern with high rates of physical and sexual abuse of children, that in a former era of disrupted parent-child relationships (when babies were boarded out to wet nurses and older children sent away to other families and boarding schools for their education) cruelty and lack of warmth were common in the relationships between marriage partners and between adults and children.

Follow-up studies of children of divorce (Hetherington *et al.* 1985; Wallerstein 1983 and 1985) indicate excessive rates of disturbance in these children, especially conduct disorders in boys, and long-lasting inner preoccupations with their family disruption which affects their own later attitudes to marriage and family life. Divorce is generally followed by remarriage and while having a step-mother does not add to the hazards of affected children, step-fathering does (Ferri 1984). The families of step-parents tend to be larger (because composite) and poorer than others, and the parental aspirations for educational achievements of step-children are lowered. Boys from such families tend to leave school earlier and with fewer qualifications; and girls are prone to make earlier marriages than comparable children from united families. Just as the children of coercive parents are more likely than others to bring up their own children coercively, so children from disrupted families are more likely themselves to lead unstable married lives.

Disruption of parent-child bonds fosters aggressiveness and children who lose parents in the setting of parental discord are much more at risk than children whose parents die, especially — in the case of boys — of antisocial disorders. Step-parents, like all substitute care-givers, have to make special efforts to establish close ties with their new children once these have outgrown infancy. And parents whose own childhood was marked by family discord and disruption, and by periods in institutional care, tend on the whole, although of course not invariably, to form early and unstable marriages, and to be less sensitive and more aggressive in the care of their own children.

Stone records that in pre-seventeenth-century England relationships between siblings were often close and rewarding (Stone 1979). Judy Dunn has pointed out that the relationship with a sibling is now the longest lasting relationship in a person's life, and that the quality of sibling relationships in early childhood persists into middle childhood and is retrospectively regarded as determining the nature of that relationship into late adult life (Dunn 1984). Even in old age certain crucial incidents occurring between siblings are vividly recalled. Dunn has shown that in early childhood lack of closeness to the mother often leads to special affection between siblings (Dunn and Kendrick 1982). We also now know (Jenkins and Smith, submitted for publication) that a good sibling relationship can protect children from the ill-effects of disharmony between their parents, as can a good relationship with another adult such as a grandparent outside the family. Whether deliberate efforts to strengthen relationships between brothers and sisters and between children and grandparents could succeed in compensating children for disrupted and frustrating relationships with their parents is an open question.

One other feature of modern family life needs to be stressed: the changing roles of mothers and fathers (Lewis and O'Brien 1987). Most married women with children go out to work at least part-time, although they remain the primary child care-giver. Despite legislative encouragement to fathers in Sweden (Sandqvist 1987), and the public fostering in that country of equal role-sharing between parents, even Swedish women still shoulder the major responsibilities for the children, and fathers fail to take up all their parental leave entitlements. There is also evidence that role reversal, with the mother as primary bread winner and the father looking after the home and children, is on the whole not comfortable for either parent. Many of the fathers in an Australian study of family role reversal (Russell 1987) suffered from loss of the status and self-esteem that are associated with paid employment, and from their neighbours' distrust and lack of respect: they were more isolated at home than mothers usually are. The women, too, found it hard to accept their husband as the primary parent and were guilty about leaving their children. Role reversal had frequently been precipitated by the father's unemployment and was often given up, with a return to more traditional roles, much sooner than the couples themselves had planned.

The changing role of women has been accompanied by a loss of the stigma formerly attached to illegitimacy and to one-parent (generally mother-headed) families. This and effective contraception has contributed

185

to a sharp drop in infant adoptions. Instead, many illegitimate children later become step-children with an increased risk of behaviour difficulties. A few of these children are then rejected in middle childhood or adolescence, when the task of finding permanent new families for them becomes more difficult.

A recent study of non-custodial fathers after divorce (Lund 1987) makes clear that mothers rather than fathers initiate divorce proceedings, generally against their husbands' wishes, knowing that the risk of losing the children is small. Only 10 per cent of divorced fathers get custody of their children. Despite greater participation of men in the care of children and the home, their role in many families is now less secure than it once was.

This chaper has briefly reviewed how children learn the attitudes and behaviour of their family, their immediate social environment, and their culture. Different beliefs and patterns of conduct characterize different cultural groups, and remarkable transformations of family life and child-rearing have occurred over the centuries. Among the current patterns of family life which arouse most concern for the affected children are family discord and marital breakdown.

Chapter ten

How can we safeguard personality development?

This final chapter is concerned with three issues: the appraisal of deviant behaviour; social policy for children; and treatment interventions.

The appraisal of social deviance

Our perceptions of abnormal behaviour, such as mental illness and crime, have undergone fluctuating changes over the years. They influence both national policies, for example, for health care, penal and welfare provisions, as well as professional approaches to the individual people affected. Knowledge about personality development in childhood and awareness of the range of possible human behaviour can modify such perceptions. Deviant behaviour which harms other people must be prevented in the light of what we know of its causes, but the perpetrators of harmful acts, often themselves parents, require to be understood, and society's necessary restrictive measures, when prevention has failed, should be the least damaging both for them and their families.

Here only two forms of deviance will be discussed: child abuse, because it has become of increasing concern in western societies; and antisocial conduct in general, because it is common and can have such detrimental effects both on the perpetrators and their victims. But first we need to consider public attitudes to antisocial behaviour and the sex differences that exist in its occurrence.

Attitudes differ towards antisocial behaviour on the part of children and adults

From the start, psychological and psychiatric services for children included provisions for aggressive and antisocial youngsters and their families. These behavioural difficulties were, and still are, regarded as part of the psychiatric morbidity of childhood and adolescence, and their causes and natural history have been much studied. But, once these conduct-disordered young people become adults, medical and psychological interest in persisting antisocial conduct, now identified as 'sociopathy', wanes. Constitutional and other organic causes, outlined in earlier chapters of this book, are overlooked and the individual sociopathic adult is often thought of as wilfully delinquent and destructive.

The compulsively repetitive, unintended nature of much antisocial, sexually perverse, or addictive behaviour in adult life, well-recognized in the past (Walker and McCabe 1973), tends to be ignored and the general public remains woefully ill-informed about the causes of both chronic petty crime and occasional acts of shocking violence. The mistaken view is prevalent that we are all equally free to choose to be friendly, law-abiding citizens and loving members of our families, and that what deters us from crime is fear of the law. In recent years especially, punitive and retributive attitudes to social deviancy have been stressed, although the evidence is that the law and its punishments, vital perhaps for the maintenance of the agreed public standards of a society, have little effect on crime prevention and should not be looked to for that purpose.

Sex differences

While among child psychiatric patients boys predominate, largely because they are most at risk of educational failure and conduct disorders, adult psychiatric services are more often used by women, the commonest disorder being a depressive illness, often in the setting of a personality disorder but short of sociopathy. Men instead are much more often delinquent and alcohol-addicted, and swell the prison populations (see also Rutter 1979). It is also now known (Robins 1986) that while about a third of seriously conduct-disordered boys follow a path into adult antisocial behaviour, the smaller numbers of seriously conduct-disordered girls are as often disturbed in adult life, but are less frequently sociopathic and more often have psychiatric symptoms, such as anxiety or depression. It is my view that, in order to improve our understanding of social deviance, antisocial conduct in childhood and in adult life needs to be viewed as part of the overall psychiatric morbidity of a population.

Child abuse

Child abuse is a particularly harrowing form of deviant behaviour. The following case histories, while not representative, aim to clarify some of the psychiatric, social and legal issues that may be involved.

Anne first entered hospital, bruised, at 2½ months, after her father had slapped her. This he admitted. The case came to a Children's Hearing, went to the sheriff court for proof and, at a further hearing, a compulsory supervision order with residence at home was made. At 6 months, more serious injuries led to a further hospitalization, and this time the father denied responsibility. He said the baby had fallen off a settee. Both parents agreed that, however the injuries had been caused, Anne had not been properly looked after and, following a further hearing, she was admitted into foster care, the parents being invited to visit regularly.

The common vicissitudes of fostering then followed: the first, excellent, foster parents suffered a bereavement, went on holiday, and gave up the baby. In the second family, the foster father was transferred by his firm to another town. By the age 13 months, when seen at a child psychiatric clinic, Anne was in her third foster home.

The family history was as follows:

The mother had been her father's 'best girl', distant from her own mother who physically assaulted her husband. The mother had a speech defect and did poorly at school. On leaving school she developed a street phobia and it took her a long time to establish herself in work. After Anne's difficult birth, she became depressed, suffering particularly because 'I didn't want to know the baby.' She lost interest in sex and the parents began to quarrel. During Anne's first year, however, the mother's depression and affection for the baby gradually improved, as did her sexual feelings for her husband.

The father had a disrupted upbringing. Both his parents drank heavily. When he was 3, the paternal grandfather discovered his wife in bed with another man, turned her out of the house, and struggled physically with her over the children who were injured in the process. Anne's father was left on the doorstep of local council offices and spent the rest of his childhood in a Dr Barnardo's Home. There he was looked after by a maiden lady to whom he was much attached and who left the home when he was 15. He was an intelligent boy and did well at school, but an older sister described him as having always been a solitary child, somewhat effeminate, and that at times the housemother dressed him as a girl.

Although gentle in manner and with much charm, he reported explosive episodes of aggression in response to minor frustrations throughout his life, and he frequently assaulted his wife. There was also a history of lapses of consciousness, at one time attributed to epilepsy.

While the mother came across as warm, of low intelligence, still much embarrassed by her speech defect, the father was remarkably detached, even callous, as he discussed his violence towards his wife and baby, with little empathic concern for either. About the attacks on his wife, he said, 'I do feel guilty. I get annoyed with her crying and I slapped her face . . . which stopped her crying.' He could not imagine how a small child might feel and think. His memories for his own childhood and for his injuries to Anne seemed genuinely incomplete.

The father's serious personality disorder was attributed to schizoid personality traits and severe early deprivations. The mother's personality was dependent, and she had in addition suffered from mild neurotic symptoms and a puerperal depressive illness.

Because her injuries had been relatively minor, the social work department was reluctant to effect a permanent separation between Anne and her parents without a well supervised trial period at home. During this, further bruising occurred while the child was alone with her father. By the age of 4, now in her fifth foster home, when social workers were applying for parental rights, Anne was emotionally withdrawn, over-cheerful, destructive of her belongings, obstinate, but also over-dependent on adults ('she'll sit on your knee 24 hours a day') and poor at playing with other children. She had a mild developmental speech delay and was still a bed wetter. She told her foster mother that her Daddy had once tied her up. The foster mother was wary of Anne's father because during one of his regular visits he had fiercely attacked the family's dog.

The local authority was granted parental rights, Anne was placed with adopters and, nine months later, when just 5 and apparently well settled in her new family, her parents signed the consent for adoption.

This case, it should be stressed, was dealt with entirely under the child care law. The police were not involved and no prosecution took place.

Janette, aged 10, had been in foster care for six months. The foster parents complained that she soiled herself and engaged in sex play with their own younger daughter. She had told her foster mother that she sometimes puts her finger in her anus, where her father had often put his penis. Psychological testing showed Janette to have an IQ of only 45 per cent and she attended a special school for handicapped children.

Her father, just 30, was illegitimate, and had been blinded in one eye since birth. He was reared by a grandmother who died when he was 10. His mother, thought to have been a prostitute, then looked after him but found him too difficult (he attacked her physically) and he spent the next six years in a children's home. Because of his aggression, he was expelled from school and spent some time in a child psychiatric unit. As a young adult he drank heavily and was in frequent fights.

The mother, also 30, from a large but united family, had always been quiet, passive, and intellectually dull.

The parents married when both were only 17. They had six children in rapid succession, two of them mentally handicapped, before the mother was finally sterilized. Family life was punctuated by crises: eviction for rent arrears; violent attacks by the father on mother and children, usually when he was drunk. One boy's arm was broken and the child placed with the grandparents. Sometimes the children were left unattended, the mother being once charged and put on probation. On another occasion the father injured two children, was charged, convicted, and imprisoned. He was in protective custody throughout because of threatened attacks from other prisoners. At various times one or other of the children were in care and, finally, all except the oldest boy were looked after in foster homes which the parents visited regularly.

At this point the couple were more harmonious. They were open about their past shortcomings. The mother blamed herself for the father's sexual assaults on Janette, because for two years (presumably again during a depressive illness) 'I stopped loving him . . . I had no time for him and he turned to Janette for loving . . . when she was 9.' The father, now facing a further court appearance, said: 'My nerves got the better of me and I'd taken it out on her all the time . . . because she's not too bright and that annoyed me.' He admitted the sexual attacks and felt appalled at his own behaviour.

The father's 'aggressive sociopathy' was attributed to his childhood deprivations, but the severity and explosiveness of his behaviour and its very early start suggested that there may have been a constitutional predisposition, such as birth injury, also. The mother was shy, inhibited, and dependent in personality. For this couple to have had six children was clearly more than they could manage. Once relieved of this great burden, they got on much better with each other. They had always looked after their eldest, normal boy well.

Although the children, still in care, were at that time well protected by the social work department and the Children's Hearings from further attacks, and despite notification to the court of the changed family circumstances, the father was none the less given a further prison sentence. This was not only hard on him and the mother, who was genuinely fond of him, but very hard on the eldest boy, loyally attached to both parents, who was now exposed for the second time to the stigma of being a prisoner's son.

During the following year the local authority assumed parental rights for Janette and she, too, was placed with adoptive parents with whom, three years later, she was found to be well settled.

These two cases illustrate physical and sexual abuse as it can occur in socio-economically deprived families with seriously personality disordered parents. Of course, not all abusing parents are socially incompetent, although it is very likely that most, if their life history is carefully examined, will be found to have long standing personality disorders.

We need to be clear that in every case the child's future safety must be the primary concern. But it is a mistake to stress, as is often done, a conflict of interests between parents and child. Very few parents *intend* to harm their children, and it helps no parent to be allowed to continue to damage his or her child. The task of professionals should be to protect the children, but also to protect parents from injuring their children with the risk of prosecution and imprisonment that follows. A second idea, commonly proclaimed, is that children are helped when the offender is brought to justice. While child molesters outside the family and people engaged in the systematic sexual exploitation of children need to be taken out of the community, in the more common cases of abuse within the family, the criminal law is not necessarily a helpful resource.

In discussions about the procedures for taking children's evidence in court, we often hear about 'balancing the interests of the child and the accused'. In fact, most children are not helped by their parents' conviction, and they are harmed when parents go to prison. Families then invariably become stigmatized and poorer. Moreover, prison is no permanent solution, and when the offending parent, usually the father, returns from his degrading experience, he is likely to be even less able than before to contribute constructively to the material and emotional welfare of his family.

Children often hesitate to reveal their sexual experiences with parents, for the very reason that they do not want to harm their families by their testimony. Many abused children love their fathers; they merely want the abuse to stop. It is possible to protect many children adequately under the child care law, except in cases where fathers deny the abuse and fail to co-operate with treatment plans, which may involve their leaving home for a period of time because their children are best rehabilitated at home and need to be kept apart from their father. In such cases, the law's coercive powers can compel compliance, and prosecution may be needed if the offender persistently denies his injurious behaviour.

Some men are genuinely relieved when their abnormal activities are revealed. For others, it is too difficult to face the enormity of their deeds: they deny them even to themselves. Abuse often occurs under the influence of alcohol or during abnormal states of consciousness when the offender is only partially aware of what he is doing. Denial should not automatically be interpreted as designed only to evade the consequences of the law. Even in cases where prosecution is needed to gain co-operation of the parent in the treatment plans for his family, the law could be used more constructively. (Lynch and Roberts (1982) have discussed these issues in relation to non-sexual child abuse.) More frequent suspended sentences and probation with a condition of treatment could be helpful; and it would be more helpful still if, perhaps in the proposed family court arrangements, the courts themselves could, like the Scottish Children's Hearings, actively monitor the progress of families over time.

New techniques of interviewing children, for example with anatomically correct dolls, can bring relief by enabling even very young children to unburden themselves. But such interviews, when video-recorded outside a court room, should not be used with the aim of collecting evidence for criminal court proceedings, unless the children themselves are fully informed of this. Small children cannot know, and can certainly not control, the use that will be made of their testimony, and we need to question the ethics of using such evidence in a way the child may, in later life, regret. There needs to be a great deal more discussion of the use of child evidence of this nature in the criminal courts (see Scottish Law Commission 1988); of the duties of professionals, whose main task is to assess and offer treatment to the child and family, in giving evidence to the courts; and of constructive sentencing of the offenders. If prison were not an ever present possibility, older children might not find giving evidence so painful, especially if they could see that the court is there to help.

The first rule in child abuse cases is 'protect the child'. The second rule must be that the results of intervention, both of diagnostic and legal procedures, should not make matters worse (Zeitlin 1987). Sometimes quite minor, although technically criminal, sexual activities between otherwise loving fathers and their small daughters are reported to the police by unhappy wives, outraged neighbours, or overzealous social workers, with destructive and totally disproportionate consequences for the fathers, the families, and especially for the children. For a balanced account of the diagnosis and management of child sexual abuse, but one that does not tackle the legal issues, see Kolvin *et al.* (1988); the report of the inquiry into the death of Jasmine Beckford (Report of the Panel of Inquiry 1985) gives helpful advice about the roles of social workers, doctors, the police, and prosecutors in cases of child abuse; and Jones' (1987) excellent book on all aspects of child abuse points to necessary changes in the child care law in England and Wales and gives guidance for medical and social work practice in this difficult field.

The appraisal of adult antisocial conduct in general

Child abuse is the form of destructive adult behaviour of most concern to professionals who look after children. Developmental influences contribute also to other, more common, types of antisocial conduct.

Constitutional factors giving rise to childhood hyperkinesis or other gross temperamental abnormalities, and to schizoid personality (see Chapter 3), are important precursors of antisocial, including violent, behaviour of all kinds. The disadvantages associated with socio-economic privations, especially large family size and ineffective parental supervision, early and severe deprivation of parental bonding and subsequent neglect, and a disrupted and violent family environment contribute to aggressive and delinquent childhood conduct, and through this to adult sociopathy (Wolff 1987). In addition, as we saw from the examples in Chapter 7, quite specific adverse childhood events, even in the setting of an affectionate and competently organized family life, can sow the seeds for later repetitive, perverse, or addictive behaviour and, more rarely, emotionally charged idiosyncratic experiences can, as in Freud's patient described in Chapter 7, mark one for life.

In the appraisal of adult antisocial and criminal behaviour, an awareness of such influences is important. The extrusion from the family, from school and peer group, and later from society of the antisocial person is a risk largely borne by men. The constitutional, social, and family factors involved tend to have later and somewhat different effects on girls. At the present time neither psychiatric and psychological nor penal interventions are at all successful in reclaiming the persistent offender (Rutter and Giller 1983). The coercive and restrictive powers of the law are necessary to protect society, and incidentally the offender too, from further crime. But a change of public attitudes from incomprehending demands for retributive and often cruel justice to a more realistic accept-ance of the failings of human nature and their causes could benefit offenders and their families, especially their children. Children inevitably identify with their parents, even with parents who have harmed them or who have failed socially in some other way. An understanding of the common fact that this harm or failure was not *intended* can help affected children come to terms with their experiences. Moreover, a less punitive response to crime would promote the extension of non-custodial penal interventions, especially for young and non-violent offenders, and would go some way towards protecting their families, especially their children, from poverty, stigma, and shame.

Child development and social policy

Policy and practice should have two aims: to reduce the occurrence of adverse, anxiety-inducing events in the lives of children; and to safeguard those ingredients in the environment in which children grow up, which are known to be necessary for optimal personality development.

These are a secure attachment to at least one parent figure especially, but not exclusively, during the earliest years of life; adequate male and female role models at least from the second or third years onwards; sensitive responsiveness not only to the children's emotional, but to their verbal and other intellectual needs, with access to interesting and rewarding educational experiences from the earliest months into adulthood. However troubled a child's family life may be, and whatever his or her intellectual abilities, self-esteem can be preserved and fostered through the acquisition and exercise of skills, and maladjustment counteracted through good relationships with people outside the family.

Here we need to be realistic. Many human failings cannot be made good. Exhortation of parents does not lead to marital harmony or better child care. But practical improvements, for example in the living environment and economic security of families, can help by reducing those traumatic life events known to precipitate socio-economically deprived mothers of young children into depressive illnesses; and improvements in the child's extra-familial environment can, at least from middle childhood onwards, compensate to some degree for what may be lacking at home.

The impact of child development research on child care and education

Research in child development has had a major, and, in the western world, universal impact on two areas of policy and practice. First, knowledge about the importance for later personality development of secure bonding with parent figures in early childhood has opened the hospital doors to parents when children are patients and to children when their parents are admitted to hospital. It has had an enormous influence, too, on the child care arrangements made by social workers when, for whatever reason, parents cannot, or cannot safely, look after their own children. It is the policy that children under 4 years are not exposed to group care, even temporarily, although this goal is not always achieved. Foster parents are sometimes in short supply; and very occasionally even such a young child may, perhaps on account of serious physical illness or handicap, or because of very severe behaviour disorders, prove too difficult for a family to look after.

Second, the discoveries of Piaget and his followers about the cognitive stage of concrete operational logic, when children learn about mathematics and practical science not from what they are told but from observing what they themselves, as active experimenters, can do, have revolutionized teaching in primary schools.

But there are many more ways in which, as a society, we could so structure the environment for our children that their development is better safeguarded, and preventable constrictions and distortions of personality are more often avoided. Some general points need emphasis: anything that is done to improve the lives of *all* children is likely to have a positive effect also on children at risk of a deviant development, when to single out for special provisions those children identified as at risk or already disturbed carries the danger of diluting the beneficial effects of the intervention with the negative impact of stigma.

This last idea has contributed to the changes in educational policy for children with special educational needs that followed the Report of the Warnock Committee in 1978. Fewer children with educational difficulties of all kinds are now taught apart from the rest in special classes or special schools. The idea has also fostered the development of various types of community care or 'intermediate treatment' for delinquent young people as an alternative to residential care in the former approved schools or the present community homes with education, and in the former Borstals, especially since the risks of further delinquency following residential training in such institutions were very high (Rutter and Giller 1983).

But there is a danger. On the face of it, both these new developments are less costly and may be favoured on that account. Yet, unless special teaching in ordinary schools for children with educational difficulties is really good (and that means well-resourced and provided by well-trained teachers), these children and their parents are not helped, but neglected. The same applies to delinquent youngsters left to roam the streets, unless the alternatives to institutional care are seriously planned by well-trained staff working in attractive premises. Restructuring the environment for the education and care of a greater number of handicapped people within the community to avoid their stigmatization requires not only genuine effort, but skilled staff and material resources. The spin-off is that such developments are likely to improve the conditions in schools and in the community for everyone.

A further point needs emphasis. Investigations that show one policy or mode of practice to be superior to another do so in statistical terms: the *majority* of individuals exposed to one set of circumstances or interventions do better, *never all*. This means that few policies can be applied across the board: a range of options must be available to cater for the special needs of individuals or minority groups. There will always be children with educational difficulties of such a nature that, however expert and accommodating the ordinary school, they will need special provisions; there will always be some youngsters who benefit most from a period of residential schooling away from disorganized and violent families, however good the educational and support services in their local community may be; and there will always be some severely ill or handicapped young people who require custodial care to protect them and society from their serious antisocial proclivities.

Lastly, even the implementation of policies known to have only small effects, for example in the prevention of juvenile aggression and crime, are worthwhile. We need to be clear that disturbed behaviour in childhood, and serious personality disorder in later life, usually follow multiple privations and traumata acting together or in sequence over time. If only one aspect of the childhood environment can be effectively improved, or one harmful event avoided, the chances of childhood psychiatric disorder or later personality difficulties are reduced.

It cannot all be left to parents

Ever since the start of compulsory schooling (in 1876 in England), the state has accepted responsibility for a large part of the upbringing of children. Despite the recent emphasis on 'parent choice' and 'parent power', no one questions that educating children requires expertise which most parents do not have. Quite apart from the formal education children get at school, the life they share there with other children in a social organization which is larger, more impersonal, and more complex than that of their own family helps them towards acquiring the social skills they will later need in their working roles and as citizens.

The care of handicapped children is also clearly recognized as in part a public responsibility. Children who are ill or have chronic physical or psychiatric disabilities are of course given medical care, and children who have lost parents or who have parents so ill or so disturbed that they cannot safely look after them of course have alternative homes found for them by the social services. But many parents, not *so* grossly disturbed that their children need public care, are nevertheless, and through no fault of their own, lacking in child-rearing skills. They have much to learn from their children's nurseries and schools, and they and their children can benefit from improved public amenities and from more positive public attitudes towards children.

The well-being of children cannot, especially in this era of changing family compositions, be left to depend entirely on what kind of parents they happen to have. Some of the public services with major effects on the lives of children — schools, housing, television, and the law — will now be considered.

What schools can achieve

We saw in Chapter 2 that good quality *pre-school education*, at least for children living in culturally unstimulating environments, can promote educational achievements and prevent adolescent delinquency.

A recent report on the long-term effects of ordinary pre-school provisions in Britain confirms some of the results of the American experimental programmes. Osborn and Milbank found that, even when social and family disadvantages were controlled for, most pre-school experiences led to significantly better educational achievements by the age of 10 years, compared with those of children who had not had such experiences (Osborn and Milbank 1987). The exceptions were early entry into primary school and attending nursery classes attached to primary schools. Even day nurseries, catering for the most disadvantaged and traumatized children, had beneficial effects on learning, and the effects of all pre-school facilities were best for the socio-economically most deprived. In contrast to the American findings, however, the children's later behaviour was not influenced beneficially by either playgroups or nursery schools, and children who had usually spent long years and long days in day nurseries were at the age of 10 found to be more conduct-disordered and more hyperactive than any other group, while children with no pre-school experiences were the least disturbed in middle childhood. The differential effects on behaviour were however small, while the effects on educational performance were large. The children in this study were all born in 1970. A disturbing finding was that those with the greatest need had the least access to pre-school facilities: 46 per cent of the socio-economically most deprived had had no such experiences, compared with only 10 per cent of the socio-economically most advantaged.

The finding that early entry into primary school, and even going to nursery classes attached to these, can be disadvantageous suggests that we should question the British tradition whereby children start formal schooling at 5 years of age, earlier than in most other developed countries. When school entry is delayed till 6 years, the chances are that more children, even the intellectually less gifted, will be able to meet their teachers' expectations and escape the sense of failure at the very start of their school career that we know can have such harmful and long-lasting effects.

Research on how different primary and secondary schools affect children's educational achievements, behaviour and later work adjustment has shown that, whatever the child's home background, school life can have effects for good or ill. Truancy, for example, has been found in a study in Wales (Reynolds *et al*. 1980) to depend not only on personal and family characteristics of the children, but on what happens at school. Truancy rates varied between different schools even when the children's intelligence and achievements at intake were similar. Schools with better attendance rates tended to be smaller; to attempt less rigid control of their pupils' lives within the school, with fewer enforced rules, for example about smoking and chewing gum; to give children more responsibilities in the organization of school life, as prefects and classroom monitors; and to have closer relationships with parents.

Michael Power and his colleagues were the first to establish that different London schools had different rates of delinquency among their children and maintained these over ten years, even when the children came from neighbourhoods with quite similar conviction rates (Power *et al.* 1972). The exceptions were schools in which a major change had occurred, such as the arrival of a new headmaster. But the definitive study of the effects of secondary schools on children was done by Rutter and his colleagues (1979). Many of their findings have now also been confirmed for primary schools (Mortimore *et al.* 1988). The first group of authors followed children of known intelligence, reading attainments, socio-economic background, and behavioural status at intake through different secondary schools in London, charting their progress but also measuring a variety of aspects of school life (Rutter *et al.* 1979). Big differences were found between schools, even when the intake features of the children were controlled, both in the educational progress and the behaviour (including truancy and delinquency) of the children. All these features were associated with each other; and truancy and poor examination success correlated with later work achievements.

The qualities of the schools in which the children did better educationally, were better behaved, truanted less, and had less recorded delinquency, included high levels of care of the children's material environment with well-decorated buildings, provision of amenities for the children, and freedom for them to move about the school, good staff co-ordination in curriculum planning, high expectations of work achievements, regular setting and checking of home work, displaying children's work, giving the children responsibilities, high rates of praise rather than reprimands in the classroom with time spent on teaching rather than keeping order. In addition, educational achievements and behaviour were better, even in less well-functioning children, when these were in a minority at school entry rather than when they made up the majority of children at a particular school. In this study, school size had no special impact on the children's progress.

As we saw earlier (p. 29) schools can have protective effects on disadvantaged children at risk of later difficulties, by providing experiences associated with a sense of competence and self-esteem.

So we can say that good schools have good attendance rates and help children towards better educational achievements and later work success. At the same time they reduce the levels of classroom misbehaviour and of juvenile delinquency. This, in turn, has important consequences for adult personality functioning, because we know that about one-third of seriously aggressive and delinquent children are destined to become sociopathic in later life (Robins 1978).

Architectural design

A study of one hundred New York corporation estates described by Oscar Newman in his book *Defensible Space* (1972), suggested that vandalism and crime, especially involving juveniles, are related to architectural features. When estates are planned so that main entrances are visible from busy streets, and residents look on internal entrances, lobbies, and garden spaces as their own and feel responsible for their care, crime rates are reduced. High-rise blocks with impersonal walkways and main entrances concealed from the street within the grounds of the estates invite criminal activity. While the social features of housing estates, such as the number of teenage children, of one-parent families, and of families on welfare, were more powerfully associated with crime, architectural design made its own contribution.

A more recent study of 38 housing estates in an inner London borough, found vandalism rates to be related to a number of housing features (Wilson 1980). The most powerful association was with the concentration of children living in a block. Landscaping and newness of the block acted as deterrents. But play areas, because so scarce, attracted children from other blocks and increased the vandalism in those blocks to which children were drawn. Only in low child-density blocks was vandalism related to the design features of 'defensible space'. Here vandalism was especially rampant when entrances to buildings gave easy and unsupervised access to outsiders.

The suggestions from this work are that families with children should be dispersed among housing estates, and that this could be achieved equitably by building dwellings of different sizes on each estate. With a lowered child-density, architectural design ensuring easy surveillance of entrances and other features of 'defensible space' will be worthwhile. Play areas for children should be plentiful, well supervised, and not too near the buildings. Families with young children should live near ground level, in buildings small enough to need no lifts, with reduced glazing, little semi-public space, and good landscaping to demarcate play areas clearly.

Vandalism may seem a nuisance rather than a serious psychological problem. Yet it does not help children to be encouraged in activities they know to be wrong and which only lead to trouble between them, their parents, and the outside world. Anything that can be done in a practical way to allow children to play outdoors freely, and without damaging their houses in the process, will help to foster self-confidence and promote personality development. It will also give their parents greater peace of mind.

The influence of television

Television is thought to have reduced the barrier of secrecy adults have had from children (Meyrowitz 1985). Greenfield, in a lively review, considers that television improves children's visual skills and enhances their grasp of social reality, but that imagination and literacy skills are fostered more by radio and reading (Greenfield 1984). The use of television and computers in school can improve children's motivation and counteract their disaffection from school life. But the most controversial and, from the point of view of personality development, the most important issue is whether television displays of violence increase the aggressive behaviour of young people.

The evidence is of two kinds. As we saw in the last chapter, young children *experimentally* exposed to films of aggressive play imitate what they see and become more aggressive in their own play, especially if previously frustrated, unfamiliar with the toys, and among their friends. Eysenck and Nias conclude firmly that television violence can provoke aggression in children of all ages, especially in boys who are socially isolated, frustrated, and culturally disadvantaged (Eysenck and Nias 1978). *Naturalistic* studies have been difficult to plan and interpret for the very reason that aggressive and maladjusted children are known to watch the screen more than other children and to prefer violent programmes. When attempts were made to control for this association, several longitudinal and one cross-sectional study did show that television violence can increase serious aggression, especially in boys (Lefkowitz *et al.* 1977;

Belson 1978; Singer and Singer 1988); another longitudinal study found only minimal effects (Milavsky *et al*. 1982). It seems likely that violent television programmes do not affect the majority of young people, but can add to the risks of aggressive behaviour for an important minority of already disadvantaged and disturbed youngsters.

The processes involved are thought to be emotional arousal, imitation, and reduction of inner constraints. The present concern of television broadcasters to limit the amounts of violence shown is greatly to be welcomed.

The law in relation to juvenile delinquency, divorce and custody

Only two topics will here be touched on: official responses to delinquent young people, and arrangements when parents divorce.

In Scotland *juvenile delinquency* has for over 15 years been largely decriminalized by the replacement of courts with Children's Hearings before panels of specially selected and trained members of the public. Up to 16 years (18 for children already within the system) most child offenders, like children in need of care, if they and their parents accept the grounds of referral, are dealt with by the panels from the declared viewpoint of what is 'in the best interests of the child'. It has been shown (Martin *et al*. 1981) that what goes on during Children's Hearings is generally understood and appreciated by the children and their families, and that individual hearings do indeed permit, as was intended, free and full discussions of the families' problems and of possible remedies. Only when there is dispute about the facts or about the panel's decision is the case referred to a court of law. This happens infrequently. A major feature of the Scottish system is that, if a child is subjected to compulsory measures of care, there are review panel Hearings until the order is discharged. This means that social workers are not left with the total responsibility for ongoing care, and also that panel members can learn from the progress they observe in the families they see over time.

The institution of this system was at times thought of as a soft option, but its introduction was not followed by an increase of referrals of delinquent children: if anything, the reverse. The point is often rightly made that the judicial services cannot be a remedy for crime. What is not often stressed is that, if a less punitive system does not make matters worse, it should be the preferred option.

Surprisingly, the Scottish legal arrangements for children, which have stood the test of time, are rarely quoted in England as an example of how society can respond to juvenile crime, with advantages for the children and their parents, no disadvantages for the community, and the lifting of a major burden of work from lawyers and the courts. The proposal of family courts in England to deal with juvenile delinquency, child care procedures, custody disputes, and divorce is to be welcomed, especially if the courts are backed, as are the Scottish hearings, by adequate social work services.

After divorce, children from middle childhood onwards need a greater voice in influencing access arrangements to the non-custodial parent, without being burdened with responsibility for the decision itself. At present custody is only rarely awarded to fathers (see also p. 186) and in up to one-half of the families there is less than yearly contact with the non-custodial parent (Lund 1987). Children are least disturbed after divorce if parents manage to share their parenting roles harmoniously and without dispute over money; children are most disturbed when there is no contact with the absent parent; while children in touch with two parents in conflict have intermediate levels of disturbance. Of course, these findings may reflect children's responses not only to the access arrangements after divorce, but to their parents' prior personality functioning during the marriage. Hodges' account of intervention for children of divorce recognizes the contribution of personality disorders of parents to their continuing conflict after the break-up; and also that access to the non-custodial parent may have to be shorter and non-residential for very young children (Hodges 1986).

In every family, custody and access arrangements must be made to suit the developmental level and individual needs of the child in the light of what the parents can manage. For a few children whose parents harmoniously organize regular residential access to the absent and remarried father, this turns out to be quite unsatisfactory. The father's new family may not be welcoming and the regular interruptions of the children's social life at weekends can interfere with their local friend-ships and out-of-school activities. Moreover, very young children, cognitively immature, and especially during the stage of primary identification (p. 150), can be made extremely anxious when shuttling between two parents in dispute, because of conflicts of loyalty and the fear that if they are too fond of the absent parent, they will lose the secure affection of the parent actually looking after them. Conciliation services attached to the courts have a vital part to play in helping parents before and after divorce make the best decisions for their children.

Treatment interventions

Treatment is often effective

In contrast to the relative failure of treatment for seriously personality disordered adults, treatments for less severe personality difficulties, for neurotic and depressive illnesses of adult life, and for all child psychiatric disorders have greatly advanced and have been shown to work, especially in the long term (Sloane *et al.* 1975; Kolvin *et al.* 1981 and 1988). Helpful treatment approaches include medication, behavioural and cognitive methods, supportive and analytic psychotherapy, group treatments, and family therapy, quite apart from the educational and social work interventions for children with special needs. While it is not yet clear which treatments are best for which particular conditions or life problems, the overall therapeutic gloom that existed some twenty years ago has lifted.

But, whether children are in treatment for physical illnesses, emotional or behavioural disorders, or because they are caught up in a social crisis demanding social-work care, effective communication is of the essence. This calls for constant awareness of the nature of childhood and the processes of development we have been considering in this book. Children are people in their own right, as well as members of their family, their school, and the wider community. Interventions need to be planned in the light of a historic understanding of each child's past development and life experiences, and of those of his or her parents, but also with an eye to the future person that child will in time become. (The principles of communicating with children and of child psychotherapy are briefly described by Wolff 1986.)

A gap in current provisions

Among the services available to children and young people in Britain today there is one gap: for the care and development of that small minority of teenagers who are too difficult to be looked after at home or in day schools, or have been exposed to such persistent stresses within their own families that they need to get away for the final years of their childhood. There is currently much pressure to keep children of whatever age at home, as if the lessons from research into the essential nature of early attachments applied to all age groups. These pressures are increased by local authority spending cuts on public services. Such a policy may not best serve the needs of children and may be uneconomical in the long term.

Andrew, described in Chapter 2, although protected against family adversity by high intelligence, relative socio-economic security, an easy temperament, and his parents' affection, benefited from boarding school at adolescence. At 16 he sent me a typed letter:

'I am undecided, at the moment, on my future career but I have decided to go on to University, I think my career will be slanted towards one of the sciences. I hope to get a pilot's licence before leaving school but due to the cost of flying lessons and the Royal Navy turning me down for a special flying award due to me having hay fever, I think it is very unlikely that I will be able to achieve this goal. I find life at . . . school very full, I always find things to do and I seem to get along with both the other pupils and the members of staff.'

A year later he came to see me. He was absolutely clear that what had helped him was being away from the parents' quarrels.

This boy had been at risk of disturbance because of the psychiatric disorders of both parents, the parental disharmony, and because of his own serious developmental learning difficulties. Boarding school helped him to distance himself from his distressed parents and to find self-enhancing opportunities for developing interests, skills and friendships.

The boy now to be described did not have this advantage.

John had more or less brought himself up amidst a most stressful family environment. He too had an 'easy child' temperament with, despite the odds, a sunny outlook on life. He too was a highly intelligent child with considerable drive. He had no educational difficulties.

At not quite 5, he had been unhappy, timid, tearful, afraid of the dark, reluctant to go to nursery school, poor at mixing with other children, and with temper tantrums at home though not at school.

Both parents had chronic schizoid personality disorders. The father was withdrawn, solitary, and lacking in empathy. The mother, attractive and more outgoing, was fanatically devoted to horticulture and wore herself out working in her large garden. Like her husband, she was rigid, but she was also somewhat paranoid. While herself hypersensitive, she lacked feelings for others and described herself as 'not awfully maternal'. She had for years felt cruelly treated, especially by her husband, had emotional outbursts and was often severely depressed. The father too felt hard done by in the marriage. When John was 11, the mother left home, taking the children with her.

John remained tense and anxious throughout his childhood, but he had a younger brother to share his troubles and the two got on exceptionally well. Both worried greatly about their parents' violent quarrels. John said 'the real problem's my dad . . . [but] it's hard to believe which side is true'. Fortunately in this family, too, the parents were not hostile to the children.

At 18, John came to see me. He wanted to become a psychologist and to work with children. Would he be suitable, he wanted to know. He had worked as a volunteer with blind children; he had done a holiday job with a housing association; he was a keen cyclist; and he had many friends. He still wished he could have helped his parents more. Each, he now reported, had tried to indoctrinate him against the other. He still spent a lot of time thinking 'why it happened; why it was so bad', and he had not 'got to the bottom of it'. He said, 'I don't want that sort of thing to happen to anyone else. I want to help people in the same boat.' When asked what in retrospect might have made it better for him as a child, he spontaneously mentioned boarding school': 'to be removed from the hostile environment'.

I told him that in my view his parents' problems were due to constitutional personality difficulties and that there was no way in which he could have made things better; but also that both his parents had always been fond of him and his brother and had coped to the best of their abilities. I thought he should go all out to get into a university psychology course, if that was what he wanted to do. Ten months later, he wrote to say he had taken this advice and was greatly enjoying his courses.

These two children were well endowed in intelligence and temperament, and had affectionate parents. Other youngsters from disharmonious families face greater hazards, especially if conduct-disordered, failing at school, rejected by their parents, and living in economically barren circumstances. They are at serious risk of maladjustment and sociopathy in later life and, in the case of girls, of depression and difficulties in bringing up their children. The consequences for the community are then costly, in terms of court proceedings, prison sentences and social-work support.

Attempts are often made to place such youngsters in foster or adoptive homes, but the obstacles to success for the young person and his or her future parents are now greater than in early childhood. Older children have to come to terms, not only with conflicts of loyalty or with lost relationships with their own parents, they often have to adapt to a change of subculture. This means that part of their own personalities, determined by the social environment in which they grew up, have to be shed if they are to succeed with new parent figures, often living in more privileged circumstances and with different attitudes from those that prevailed in the children's past families and neighbourhoods.

Many such young people spend time in children's homes. It is a sad fact that at present few such homes, unlike residential schools, have the resources to provide the sort of care that could compensate the youngsters for their past traumata and privations and help them towards an improved personality development There are two main reasons for this. Care staff without very special training are at a loss to know how to cope with difficult adolescents. Their problems are increased because they lack the material resources and often the autonomy needed to develop the children's interests and competencies to the full. A case has recently been made for good residential care for that small minority of adolescents who need to live away from their own parents, may still have close ties with them, and may not want to become members of other people's families (Waterhouse 1987). Alternative or 'auxiliary' residential care or schooling can, by relieving the young people and their parents from the everyday frustrations of mutually coercive interactions, preserve the relationships between them, while providing for the youngsters emotional security and stimulating life experiences to widen their horizons, enhance their self-esteem, and, hopefully, contribute to an improved future life adjustment.

Even when change is not possible, understanding helps

We have seen that there are a few children, especially boys, with such serious and long-lasting constitutional or environmental disadvantages and such major childhood disorders that their future path leads them into an unhappy and often repeatedly antisocial life. For girls, who are less frequently constitutionally impaired, the same environmental hazards and childhood disorders may lead to early motherhood, lack of a supportive husband, anxiety, and depression. Treatments based on psychoanalytic understanding, helpful for more minor disorders, have failed as an effective method to prevent and remedy such developments. More active interventions — behavioural, family therapy, environmental — bring better results. But, even when no treatment has succeeded, an understanding of how the other person has come to be as he is and a psychodynamic grasp of his inner world can effectively overcome the barriers imposed on relationships by antisocial behaviour and prevent the extrusion of the delinquent person from his family and social group, wherever he may need to live.

If one can retrospectively understand why an action occurred, empathy and affiliation are re-established. To recognize the childhood origins of later deviancy helps one to understand and empathize even with people who have committed a crime. However gloomy the future outlook, everyone feels better if the roots of their troubles are recognized. In the case of children, both they and their parents benefit from such understanding, although the main treatment may be a family-based behavioural approach or a planned change in the child's environment, with or without special educational help or social work support.

Understanding of the other person is essential in all helping relationships

Fortunately, most psychiatric disorders of childhood and adult life are transient and respond well to a variety of interventions. Psychoanalytic understanding and a more general developmental approach to unravelling the causes of disturbance may not be the essential ingredients of effective treatment. But everyone is comforted if the person to whom they turn for help understands their inner world, whatever the treatment plan. What is more, the professional intervention becomes more interesting and rewarding if some real developmental understanding accompanies what may otherwise be a routine therapeutic task.

Understanding the life history and conveying accurate empathy create intimacy between the therapist and the person who comes for help. This strengthens the essential bond between them which helps them tolerate delays to improvement, persevere in the face of setbacks, and is the basis for all treatment.

References

Introduction

Hoffman, M.L. (1975) 'Developmental synthesis of affect and cognition and its implications for altruistic motivation', *Developmental Psychology* 11, 607–22.
—— (1984) 'Moral Development', in M.H. Bornstein and M.E. Lamb (eds) *Developmental Psychology: An Advanced Text Book*, 279–324, New Jersey: Lawrence Erlbaum.
Toulmin, S. (1970) 'Reasons and Causes', in R. Borger and F. Cioffi (eds) *Explanation in the Behavioural Sciences*, Cambridge: Cambridge University Press.

Chapter 1

Allport, G. (1961) *Pattern and Growth in Personality*, New York: Holt, Rinehart and Winston.
Clarke, A.M. and Clarke, A.D.B. (1976) *Early Experience: Myth and Evidence*, London: Open Books.
Erikson, E.H. (1968) *Identity, Youth and Crisis*, London: Faber & Faber.
Magnusson, D. (1988) *Individual Development from an Interactional Perspective*, 132–52, Hillsdale, NJ: Lawrence Erlbaum.
Plomin, R., DeFries, J.C., and McClearn, G.E. (1980) *Behavioral Genetics: a Primer*, San Francisco: W.H. Freeman and Co.
Rutter, M. (1981) *Maternal Deprivation Reassessed*, 2nd edn, Harmondsworth: Penguin.
Rutter, M., Tizard, J., and Whitmore, L. (1970) *Education, Health and Behaviour*, London: Longman.
Scarr, S. and Kidd, K. (1983) 'Developmental Behavior Genetics', in M.M. Haith and J.J. Campos (volume eds) *Vol II Infancy and Developmental Psychobiology*, 345–433, of P.H. Mussen (ed.) *Handbook of Child Psychology*, New York and Chichester: John Wiley and Sons.
Scarr, S. and McCartney, K. (1983) 'How people make their own environments: a theory of genotype-environment effects', *Child Development* 54, 424–35.

Shields, R. (1962) *Monozygotic Twins Brought Up Apart and Brought Up Together*, 58–64 and 65–76, London: Oxford University Press.

Chapter 2

Berrueta-Clement, J.R., Schweinhart, L.J., Barnett, W.S., Epstein, A.S. and Weikhart, D.P. (1984) *Changed Lives: the Effects of the Perry Preschool Program on Youths through 19*, Monographs of the High/Scope Educational Research Foundation No 8, High/Scope Educational Research Foundation, Ypsilanti, Michigan.

Bronfenbrenner, U. (1974) *Is Early Intervention Effective? A Report on Longitudinal Evaluations of Preschool Programs, Vol. II*, Office of Child Development, US Department of Health, Education and Welfare.

Burt, C. (1946) *The Backward Child*, London: University of London Press.

—— (1975) *The Gifted Child*, London: Hodder & Stoughton.

Douglas, W.J.B. (1964) *The Home and the School*, London: MacGibbon & Kee

Douglas, W.J.B., Ross, J.M., and Simpson, H.R. (1968) *All Our Future*, London: Peter Davies.

Eysenck, H.J. (1962) *Know Your Own IQ*, Harmondsworth: Pelican Books.

Farrington, D. (1985) 'Delinquency prevention in the 1980s', *Journal of Adolescence* 8, 3–16.

Freeman, J. (1983) 'Annotation: Emotional problems of the gifted child', *Journal of Child Psychology and Psychiatry*, 24, 481–5.

Gottfried, A.W. (1984) *Home Environment and Early Cognitive Development: Longitudinal Research*, New York, London: Academic Press Inc.

Henderson, N.D. (1982) 'Human behavior genetics', *Annual Review of Psychology* 33, 403–40.

Jensen, A.R. (1980) *Bias in Mental Testing*, New York: The Free Press, Macmillan.

—— (1981) *Straight Talk about Mental Tests*, 191–232, London: Methuen.

Plomin, R., DeFries, J.C., and McClearn, G.E. (1980) *Behavioral Genetics: A Primer*, San Francisco: W.H. Freeman & Co.

Quinton, D. and Rutter, M. (1988) *Parenting Breakdown: the Making and Breaking of Intergenerational Links*, Aldershot: Averbury.

Robins, L. (1966) *Deviant Children Grown Up*, Baltimore: Williams & Wilkins.

Rutter, M. (1970) 'Psychological development: predictions from infancy', *Journal of Child Psychology and Psychiatry* 11, 49–62.

—— (1985) 'Family and school influences on cognitive development', *Journal of Child Psychology and Psychiatry* 26, 683–704.

Rutter, M., Tizard, J., and Whitmore, L. (1970) *Health, Education and Behaviour*, London: Longman.

Rutter, M., Maughan, B., Mortimore, P., and Ousten, J. (1979) *Fifteen Thousand Hours: Secondary Schools and their Effects on Children*, London: Open Books.

Rutter, M., Yule, B., Quinton, D., Rowlands, O., Yule, W., and Berger, M. (1975) 'Attainment and adjustment in two geographic areas: III. Some factors accounting for area differences', *British Journal of Psychiatry* 126, 520–33.

Stevenson, H.W., Stigler, J.W., Shin-Ying Lee, and Lucker, G.W. (1985) 'Cognitive performance and academic achievement of Japanese, Chinese and American children', *Child Development* 56, 718–34.

Stevenson, J., Graham, P., Fredman, G., and McLoughlin, V. (1987) 'A twin study of genetic influences on reading and spelling ability and disability', *Journal of Child Psychology and Psychiatry* 28, 229–47.

Tanner, J.M. (1984) 'Physical growth and development', in J.O. Forfar and G.C. Arneil (eds) *Textbook of Paediatrics*, 3rd edn, vol. I, 278–330, Edinburgh: Churchill Livingstone.

Terman, L.M. and Oden, M.H. (1959) *The Gifted Group at Mid-Life: Thirty-Five Years' Follow-Up of the Superior Child*, Stanford, California: Stanford University Press.

Tizard, B. and Hughes, M. (1984) *Young Children Learning: Talking and Thinking at Home and at School*, London; Fontana Press.

Tizard, J. (1975) 'Race and IQ: the limits of probability', *New Behaviour* 1, 6–9.

Chapter 3

Ackerknecht, E.G. (1968) *Short History of Psychiatry*, 10–11, New York and London: Hafner.

Chess, S. and Thomas, A. (1984) *Origins and Evolution of Behavior Disorders*, New York: Raven Press.

Claridge, G. (1985) *Origins of Mental Illness*, Oxford: Basil Blackwell.

Eysenck, H.J. (1967) *The Biological Basis of Personality*, Springfield, Illinois: C.D. Thomas.

—— (1970) *The Structure of Human Personality*, 3rd edn, London: Methuen

Freedman, D.G. (1979) *Human Sociobiology*, New York: Free Press.

Glueck, S. and Glueck, E. (1950) *Unravelling Juvenile Delinquency*, New York: The Commonwealth Fund.

Hutt, C. (1972) *Males and Females*, Harmondsworth: Penguin Books.

Kagan, J., Reznick, J.S., and Snidman, N. (1986) 'Temperamental inhibition in early childhood', in R. Plomin and J. Dunn (eds) *The Study of Temperament: Changes, Continuities and Challenges*, 53–65, Hillsdale, New Jersey and London: Lawrence Erlbaum Associates.

—— (1988) 'Biological bases of childhood shyness', *Science* 240, 167–71.

Kretschmer, E. (1925) *Physique and Character: an Investigation of the Nature of Constitution and the Theory of Temperament*, 2nd edn, London: Kegan Paul, Trench and Trubner.

McDevitt, S.C. (1986) 'Continuity and discontinuity of temperament in infancy and early childhood: a psychometric perspective', in R. Plomin and J. Dunn (eds) *The Study of Temperament: Changes, Continuities and Challenges*, 27–38, Hillsdale, New Jersey and London: Lawrence Erlbaum Associates.

Manning, M., Heron, J., and Marshall, C. (1977) 'Styles of hostility and social interactions at nursery, at school and at home: an extended study of children', in L.A. Hersov and M. Berger (eds) *Aggression and Anti-Social Behaviour in Childhood and Adolescence*, Oxford: Pergamon Press.

Mednick, S.A., Moffitt, T., Gabrielli, W., and Hutchings, B. (1986) 'Genetic factors in criminal behavior: a review', in D. Olsweus, J. Block, and M. Radke-Yarrow (eds) *Development of Antisocial and Prosocial Behavior: Research, Theories and Issues*, 33–55, Orlando, Florida: Academic Press.

Meyer-Bahlburg, H.F.F., Ehrhardt, A., and Feldman, J.F. (1986) 'Long-term implications of the prenatal endocrine milieu for sex-dimorphic behavior', in L. Erlenmeyer-Kimling and N.E. Miller (eds) *Life-Span Research on the Prediction of Psychopathology*, 17–30, Hillsdale, New Jersey: Lawrence Erlbaum Associates.

Olweus, D. (1986) 'Aggression and hormones: behavioral relationship with testosterone and adrenaline', in D. Olweus, J. Block, and M. Radke-Yarrow (eds) *Development of Antisocial and Prosocial Behavior: Research, Theories and Issues*, 51–72, Orlando, Florida: Academic Press.

Patterson, G.R., Littman, R.A., and Bricker, W. (1967) 'Assertive behavior in children: a step toward a theory of aggression', *Monographs of the Society for Research in Child Development*, 32, No. 5.

Plomin, R. and Dunn, J. (eds) (1986) *The Study of Temperament: Changes, Continuities and Challenges*, Hillsdale, New Jersey and London: Lawrence Erlbaum Associates.

Rutter, M. (1987) 'Temperament, personality and personality disorder', *British Journal of Psychiatry* 150, 443–58.

Rutter, M., Birch, H.S., Thomas, A., and Chess, S. (1964) 'Temperamental characteristics in infancy and later development of behavioural disorders', *British Journal of Psychiatry* 110, 651–61.

Scarr, S. and Kidd, K.K. (1983) 'Developmental Behavior Genetics', in M.M. Haith and J.J. Campos (volume eds) *Infancy and Developmental Psychobiology*, II, of P.H. Mussen (ed.) *Handbook of Child Psychology*, 345–433, New York and Chichester: John Wiley and Sons.

Sheldon, W.H. (1942) *The Varieties of Temperament*, New York: Harper.

Stevenson-Hinde, J. and Hinde, R.A. (1986) 'Changes in associations between characteristics and interactions', in R. Plomin and J. Dunn (eds) *The Study of Temperament: Changes, Continuities and Challenges*, 115–29, Hillsdale, New Jersey and London: Lawrence Erlbaum Associates.

Taylor, E.A. (ed.) (1986) *The Overactive Child*, Clinics in Developmental Medicine No. 97, Oxford: Spastics International Medical Publications and Blackwell Scientific Publications Ltd.

Thomas, A., Chess, S., Birch, H.G., Hertzig, M., and Korn, S. (1963) *Behavioral Individuality in Early Childhood*, New York: New York University Press.

Wallace, M. (1986) *The Silent Twins*, Harmondsworth: Penguin Books.

Weiss, G., Hechtman, L., Milroy, T., and Perlman, T. (1985) 'Psychiatric status of hyperactives as adults: a controlled prospective 15-year follow-up of 63 hyperactive children', *Journal of the American Academy of Child Psychiatry* 24, 211–20.

Wing, L. (1981) 'Asperger's syndrome: a clinical account', *Psychological Medicine* 11, 115–30.

Wolff, S. (1989) 'Schizoid personality disorders of childhood and adolescence', in C. Last and M. Hersen (eds) *Handbook of Child Psychiatric Diagnosis*, New York: Wiley (in press).

Wolff, S. and Chick, J. (1980) 'Schizoid personality in childhood: a controlled follow-up study', *Psychological Medicine* 10, 85–100.

Wolff, S. and Cull, A. (1986) '''Schizoid'' personality and antisocial conduct: a retrospective case note study', *Psychological Medicine* 16, 677–87.

Chapter 4

Ainsworth, M.D.S., Bell, S.M., and Stayton, D.J. (1974) 'Infant-mother attachment and social development: "socialization" as a product of reciprocal responsiveness to signals', in M.P.M. Richards (ed.) *The Integration of a Child into a Social World*, Cambridge: Cambridge University Press.

Baldwin, J.M. (1897) *Social and Ethical Interpretations of Mental Development: A Study in Social Psychology*, 4th edn 1906, New York: Macmillan.

Bell, R.Q. (1974) 'Contribution of human infants to caregiving and social interaction', in M. Lewis and L.A. Rosenblum (eds) *The Origins of Behavior, Vol I: the Effect of the Infant on its Caregiver*, New York and London: Wiley.

Bernal, J.F. (1973) 'Night waking of infants during the first 14 months', *Developmental Medicine and Child Neurology* 15, 760–9.

Bower, T.G.R. (1974) *Development in Infancy*, San Francisco: Freeman and Co.

Bowlby, J. (1951) *Maternal Care and Mental Health*, WHO Monograph 2, Geneva.

—— (1979) 'Effects on behaviour of disruption of an affectional bond', in J. Bowlby *The Making and Breaking of Affectional Bonds*, 67–80, London: Tavistock.

—— (1982) *Attachment and Loss, Vol. I: Attachment*, 2nd edn, London: The Tavistock Institute of Human Relations and The Hogarth Press. Also published by Penguin Books, 1984.

Brown, G.W. (1982) 'Early loss and depression', in C.M. Parkes and J. Stevenson-Hinde (eds) *The Place of Attachment in Human Behaviour*, 232–68, London: Tavistock Publications.

Bruner, J. (1972) 'Nature and uses of immaturity', *American Psychologist* 27, 687–708.

Bruner, J. (1973) 'Organization of early skilled action', *Child Development* 44, 1–11.

Campos, J.J., Barrett, K.C., Lamb, M.E., Goldsmith, H.H., and Stenberg, C. (1983) 'Socioemotional Development', in M.M. Haith and J.J. Campos (volume eds) *Infancy and Developmental Psychobiology*, vol. II of P.H. Mussen (ed.) *Handbook of Child Psychology*, New York and Chichester: John Wiley and Sons.

Clarke, A.M. and Clarke, A.D.B. (1976) *Early Experience: Myth and Evidence*, London: Open Books.

Cutrona, C.E. and Troutman, B.R. (1986) 'Social support, infant temperament, and parenting self-efficacy: a mediation model of postpartum depression', *Child Development* 57, 1507–18.

Darwin, C. (1877) 'A biographical sketch of an infant', *Mind* 2, 285–94.

Douglas, J. (1975) 'Early hospital admissions and later disturbances of behaviour and learning', *Developmental Medicine and Child Neurology* 17, 456–78.

Etzel, B.D. and Gewirtz, J.L. (1967) 'Experimental modification of caretaker-maintained high-rate operant crying in a 6- and a 20-week-old infant (infans tyrannotearus): extinction of crying with reinforcement of eye contact and smiling', *Journal of Experimental Child Psychology* 5, 303–17.

Feinman, S. and Lewis, M. (1983) 'Social referencing at ten months: a second-order effect on infants' responses to strangers', *Child Development* 54, 878–87.

Fraiberg, S. (1974) 'Blind infants and their mothers: an examination of the sign system', in M.M. Lewis and L.A. Rosenblum (eds) *The Origins of Behavior, Vol. I: The Effect of the Infant on its Caregiver*, New York and London: Wiley.

Freedman, D. and Keller, B. (1963) 'Inheritance of behaviour in infants', *Science* 140, 196–8.

Goldfarb, W. (1945) 'Effects of psychological deprivation in infancy and subsequent stimulation', *American Journal of Psychiatry* 102, 18–33.

Grossman, K., Grossman, K.E., Spangler, G., Suess, G., and Unzner, L. (1985) 'Sensitivity and newborns' orientation responses as related to quality of attachment in northern Germany', in I. Bretherton and E. Waters (eds) *Growing Points of Attachment Theory and Research*, Monographs of the Society for Research in Child Development 50, Nos 1–2, 233–56.

Harlow, H.F. and Zimmerman, R.R. (1959) 'Affectional responses in infant monkeys', *Science* 130, 421–32.

Hinde, R.A. (1976) 'On describing relationships', *Journal of Child Psychology and Psychiatry* 17, 1–19.

Hinde, R.A., Leighton-Shapiro, M.E., and McGinnis, L. (1978) 'Effects of various types of separation experience on rhesus monkeys 5 months later', *Journal of Child Psychology and Psychiatry* 19, 199–211.

Klaus, M.H., Trause, M.A., and Kennell, J.H. (1975) 'Does human maternal behavior after delivery show a characteristic pattern?', in *CIBA Foundation Symposium, 33: Parent-Infant Interaction*, 69–78, Amsterdam, Oxford, New York: Elsevier.

Lamb, M.E. (1983) 'Early mother-neonate contact and the mother-child relationship', annotation, *Journal of Child Psychology and Psychiatry* 24, 487–94.

Lorenz, K.(1935), quoted in Schaffer, R.H. (1971) *The Growth of Sociability*, 101–3, Harmondsworth: Penguin Books.

McFarlane, A. (1975) 'Olfaction in the development of social preferences in the human neonate', in *CIBA Foundation Symposium, 33: Parent-Infant Interaction*, 103–17, Amsterdam, Oxford, New York: Elsevier.

Marris, P. (1982) 'Attachment and Society', in C.M. Parkes and J. Stevenson-Hinde (eds) *The Place of Attachment in Human Behaviour*, 185–201, London: Tavistock Publications.

Newson, J. (1979) 'Intentional behaviour in the young infant', in D. Shaffer and J.Dunn (eds) *The First Year of Life: Psychological and Medical Implications of Early Experience*, 91–6, Chichester: John Wiley and Sons.

Parke, R.D. (1981) *Fathering*, Glasgow: Fontana Paperbacks.

Preyer,W. (1888) *Mind of the Child*, Transl., H.W. Brown, New York: Appleton.

Robertson, J. and Robertson, J. (1967–72) *Young Children in Brief Separations* (film series), London: Tavistock Institute of Human Relations.

Ruppenthal, G.C., Arling, G.L., Harlow, H.F., Sacket, G.P., and Suomi, S.J. (1976) '10-year perspective of motherless-mother monkey behavior', *Journal of Abnormal Psychology* 85, 341–9.

Rutter, M. (1981) *Maternal Deprivation Reassessed*, 2nd edn, Harmondsworth: Penguin Books.

Schaffer, H.R. (1965) 'Changes in developmental quotient under two conditions of maternal separation', *British Journal of Social and Clinical Psychology* 4, 39–46.

—— (1966) 'Activity level as a constitutional determinant of infantile reaction to deprivation', *Child Development* 37, 595–602.

—— (1971) *The Growth of Sociability*, Harmondsworth: Penguin Books.

—— (1977a) *Mothering*, London: Fontana Open Books.

—— (1977b) 'Early interactive development', in H.R. Schaffer (ed.) *Studies in Mother-Infant Interaction*, 3–16, London, New York, San Francisco: Academic Press.

Schaffer, H.R. and Callender, W.M. (1959) 'Psychological effects of hospitalisation in infancy, *Pediatrics* 24, 528–39.

Schaffer, H.R. and Emerson, P.E. (1964) 'The development of social attachments in infancy', *Monographs of the Society for Research in Child Development* 29, No. 3.

Spitz, R.A. (1945)'Anaclytic depression', *Psychoanalytic Study of the Child* 1, 313–42.

Sroufe, L.A. (1985) 'Attachment classification from the perspective of infant-caregiver relationships and infant temperament', *Child Development* 56, 1–14.

Sroufe, L.A., Fox, N.E., and Pancake, V.R. (1983) 'Attachment and dependency in developmental perspective', *Child Development* 54, 1615–27.

Taine, M. (1877) from *Revue Philosophique*, No. 1, January 1876, translated and reported in *Mind* 2, 252–9.

Tizard, B. (1972) *Adoption: a Second Chance*, London: Open Books.

—— (1979) 'Early experience and later social behaviour', in D. Shaffer and J. Dunn (eds) *The First Year of Life: Psychological and Medical Implications of Early Experience*, 197–211, Chichester: John Wiley and Sons.

Tizard, B., Cooperman, O., Joseph, A., and Tizard, J. (1972) 'Environmental effects on language development: a study of young children in long-stay residential nurseries', *Child Development* 43, 337–58.

Tizard, B. and Rees, J. (1976) 'A comparison of the effects of adoption, restoration to the natural mother, and continued institutionalization on the cognitive development of four-year-old children', in A.M. Clarke and A.D.B. Clarke (eds) *Early Experience: Myth and Evidence*, London: Open Books.

Trevarthen, C. (1974) 'Conversations with a two-month-old', *New Scientist* 62, 230–5.

Werner, E.E. and Smith, R.S. (1982) *Vulnerable But Invincible: A Longitudinal Study of Resilient Children and Youth*, New York and London: McGraw-Hill Book Co.

Yarrow, L.J. (1972) 'Attachment and dependency: a developmental perspective', in J.L. Gewirtz (ed.) *Attachment and Dependency*, New York: V.H. Winston and Sons, Inc.

Chapter 5

Anderson, J.W. (1974) 'Attachment behaviour out of doors', in N. Blurton Jones (ed.) *Ethological Studies of Child Behaviour*, Cambridge: Cambridge University Press.

Baldwin, J.M. (1897) *Social and Ethical Interpretations of Mental Development: A Study in Social Psychology*, 4th edn, 1906, New York: Macmillan.

Bowlby, J. (1951) *Maternal Care and Mental Health*, Geneva: World Health Organisation.

Brown, G.W. (1982) 'Early loss and depression', in C.M. Parkes and J. Stevenson-Hinde (eds) *The Place of Attachment in Human Behaviour*, London: Tavistock Publications.

Campos. J.J., Barrett, K.C., Lamb, M.E., Goldsmith, H.H., and Stenberg, C. (1983) 'Socioemotional Development', in M.M. Haith and J.J. Campos (volume eds) *Infancy and Developmental Psychobiology*, vol. II of P.H. Mussen (ed) *Handbook of Child Psychology*, 783–915, New York and Chichester: John Wiley and Sons.

Dowdney, L., Skuse, D., Rutter, M., and Mrazek, D. (1985) 'Parenting qualities: concepts, measures and origins', in J.E. Stevenson (ed.) *Recent Research in Developmental Psychopathology*, 19–42, Oxford: Pergamon Press.

Dunn, J. and Kendrick, C. (1982) *Siblings: Love, Envy and Understanding*, London: Grant McIntyre.

Dunn, J. and Munn, P. (1985) 'Becoming a family member: family conflict and the development of social understanding in the second year', *Child Development* 56, 480–92.

Hartup, W.W. (1980) 'Peer relations and family relations: two social worlds', in M. Rutter (ed.) *Scientific Foundations of Developmental Psychiatry*, 280–92, London: Heinemann Medical Books.

Hinde, R.A., Easton, D.F., Meller, R.E., and Tamplin, A. (1983) 'Nature and determinants of preschoolers' differential behaviour to adults and peers', *British Journal of Developmental Psychology* 1, 3–19.

Hinde, R.A. and McGinnis, L. (1977) 'Some factors influencing the effects of temporary mother-infant separation — some experiments with rhesus monkeys', *Psychological Medicine* 7, 187–212.

Hinde, R.A. and Tamplin, A. (1983) 'Relations between mother-child interaction and behaviour in school', *British Journal of Developmental Psychology* 7, 231–57.

Hodges, J. (1989) 'Social and family relations of ex-institutional children', *Journal of Child Psychology and Psychiatry* (in press).

Hoffman, M.L. (1984) 'Moral Development', in M.H. Bornstein and M.E. Lamb (eds) *Developmental Psychology: An Advanced Textbook*, 279–324, New Jersey: Lawrence Erlbaum Associates.

Kagan, J. (1981) *The Second Year: The Emergence of Self-Awareness*,

Cambridge, Mass. and London: Harvard University Press.

McGrew, W.C. (1974) 'Aspects of social development in nursery school children, with emphasis on introduction to the group', in N. Blurton Jones (ed.) *Ethological Studies of Child Behaviour*, 129–56, Cambridge: Cambridge University Press

Main, M. and Kaplan, N. (1985) 'Security in infancy, childhood, and adulthood: a move to the level of representation', in I. Bretherton and E. Waters (eds) *Growing Points of Attachment Theory and Research*, Monographs of the Society for Research in Child Development, vol. 50, nos 1–2, 66–104.

Mills, M., Puckering, C., Pound, A., and Cox, A. (1985) 'What is it about depressed mothers that influences their children's functioning?', in J.E. Stevenson (ed.) *Recent Research in Developmental Psychopathology*, 11–17, Oxford: Pergamon Press.

Pound, A., Cox, A.D., Puckering, C., and Mills, M. (1985) 'The impact of maternal depression on young children', in J.E. Stevenson (ed.) *Recent Research in Developmental Psychopathology*, 3–10, Oxford: Pergamon Press.

Quinton, D. and Rutter, M. (1988) *Parenting Breakdown: the Making and Breaking of Intergenerational Links*, Aldershot: Avebury.

Radke-Yarrow, M., Cummings, E.M., Kuczynski, L., and Chapman, M. (1985) 'Patterns of attachment in two- and three-year-olds in normal families and families with parental depression', *Child Development* 56, 884–93.

Richman, N., Stevenson, J., and Graham, P. (1982) *Pre-School to School: a Behavioural Study*, London: Academic Press.

Rutter, M. (1981) *Maternal Deprivation Reassessed*, 2nd edn, Harmondsworth: Penguin.

Schaffer, H.R. (1971) *The Growth of Sociability*, Harmondsworth: Penguin Books.

—— (1984) *The Child's Entry into a Social World*, London: Academic Press.

Skuse, D. and Cox, A. (1985) 'Parenting the pre-school child: clinical and social implications of research into past and current disadvantage', in J.E. Stevenson (ed.) *Recent Research in Developmental Psychopathology*, Oxford: Pergamon Press.

Stevenson-Hinde, J. and Hinde, R.A. (1986) 'Changes in associations between characteristics and interactions', in R. Plomin and J. Dunn (eds) *The Study of Temperament: Changes, Continuities and Challenges*, 115–29, Hillsdale, New Jersey and London: Lawrence Erlbaum Associates.

Tizard, B. (1977) *Adoption: A Second Chance*, London: Open Books.

Tizard, B., Cooperman, O., Joseph, A., and Tizard, J. (1972) 'Environmental effects on language development: a study of young children in long-stay residential nurseries', *Child Development* 43, 337–58.

Tizard, B. and Hodges, J. (1978) 'The effect of early institutional rearing on the development of eight-year-old children', *Journal of Child Psychology and Psychiatry* 19, 99–118.

Turiel, E. (1983) *The Development of Social Knowledge: Morality and Convention*, Cambridge: Cambridge University Press.

Wolkind, S. and Krug, S. (1985) 'From child to parent: early separation and adaptation to motherhood', in A.R. Nicol (ed.) *Longitudinal Studies in Child*

Psychology and Psychiatry: Practical Lessons from Research Experience,
53–74, New York, Chichester: John Wiley and Sons.

Chapter 6

Boden, M. (1979) *Piaget,* London: Fontana Paperbacks.
Bower, T.G.R. (1974) *Development in Infancy,* San Francisco: W.H. Freeman.
Bruner, J. (1972) 'Nature and uses of immaturity', *American Psychologist* 27, 687–708.
—— (1978) 'Learning how to do things with words', in J.S. Bruner and A. Garton (eds) *Human Growth and Development: Wolfson College Lectures 1976,* 62–84, Oxford: Clarendon Press.
Cazden, C.B. (1974) 'Two paradoxes in the acquisition of language structure and function', in K.J. Connolly and J.S. Bruner (eds) *The Growth of Competence,* London: Academic Press.
Chomsky, N. (1976) *Reflections on Language,* London: Temple Smith/Fontana.
Clark, E.V. (1983) 'Meanings and Concepts', in J.H. Flavell and E.M. Markman (eds) *Cognitive Development,* vol. III of P.H. Mussen (ed) *Handbook of Child Psychology,* New York: Wiley.
Colby, A., Kohlberg, L., Gibbs, J., and Lieberman, M. (1983) *A Longitudinal Study of Moral Judgement,* Monographs of the Society for Research in Child Development 48, Serial No. 200.
Darwin, C.A. (1877) 'A biographical sketch of an infant', *Mind* 2, 285–94.
Dixon, R.A. and Lerner, R.M. (1984) 'A history of systems in developmental psychology', in M.H. Bornstein and M.E. Lamb (eds) *Developmental Psychology: An Advanced Textbook,* chapter 1, New Jersey: Lawrence Erlbaum Associates.
Donaldson, M. (1978) *Children's Minds,* Glasgow: Fontana/Collins.
Gelman, R. and Baillargeon, N. (1983) 'A review of some Piagetian concepts', in J.H. Flavell and E.M. Markman (eds) *Cognitive Development,* vol. III of P.H. Mussen (ed) *Handbook of Child Psychology,* New York: John Wiley.
Howlin, P. (1980) 'Language', in M. Rutter (ed.) *Scientific Foundations of Developmental Psychiatry,* 198–220, London: Heinemann Medical Books.
Kohlberg, L. (1963) 'The development of children's orientations towards a moral order, I: sequence in the development of moral thought', *Vita Humana* 6, 11–33.
Luria, A. (1957) 'The role of language in the formation of temporary connections', in B. Simon (ed.) *Psychology in the Soviet Union,* California: Stanford University Press.
Macnamarra, J. (1972) 'Cognitive basis of language learning in infants', *Psychological Review* 79, 1–13.
Meadows, S. (1986) *Understanding Child Development,* London: Hutchinson.
Penner, S.G. (1987) 'Parental responses to grammatical and ungrammatical child utterances', *Child Development* 58, 376–84.
Piaget, J. (1929) *The Child's Conception of the World,* London: Routledge and Kegan Paul. Reprinted 1964.

—— (1932) *The Moral Judgement of the Child*, London: Routledge and Kegan Paul, and Harmondsworth: Penguin Books.

—— (1951) *Judgement and Reasoning in the Child*, London: Routledge and Kegan Paul.

—— (1960) *Language and Thought of the Child*, London: Routledge Paperbacks.

—— (1967) *The Construction of Reality in the Child*, London: Routledge and Kegan Paul.

—— (1971) *The Science of Education and the Psychology of the Child*, London: Longman.

Piaget, J. and Inhelder, B. (1969) *The Psychology of the Child*, London: Routledge and Kegan Paul.

Pinchbeck, I. and Hewitt, M. (1969) *Children in English Society*, I, London: Routledge and Kegan Paul.

Preyer, W. (1888) *Mind of the Child*, Transl. H.W. Brown, New York: Appleton.

Sandler, A.M. (1975) 'Comments on the significance of Piaget's work for psychoanalysis', *International Review of Psychoanalysis* 2, 305–78.

Taine, M. (1877) From *Revue Philosophique* No. 1, January 1876, translated and reported in *Mind* 2, 252–9.

Tanner, J.M. (1984) 'Physical growth and development', in J.O. Forfar and G.C. Arneil (eds) *Textbook of Paediatrics*, 3rd edn, vol. I, 278–330, Edinburgh: Churchill Livingstone.

Tapp, J.L. and Levine, F.J. (1972) 'Compliance from kindergarten to college: A speculative research note', *Journal of Youth and Adolescence* I, 233–49.

Vigotsky, L.S. (1962) *Thought and Language*, edited and translated by E. Haufmann and G. Vakar, Cambridge, Mass: M.I.T. Press.

Weir, R.H. (1962) *Language in the Crib*, The Hague, Holland: Mouton & Co.

Wolff, S. (1981) *Children Under Stress*, 2nd edn, Harmondsworth: Penguin Books.

Chapter 7

Beloff, H. (1957) 'The Structure and Origin of the Anal Character', *Genetic Psychology Monographs* 55, 141–72.

Bowlby, J. (1975) *Attachment and Loss, Vol. II: Separation, Anxiety and Anger*, London: Penguin.

—— (1980) *Attachment and Loss, Vol. III: Loss*, London: The Tavistock Institute of Human Relations and The Hogarth Press.

Breuer, J. and Freud, S. (1893) 'On the Psychical Mechanisms of Hysterical Phenomena: Preliminary communication', in *The Standard Edition of the Complete Psychological Works of Sigmund Freud*, vol. II, (1955), 1–17, London, Hogarth Press and the Institute of Psychoanalysis.

—— (1893–1895) 'Studies on Hysteria I', in *The Standard Edition of the Complete Psychological Works of Sigmund Freud*, vol. II, (1955), London: The Hogarth Press and the Institute of Psychoanalysis.

Brown, G.W. and Harris, T. (1978) *Social Origins of Depression: A Study of Psychiatric Disorders in Women*, London: Tavistock Publications.

Freud, A. (1961) *The Ego and the Mechanisms of Defence*, London: The Hogarth

Press and the Institute of Psychoanalysis.

—— (1966) *Normality and Pathology in Childhood*, London: The Hogarth Press and the Institute of Psychoanalysis.

Freud, S. (1905) 'Three Essays on the Theory of Sexuality', in *The Standard Edition of the Complete Psychological Works of Sigmund Freud*, vol. VII, (1953), London: The Hogarth Press and the Institute of Psychoanalysis.

—— (1913) 'Two lies told by children', in *The Standard Edition of the Complete Psychological Works of Sigmund Freud*, vol. XII, (1958), 305–9, London: The Hogarth Press and the Institute of Psychoanalysis.

—— (1923) 'The Ego and the Id I', in *The Standard Edition of the Complete Psychological Works of Sigmund Freud*, vol. XIX, (1961), London: The Hogarth Press and the Institute of Psychoanalysis.

Hartmann, H. (1951) 'Ego psychology and the problems of adaptation', in D. Rapaport (ed.) *Organization and Pathology of Thought*, New York: Columbia University Press.

Kagan, J. (1981) *The Second Year: The Emergence of Self-Awareness*, Cambridge, Mass., and London: Harvard University Press.

Kräupl Taylor, F. (1987) 'Editorial: Psychoanalysis: a philosophical critique', *Psychological Medicine* 17, 557–60.

Laplanche, J. and Pontalis, J.B. (1973) *The Language of Psychoanalysis*, London: The Hogarth Press and the Institute of Psychoanalysis.

Liotti, G. (1987) 'The resistance to change of cognitive structures: a counter-proposal to Psychoanalytic Metapsychology', *Journal of Cognitive Psychotherapy: An International Quarterly* 1, 87–104.

Macdougall, W. (1924) *An Outline of Psychology*, 2nd edn, 121–76, London: Methuen & Co. Ltd.

Mitchell, J. (ed.) (1986) *The Selected Melanie Klein*, Harmondsworth: Penguin.

Munroe, R. (1957) *Schools of Psychoanalytic Thought*, 86, London: Century Hutchinson Ltd.

Oatley, K. (1985) 'Experimental method and psychodynamic theory: discussion paper', *Journal of the Royal Society of Medicine* 78, 729–38.

Segal, H. (1979) *Klein*, Glasgow: Fontana/Collins.

Whiting, J.W.M. and Child, I.L. (1953) *Child Training and Personality: A Cross-Cultural Study*, New Haven, CT: Yale University Press.

Will, D. and Wrate, R.M. (1985) *Family Therapy: A Problem-Centred Psychodynamic Approach*, London: Tavistock.

Wolff, S. (1981) *Children Under Stress*, 2nd edn, Harmondsworth: Penguin.

—— (1987) 'Antisocial conduct: whose concern?', *Journal of Adolescence* 10, 105–18.

Chapter 8

Bowlby, J.(1982) *Attachment and Loss, Vol. I: Attachment*, 2nd edn, The Hogarth Press and the Institute of Psychoanalysis; also published by Penguin Books, 1984

Capsi, A. and Elder, G.H. (1988) 'Emergent family patterns: the intergenerational construction of problem behaviour and relationships', in R.A. Hinde and J. Stevenson-Hinde (eds) *Relationships within Families: Mutual Influences*, 218–40 Oxford: Clarendon Press.

Elder, G.H., Liker, J.K., and Cross, C.E. (1984) 'Parent-child behavior in the Great Depression: life course and intergenerational influences', in P.B. Baltes and O.G. Brim (eds) *Life-Span Development and Behavior*, 109–58, New York and London: Academic Press.

Erikson, E.H. (1965) *Childhood and Society*, Harmondsworth: Penguin.

—— (1968) *Identity, Youth and Crisis*, London: Faber and Faber, first published by W.W. Norton & Company Inc, New York.

Pinchbeck, I. and Hewitt, M. (1969) *Children in English Society: Vol. I, from Tudor Times to the Eighteenth Century*, London: Routledge and Kegan Paul.

Quinton, D., Rutter, M.L., and Liddle, C. (1984) 'Institutional rearing, parenting difficulties and marital support', *Psychological Medicine* 14, 107–24.

Rycroft, C. (1968) 'Introduction: causes and meaning', in C. Rycroft (ed.) *Psychoanalysis Observed*, Harmondsworth: Penguin.

West, D.J. and Farrington, D.P. (1973) *Who Becomes Delinquent?*, London: Heinemann Educational Books.

Chapter 9

Ariès, P. (1973) *Centuries of Childhood*, translated by R. Baldick, Harmondsworth: Penguin; first published in 1962 by Jonathan Cape, London.

Baldwin, A.L., Kalhorn, J., and Breese, F.H. (1949) 'The appraisal of parent behavior', *Psychological Monographs* 63, 299.

Bandura, A. (1977) *Social Learning Theory*, New Jersey: Prentice-Hall.

Bandura, A. and Walters, R.H. (1963) *Social Learning and Personality Development*, New York: Holt, Rinehart and Winston.

Briggs, J.L. (1973) 'The issue of autonomy and aggression in the three year old: the Utku Eskimo case', *Seminars in Psychiatry* 4, 317–29; also in S. Chess and A. Thomas (eds) *Annual Progress in Child Psychiatry and Child Development*, 139–55, New York: Bruner/Mazel.

Burke, P. (1976) 'The Discovery of Childhood', unpublished manuscript of lecture delivered to The Association for Child Psychology & Psychiatry 1976.

Caudhill, W. and Weinstein, H. (1969) 'Maternal care and infant behavior in Japan and America', *Psychiatry* 32, 12–43.

Dunn, J. (1984) 'Sibling Studies and the Developmental Impact of Critical Incidents', in P.B. Baltes and O.G. Brim (eds) *Life-Span Development and Behavior*, 335–53, New York and London: Academic Press.

Dunn, J. and Kendrick, C. (1982) *Siblings: Love, Envy and Understanding*, Cambridge, Mass: Harvard University Press.

Elder, G.H., Liker, J.K., and Cross, C.E. (1984) 'Parent-Child Behavior in the Great Depression: Life Course and Intergenerational Influences', in P.B. Baltes and O.G. Brim (eds) *Life-Span Development and Behavior*, 109–58, New York and London: Academic Press.

Ferri, E. (1984) *Step Children: A National Study*, London: National Foundation for Educational Research and Nelson.

Freedman, D.G. (1975) 'Culture, inbreeding and behaviour, with some thoughts on inter-ethnic communication', in L. Levi *Society, Stress and Disease: vol II, Childhood and Adolescence*, London: Oxford University Press.

Hetherington, E.M., Cox, M., and Cox, R. (1985) 'Long-term effects of divorce and remarriage on the adjustment of children', *Journal of the American Academy of Child Psychiatry*, 24, 518–30.

Jenkins, J. M. and Smith, M.A. 'Factors protecting children in disharmonious homes', submitted for publication.

Jonsson, G. (1975) 'Negative Social Inheritance', in L. Levi (ed.), *Society, Stress and Disease, vol. II: Childhood and Adolescence*, London: Oxford University Press.

Keesing, R.M. (1981) *Cultural Anthropology: A Contemporary Perspective*, New York: Holt, Rinehart and Winston.

Lamb, M.E. (ed.) (1981) *The Role of the Father in Child Development*, 2nd edn, New York: Wiley.

—— (ed.) (1986a) *The Father's Role: Applied Perspectives*, New York: Wiley.

—— (1986b) 'The changing roles of fathers', in M.E. Lamb (ed.) *The Father's Role: Applied Perspectives*, 3–27, New York: Wiley.

Levine, R.A. and Levine, B.B. (1963) 'Nyansongo: A Gusil community in Kenya', in B.B. Whiting (ed.) *Six Cultures: Studies of Child Rearing*, 15–202, New York: Wiley.

Lewis, C. and O'Brien, M. (1987) *Reassessing Fatherhood: New Observations on Fathers and the Modern Family*, London: Sage.

Lund, M. (1987) 'Common Challenges in Parenting after Divorce', in C. Lewis and M. O'Brien (eds) *Reassessing Fatherhood: New Observations on Fathers and the Modern Family*, 212–24, London: Sage.

Maretzki, T.W. and Maretzki, H. (1963) 'Taira: an Okinawan village', in B.B. Whiting (ed.) *Six Cultures: Studies of Child Rearing*, 363–539, New York: Wiley.

Marshall, R.K. (1976) *Childhood in Seventeenth Century Scotland*, Edinburgh: Scottish National Portrait Gallery.

De Mause, L.E. (ed.) (1976) *The History of Childhood*, London: Souvenir Press.

Newson, J. and Newson, E. (1976) *Seven Years Old in the Home Environment*, London: Allen & Unwin.

—— (1977) *Perspectives on School at Seven Years Old*, London: Allen & Unwin.

Patterson, G.R. (1982) *Coercive Family Process*, Eugene, Oregon: Castalia.

—— (1986) 'Performance models for antisocial boys', *American Psychologist* 41, 432–44.

Patterson, G.R., Littman, R.A., and Bricker, W. (1967) 'Assertive behavior in children: a step toward a theory of aggression', *Monographs of the Society for Research in Child Development*, vol. 32, No. 5.

Pinchbeck, I. and Hewitt, M. (1969) *Children in English Society: Vol. I.*

From Tudor Times to the Eighteenth Century, London: Routledge and Kegan Paul.

Pinchbeck, I. and Hewitt, M. (1973) *Children in English Society: Vol. II. From the Eighteenth Century to the Children's Act, 1948*, London: Routledge and Kegan Paul.

Pollock, L.A. (1983) *Forgotten Children: Parent-Child Relations from 1500 to 1900*, Cambridge: Cambridge University Press.

Robins, L. (1966) *Deviant Children Grown-Up*, Baltimore: Williams and Wilkins.

Russell, G. (1987) 'Problems in role-reversed families', in C. Lewis and M. O'Brien (eds) *Reassessing Fatherhood: New Observations on Fathers and the Modern Family*, 161-79, London: Sage.

Rutter, M., Tizard, J., and Whitmore, L. (1970) *Education, Health and Behaviour*, London: Longman.

Sandqvist, K. (1987) 'Swedish Family Policy and the Attempt to Change Paternal Roles', in C. Lewis and M. O'Brien (eds) *Reassessing Fatherhood: New Observations on Fathers and the Modern Family*, 144-60, London: Sage.

Schaffer, H.R. (1989) 'Language Development in Context', in S. von Tetzchner, L. Siegel, and L. Smith (eds) *The Social and Cognitive Aspects of Normal and Atypical Language Development*, New York: Springer (in press).

Sears, R.R., Maccoby, E.E., and Levin, H. (1957) *Patterns of Child Rearing*, Illinois and New York: Row, Peterson & Co.

Stone, L. (1977) *The Family, Sex and Marriage in England 1500-1800*, London: Weidenfeld & Nicolson; abridged version (1979), Harmondsworth: Pelican Books.

—— (1983) 'Children of divorce: the psychological tasks of the child', *American Journal of Ortho-psychiatry* 53, 230-43.

Wallerstein, J.S. (1985) 'Children of divorce: preliminary report of a ten-year follow-up of older children and adolescents', *Journal of the American Academy of Child Psychiatry* 24, 545-53.

Zigler, E. (1971) 'Social class and socialisation process', in S. Chess and A. Thomas (eds) *Annual Progress in Child Psychiatry and Child Development*, 185-209, London: Butterworths.

Chapter 10

Belson, W.A. (1978) *Television Violence and the Adolescent Boy*, Farnborough: Saxon House.

Eysenck, H.J. and Nias, D.K.B. (1978) *Sex, Violence and the Media*, London: Granada.

Greenfield, P.M. (1984) *Mind and Media: the Effects of Television, Computers and Video Games*, Aylesbury, Bucks: Fontana.

Hodges, W.F. (1986) *Intervention for Children of Divorce: Custody, Access and Psychotherapy*, Chichester and New York: John Wiley and Sons.

Jones, D.N. (1987) *Understanding Child Abuse*, 2nd edn, London and Basingstoke: Macmillan.

Kolvin, I., Garside, R.F., Nicol, A.R., Macmillan, A., Wolstenholme, F., and Leitch, I. (1981) *Help Starts Here: the Maladjusted Child in the Ordinary School*, London: Tavistock.

Kolvin, I., Macmillan, A., Nicol, A.R., and Wrate, R.M. (1988) 'Psychotherapy is effective', *Journal of the Royal Society of Medicine* 81, 261–6.

Kolvin, I., Steiner, H., Bamford, F., Taylor, M., Wynne, J., Jones, D., and Zeitlin, H. (1988) 'Child sexual abuse: some principles of good practice', *British Journal of Hospital Medicine* 39, 54–62.

Lefkowitz, M.M., Eron, L.D., Walder, L.O., and Huesmann, L.R. (1977) *Growing Up to be Violent: a Longitudinal Study of the Development of Aggression*, Oxford: Pergamon.

Lund, M. (1987) 'The non-custodial father: common challenges in parenting after divorce', in C. Lewis and M. O'Brien (eds) *Reassessing Fatherhood: New Observations on Fathers and the Modern Family*, London: Sage.

Lynch, M.A. and Roberts, J. (1982) *Consequences of Child Abuse*, London: Academic Press.

Martin, F.M., Fox, S.J., and Murray, K. (1981) *Children Out of Court*, Edinburgh: Scottish Academic Press.

Meyrowitz, J. (1985) *No Sense of Place: the Impact of Electronic Media on Social Behaviour*, Oxford: Oxford University Press.

Milavsky, J.R., Kessler, R.C., Stipp, H.H., and Rubens, W.S. (1982) *Television and Aggression: A Panel Study*, New York and London: Academic Press.

Mortimore, P., Sammons, P., Stoll, L., Lewis, D., and Etob, R. (1988) *School Matters: the Junior Years*, Wells: Open Books.

Newman, O. (1972) *Defensible Space: People and Design in the Violent City*, London: Architectural Press.

Osborn, A.F. and Milbank, J.E. (1987) *The Effects of Early Education: a Report from the Child Health and Education Study*, Oxford: Clarendon Press.

Power, M.J., Benn, R.T., and Morris, J.N. (1972) 'Neighbourhood, school and juveniles before the court', *British Journal of Criminology* 12, 111–32.

Report of the Panel of Inquiry into the Circumstances surrounding the Death of Jasmine Beckford: *A Child in Trust* (1985), Brent Borough Council, HMSO.

Reynolds, D., Jones, D., St Leger, S., and Murgatroyd, S. (1980) 'School factors and truancy', in L. Hersov and I. Berg (eds) *Out of School: Modern Perspectives in Truancy and School Refusal*, 85–110, London: John Wiley and Sons.

Robins, L.N. (1978) 'Sturdy childhood predictors of adult antisocial behaviour: replications from longitudinal studies', *Psychological Medicine* 8, 611–22.

—— (1986) 'The consequences of conduct disorders in girls', in D. Owens, J. Block, and M. Radke-Yarrow (eds) *Development of Antisocial and Prosocial Behavior: Research, Theories and Issues*, Orlando, Florida: Academic Press.

Rutter, M. (1979) *Changing Youth in a Changing Society: Patterns of Adolescent Development and Disorder*, Abingdon: The Rock Carling Fellowship, The Nuffield Provincial Hospitals Trust.

Rutter, M. and Giller, H. (1983) *Juvenile Delinquency: Trends and Perspectives*, Harmondsworth: Penguin.

Rutter, M., Maughan, B., Mortimore, P., and Ousten, B. (1979) *Fifteen Thousand Hours: Secondary Schools and their Effects on Children*, London: Open Books.

Scottish Law Commission (1988) *Discussion Paper No. 75: The Evidence of*

Children and Other Potentially Vulnerable Witnesses, Edinburgh: S.L.C.

Singer, J.L. and Singer, D.G. (1988) ' Some hazards of growing up in a television environment: children's aggression and restlessness', in S. Oskamp (ed.) *Television as a Social Issue*, Newbury Park: Sage.

Sloane, R.B., Staples, E.R., Cristol, A.H., Yorkston, N.J., and Whipple, K. (1975) *Psychotherapy Versus Behavior Therapy*, Cambridge, Mass: Harvard University Press.

Walker, N. and McCabe, S. (1973) *Crime and Insanity in England, Vol. II: New Solutions and New Problems*, Edinburgh: Edinburgh University Press.

The Warnock Report (1978) *Special Educational Needs: Report of the Enquiry into the Education of Handicapped Children and Young People*, London: HMSO.

Waterhouse, L. (1987) 'In defence of residential care', *Maladjustment and Therapeutic Education* 5, 39–53.

Wilson, S. (1980) 'Vandalism and "Defensible Space" in London's housing estates', in R.V.G. Clarke and P. Mayhew (eds) *Designing Out Crime*, 39–66, London: Home Office Research Unit, HMSO.

Wolff, S. (1986) 'Child psychotherapy', in S. Bloch (ed.) *An Introduction to the Psychotherapies*, 2nd edn, Oxford: Oxford University Press.

—— (1987) 'Antisocial conduct: whose concern?', *Journal of Adolescence* 10, 105–18.

Zeitlin, H. (1987) 'Investigation of the sexually abused child', *The Lancet* II, 842–5.

Name Index

Subject Index

abnormality, concepts of 16-17, 126-7

abstract operational stage *see* formal operational stage

accommodation, Piaget's concept of 99-101

activity level 37; and aggression 41, 170; correlates of in boys and girls 39; ethnic differences in 40; sex differences in 40; *see also* hyperactivity; hyperkinesis

adaptability 4, 9, 15, 37

addiction 140, 188, 194-5; alcohol 145-7, 188

adolescence: Erikson's stage of 157-9; experimentation at 160, 161; Freudian view of 137-8, 149; historical changes of 181, 183; rehearsal for 151-9; special hazards of 160-2

adoption: in adolescence 207-8; after institutional care 55, 84-5; late 85

adoption studies: of delinquency 41; intelligence 23

adualism 101

aggression: and activity level 41, 42; at adolescence 159; in animals 169; and child rearing 171-2, 181-3; constitutional determinants 41-2, 169; disorders 170; drive 127; and family disruption 184-5; and

hormones 40, 41; sex differences 40; social causes 170; and social learning 170-6, 181-3; stability of 171; sublimation of 132; *see also* antisocial behaviour; crime; violence

Ainsworth 'strange situation' 65-6, 78, 80

ambivalence 146

amnesia for early childhood 53, 137

anal: character 122; eroticism 133-4; stage 85, 136, 147-9

animism 107-8, 114, 151, 155, 161, 183

animistic stage 105-12, 115, 129, 136

anthropology 176-8

antisocial behaviour: and academic failure 171, 194; appraisal of 194-5; attitudes towards 187-8; and family discord and disruption 184-5; and family size 194; and hyperactivity 42; and hyperkinesis 42, 43-45, 194; and peer rejection 171; and schizoid personality 194; and low self-esteem 171; and social class 175; and socio-economic privation 194; *see also* aggression; conduct disorder; crime; delinquency

anxiety: behavioural treatment of 168; in boys 150; castration 129,

vandalism and housing 201-2
violence 140, 188, 194; in former
    times 181-3; and gangs 160;
    intrafamilial 171-2; and
    television 202-3
vulnerability factors for depression

78-9

Warnock Report (1978) 197
wet nursing 180-1, 184
working models *see* internal, models
    of people
working mothers 185